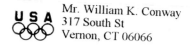

Informed Choices

FOR Struggling Adolescent Readers

A Research-Based Guide to Instructional Programs and Practices

Donald D. Deshler

Annemarie Sullivan Palincsar

Gina Biancarosa

Marnie Nair

Commissioned by Carnegie Corporation of New York

INTERNATIONAL
Reading Association
800 BARKSDALE ROAD, PO BOX 8139
NEWARK, DE 19714-8139, USA
www.reading.org

Carnegie Corporation's Advancing Literacy program is dedicated to the issues of adolescent literacy and the research, policy, and practice that focus on the reading and writing competencies of middle and high school students. Advancing Literacy reports and other publications are designed to encourage local and national discussion, explore promising ideas, and incubate models of practice, but do not necessarily represent the recommendations of the corporation. For more information, visit www.carnegie.org/literacy.

Written by Donald D. Deshler, Annemarie Sullivan Palincsar, Gina Biancarosa, and Marnie Nair for Carnegie Corporation of New York.

Published by the International Reading Association.

The International Reading Association attempts, through its publications, to provide a forum for a wide spectrum of opinions on reading. This policy permits divergent viewpoints without implying the endorsement of the Association.

Executive Editor, Books   Corinne M. Mooney
Developmental Editor   Charlene M. Nichols
Developmental Editor   Tori Mello Bachman
Developmental Editor   Stacey Lynn Sharp
Editorial Production Manager   Shannon T. Fortner
Production Manager   Iona Muscella
Supervisor, Electronic Publishing   Anette Schuetz

Cover   Linda Steere

The publisher would appreciate notification where errors occur so that they may be corrected in subsequent printings and/or editions.

Library of Congress Cataloging-in-Publication Data
Informed choices for struggling adolescent readers : a research-based guide to
instructional programs and practices / Donald D. Deshler ... [et al.].
     p. cm.
 Includes bibliographical references and index.
 ISBN 978-0-87207-465-1
 1. Reading (Middle school)--United States. 2. Literacy--United States. 3.
Literacy programs--United States--Directories. I. Deshler, Donald D.
 LB1632.P75 2007
 428.4071'2--dc22
                                                                                        2007009442

CONTENTS

Program Summaries 130

ABOUT THE AUTHORS

Donald D. Deshler, School of Education, University of Kansas
Don Deshler taught adolescents in secondary schools in rural Alaska. Currently, he is the director of the Center for Research on Learning and professor in the School of Education at the University of Kansas. His research and development work focuses on the design and validation of instructional strategies for use in academically diverse secondary classrooms. Don is a member of several advisory boards dealing with issues related to adolescent literacy, including the National Institute for Literacy, the Carnegie Corporation of New York, the Alliance for Excellent Education, and the National Governors Association.

Annemarie Sullivan Palincsar, School of Education, University of Michigan
Annemarie Sullivan Palincsar is the Jean and Charles Walgreen Jr. Chair of Reading and Literacy and a teacher educator in Educational Studies at the University of Michigan. Her research focuses on the design of learning environments that support self-regulation in learning activity, especially for students who experience difficulty learning in school. She studies how students use literacy in the context of guided inquiry science instruction, what types of text support students' inquiry, and the use of digital texts to support learning from graphics-rich informational text. Annemarie has served as a member of the National Academy's Research Council on the Prevention of Reading Difficulty in Young Children, the OERI/RAND Reading Study Group, and the National Research Council's Panel on Teacher Preparation. She is co-editor of the journal *Cognition and Instruction*.

Gina Biancarosa, School of Education, Stanford University
Gina Biancarosa is a postdoctoral fellow at the Stanford University School of Education's Institute for Research on Education Policy and Practice. She has taught struggling adolescent readers in school-sponsored after-school and summer programs. Her research focuses on understanding the heterogeneity of struggling adolescent readers and on the design of better measures for research and educational purposes.

Marnie Nair, Graduate School of Education, Harvard University
Marnie Nair received her doctoral degree in Language and Literacy at the Harvard Graduate School of Education. Previously, she worked as a teacher and reading specialist in middle and high schools in Oakland, New York City, and Washington, DC, and as a secondary school principal in New Orleans. Her research focuses on improving the supports offered to struggling adolescent

readers in urban schools, with a current emphasis on vocabulary teaching and learning in the content area classroom.

With contributions from:

Doran Catlin
Teachers College
Columbia University

Reed T. Deshler
AlignOrg Solutions, LLC

Alex Elson
Teachers College
Columbia University

Henry M. Levin
Teachers College
Columbia University

ACKNOWLEDGMENTS

WE ARE DEEPLY APPRECIATIVE of the thoughtful feedback and input from many of our colleagues during the writing process. First, the inspiration for this book came from Andrés Henríquez, program officer in Carnegie Corporation of New York's Education Division. Through his visionary leadership, Andrés has guided the work of the corporation's Advancing Literacy program. He has had a profound impact on improving programs and influencing policies related to adolescent literacy in our country. Our work was also shaped by insightful suggestions from members of the Carnegie Corporation of New York's Advisory Council on Advancing Adolescent Literacy. We would like to thank Catherine Snow, chairperson of the Advisory Council and advisor to two of the authors (Gina Biancarosa and Marnie Nair) during their doctoral studies; in both of these roles she provided ongoing support of and insight into this work. Finally, we appreciate the guidance and assistance of Daniel Mangan, director of publications for the International Reading Association.

This work was partly made possible by support from the Spencer Foundation's Research Training Grant Program at Harvard Graduate School of Education and primarily through support from the Carnegie Corporation of New York.

INTRODUCTION

Gina Biancarosa, Marnie Nair, Donald D. Deshler,
& Annemarie Sullivan Palincsar

A MONG MIDDLE AND SECONDARY school administrators and teachers, there has long been great concern about adolescent literacy, as well as frustration at the lack of attention, information, and resources being directed at this very real concern. We hope the discussion here will make it clear not only that this concern is well-placed but also that the struggles many adolescent readers face are serious. Many adolescents fail and/or drop out of school because of their inability to read in school. Others stay in school and even appear to meet current standards only to find that their literacy skills do not meet the demands placed on them when they enter college or the workforce. Addressing the needs of these struggling readers is by no means a simple task. The reading "profile" of a school and even of students within that school can differ dramatically based on the school's context, which makes addressing the needs of struggling readers a complex task and highlights the need to individually tailor a reading program to meet the particular needs of each setting.

This book is our attempt to arm educators with information and resources for addressing adolescent literacy within their own contexts. We hope this book will speak to your concerns whether your role is that of teacher, specialist, principal, or district administrator. Wherever you serve your students, be it a rural, suburban, or urban locale, the *process* you must go through to enact effective change in adolescent literacy achievement is much the same. At the same time, because the students you serve are unique, the *program* you develop will be unique. This book attempts to provide you with insight into the process in order to enable you to choose wisely among the extremely wide array of instructional programs currently available.

Getting the Lay of the Land: The Condition of Adolescent Literacy

In any adolescent literacy effort, it pays to be mindful not only of your local context but also of the larger national picture. Too often educators work in isolation from one another, not knowing that their colleagues in very different places are facing similar challenges or that they may have discovered some very effective means for dealing with those challenges. We begin by considering adolescent literacy achievement broadly and then consider the ramifications of poor literacy.

Poor literacy skills are all too common in America's schools, with students in schools in both urban and rural low-income neighborhoods most at risk of failing to learn to read well. While there has been increased attention given to reading instruction in the last few years, accompanied by a louder call for standards-based learning, testing, and funding, currently most of the attention and resources have been focused on the reading needs of learners through grade 3.

Meanwhile, the well-documented "reading slump" that occurs in U.S. schools after fourth grade persists (Chall & Jacobs, 2003; Chall, Jacobs, & Baldwin, 1990). Since the gap between proficient and struggling readers increases over time (Stanovich, 1986), the end result—as nationally mandated assessment data continue to attest—is that at-risk high school students across the United States are failing on measures of reading at epidemic rates (Perie, Grigg, & Donahue, 2005).

Comparing the most recent National Assessment of Educational Progress (NAEP) reading results for 4th-, 8th-, and 12th-grade levels with those from 1992 reveal that although the percentage of students scoring proficient has significantly improved among 4th graders, the percentage of 8th and 12th graders scoring proficient has remained stagnant (Donahue, Voelkl, Campbell, & Mazzeo, 1999; Perie, Grigg, et al., 2005; Perie, Moran, & Lutkus, 2005). Despite improvements in 4th-grade proficiency rates, 70% of students entering the 5th and 9th grades in 2005 are reading below grade level (Perie, Grigg, et al., 2005). In fact, both dropouts and high school graduates are demonstrating significantly worse reading skills than 10 years ago (Kutner, Greenberg, & Baer, 2006).

In the U.S. capital in 2005, only 11% of eighth-grade students were found to be proficient readers (Perie, Grigg, et al., 2005). In 2004, in approximately 20% of Orleans Parish, Louisiana, schools, not a single eighth-grade student passed the state English Language Arts exam in 2004, and in another 57% of these schools less than 10% of students passed the same exam (LEAP for the 21st Century, n.d.). In 2005, in California, only 20% of students were proficient readers by the eighth grade (Perie, Grigg, et al., 2005). While poor literacy skills are more acute in some locales than in others, across the United States it is youths living in poverty who are most at risk of failing to learn to read well, and these statistics reflect the performance of adolescents living in poverty across the country. Even so, poor literacy skills are found in every corner of U.S. society.

Today, graduation rates range from 89% in New Jersey to 53% in South Carolina (Greene & Winters, 2005), with a disproportionate number of the students who drop out being poor and of color (Orfield, 2004). In general, students entering ninth grade in the lowest 25% of achievement are 20 times more likely to drop out than their higher performing peers (Carnevale, 2001). It should not be surprising then that some 30% of students drop out (Greene & Winters, 2005).

Of those students who do graduate from high school, approximately 32% are not ready for college-level English composition courses (ACT, 2005) and approximately 40% lack the literacy skills employers seek (Achieve, 2005). Moreover, the data reveal geographic and racial disparities in preparedness for higher education (Greene & Winters, 2005). About 38% of students in the northeast region of the country (Connecticut, Delaware, Maine, Maryland, Massachusetts, New Hampshire, New Jersey, New York, Pennsylvania, Rhode Island, and Vermont) graduate prepared for college, but the northeast also shows the greatest disparity in preparedness between white students (44% prepared) and Hispanic students (12% prepared). Students in the central region of the country (Illinois, Indiana, Iowa, Kansas, Michigan, Minnesota, Missouri, Nebraska, North Dakota, Ohio, South Dakota, and Wisconsin) have the lowest average rate of preparedness (31%) and the largest disparity between white students (35%) and African American students (15%). However, on average, half as many Hispanic and African American students graduate from high school prepared for college. With both college professors and employers reporting nearly equal dissatisfaction with the literacy skills of high school graduates (Achieve, 2005), we have strong evidence that similar numbers of high school graduates are unprepared to meet the literacy demands of the workplace.

The Real-World Demands for Advanced Literacy

Even youth who have successfully navigated the U.S. K–12 education system clearly have no guarantee that they will be able to perform competitively in higher education or employment. Community colleges and even four-year institutions find themselves unable to keep up with the demand for remedial reading and writing courses, yet students who need these courses and are unable to complete them are less likely to complete a vocational program at a community college and even less likely to go on to graduate from a four-year program (Bettinger & Long, 2005).

This fact is even more alarming when you consider that between 1973 and 1998 alone, the percentage of workers who were high school dropouts fell by at least half, whereas the percentage of workers with some college or a college degree more than doubled—not only in skilled blue-collar, clerical, and related professions but also in less-skilled blue-collar, service, and related professions (Carnevale, 2001). Not surprisingly, as the demand for unskilled labor has decreased, unemployment has increased at the fastest pace for those with low educational attainment (Organisation for Economic Co-operation and Development [OECD], 2000, Tables 2.4, 2.5, & 3.1).

The end result is that the 70% of high school students who manage to graduate from high school (Greene & Winters, 2005) often find themselves unprepared to compete for the more lucrative jobs that require not only postsecondary education but an ongoing ability to read in order to keep abreast of new developments in a rapidly changing global economy (Biancarosa & Snow, 2004; Levy & Murnane, 2004; OECD, 2000).

More worrisome still, the abysmal performance of America's adolescents is not due to inflated or unreasonable standards. International comparisons have found that U.S. 11th-grade students rank close to the bottom and behind Philippine, Indonesian, and Brazilian students (RAND Reading Study Group, 2002). Moreover, U.S. dropouts rank lower than dropouts in most industrialized nations, performing comparably only with Chile, Poland, Portugal, and Slovenia (OECD, 2000). In addition, the range between the highest and lowest literacy levels in America is much wider than in almost any other nation, whether or not education is taken into account (OECD, 2000).

Certainly, poor literacy skills have far-reaching consequences in the lives of individual students. A large percentage of young dropouts are unemployed. Many end up in prison. The relatively small proportion who do find work can expect to make significantly less than their counterparts who do graduate from high school (Barton, 2005; OECD, 2000; Orfield, 2004). In 2002, the national average income for those dropouts who did find employment was only US$18,800 per year (Orfield, 2004).

Students who do graduate from high school but are not prepared to complete college are often screened out of employment on the basis of low literacy skills (Achieve, 2005), and those who do find employment will earn on average US$20,000 a year less than their counterparts with a bachelor's degree (Day & Newburger, 2002). Considering that this disparity has grown yearly over the past 25 years and that an increasingly technology-driven workplace demands more literacy skills than ever before, the economic impact for failing to learn to read well only heightens the need to address this pressing issue.

How This Book Can Help

Much of what we report in the preceding sections will not be news to educators who work daily with adolescents. We want to encourage you that the tide seems to be turning: The larger educational community seems to be responding to the needs of the adolescent reader. This is evidenced by policymakers and educational researchers who are increasingly turning their attention to addressing the needs of the struggling adolescent reader. Our purpose in writing this book is twofold.

The first purpose in writing this book is to offer an overview of what the latest research in adolescent literacy has shown to work best. We believe this overview will provide critical background information, not only for those who are responsible for making literacy curriculum choices for students but also for those who may be specialists in subjects other than reading and want to better understand both the reading process and their struggling students.

The second purpose is to offer information to educators about specific literacy programs. In response to heavy demand, the availability of resources, programs, and curriculum that can be implemented in the classroom is growing by the day. This is a mixed blessing to the extent that with this increase comes a great deal of variability in the type and quality of programs available.

As such, the book is divided into two parts. Part I takes you through the process, from understanding the nature of adolescent literacy to considering the costs of instructional changes, while Part II provides a directory of adolescent literacy curriculum and programming options. We hope that this information will generate new insights and enable educators to make informed choices when attempting to address adolescent literacy, and this book has been structured to maximize this likelihood.

Although challenges will naturally differ from school to school, district to district, and even state to state, we believe strongly that a common base of understanding about the nature of adolescent literacy and the variation in adolescents' struggles with literacy is required to effect positive and lasting change. These are the topics of Chapter 1. We also assert that good adolescent literacy instruction, and especially good intervention, attends not just to a checklist of elements but to the specific needs and challenges of the local context. Chapter 2 reviews the potential content of adolescent literacy instruction and Chapter 3 the characteristics and supports of effective adolescent literacy instruction. In addition, we try to provide you with a way to plan for the real costs of any program you choose and how decisions about implementation can affect those costs. Thus, Chapter 4 estimates the costs of three very different programs for several different implementations, both actual and ideal. Finally, effective change should be guided by an appreciation for how instructional change requires organizational change and how you can look for the signs of readiness in your school. Consequently, Chapter 5 delves into the distinct challenges of making change—especially as it relates to implementing a new literacy program—in middle and high schools.

Part II contains a directory of adolescent literacy programs. The directory listings are preceded by a brief review of the process by which we located and checked our information on the included programs. Although the directory has a large selection of programs, we make no claims that it is exhaustive. In fact, the somewhat baffling quantity of curricula and professional development programs and the great variation among them is in part what inspired this book. Moreover, the proliferation of new programs, especially those being designed through renewed research interest in adolescent literacy, inspired us to include an appendix listing programs that are currently emerging through research. Hence, we strongly urge you to resist the temptation to skip right to the directory, which includes comparative matrixes, descriptive information, and sources. Rather, please take the time to study the first part of the book because of the information it provides to guide you in determining the specific needs of your students and how to meet them most effectively. It is in the inclusion of these chapters that this book differs from other excellent reviews of adolescent literacy programs (Florida Center for Reading Research, 2006; Shanahan, 2005). It is our hope that armed with the information found in the first five chapters, you will approach this overview as simply a starting point for digging deeper and finding a literacy solution that is uniquely suited to your situation—your school, your administration, your teachers, and most of all, your students.

Contextualizing the Facts

To aid you in the process of finding a literacy solution, we have woven examples of how the facts we present might work themselves out in practice in several real schools that we have come to know in our research and practice. We hope that our discussion of these very real cases as we work through the issues in the following chapters will help you to imagine how you might do the same. Although we will cite a number of actual examples, we will focus more closely on the three schools we introduce here. (All names of institutions and people have been changed to maintain anonymity, but as much information as possible on each school's context has been preserved in order to make the examples as useful to the reader as possible.)

Hampshire Middle School

Hampshire Middle School is a public, urban school in Boston, Massachusetts, that serves 560 students in grades 6 through 8. Over three-quarters qualify for free or reduced-cost lunches, which is not unusual in Boston. About a third of Hampshire students are identified as English-language learners (ELLs), but only 6% (or 35 students) are identified as limited English proficient (LEP). LEP students do not receive services for developing their English proficiency as there are no teachers of English as a second language in the school. Hampshire is unusual in that a third of its students are in special education, and many of these students are not integrated into regular education classrooms. The school was declared underperforming by the State Department of Education in 2004–2005 when state tests revealed that less than a quarter of students were performing at grade level on the state test, with half needing improvement and almost a third in danger of failing. Moreover, the results were worse for other subject areas such as math. In addition to its literacy woes, the school has a higher than average out-of-school suspension rate (18 versus the city's average of 8) and absentee rate (19 days versus the city's average of 13).

Hope Academy

Hope Academy was a private, urban middle and high school for boys in New Orleans, Louisiana. Sad to say, it was destroyed in Hurricane Katrina. While in operation, Hope Academy served approximately 140 boys in grades 7 through 10. One hundred percent of the students were African American, native English speakers; all but two students qualified for free or reduced-cost lunch. Although the school was a private school, students paid only a small amount of tuition (on average US$20 per month) with the rest of the funding provided by scholarships. This being a new school, teachers were flexible and ready for change, although the level of teacher preparation was varied. While the school's status as a private school meant that teachers had three years after hiring to meet certification requirements, the lack of certified teachers was very reflective of schools in the area. Although only a small number of the students were identified as special education students, the teachers readily acknowledged their students' reading difficulties and that many students at each grade level were unable to decode even single-syllable words.

Bernadine High School

Bernadine High School (BHS) is a public, rural high school in the Midwest. BHS serves approximately 1,200 students, about 60% of whom are Caucasian, about 30% Hispanic, and 8% African American. Almost half of the students qualify for free and reduced-cost lunches, and an increasing number of ELLs have been enrolling at BHS. Most of these ELLs come from migrant-worker families. In the 1970s and 1980s the school had one of the best academic records of comparable schools in the state. But with its shifting demographics, academic performance began to fall rapidly in the early 1990s, which led to a 10-year string of failed short-term reform efforts that did little to reverse the school's decline. Recent assessments have revealed that half of the school's 390 ninth-graders read below grade level, with one-third of them performing two or more years below grade level. With a staff weary of the turnstile of reform, BHS faces an uphill battle to regain its former glory as a place where adolescents learn, read, and write proficiently.

Some Final Food for Thought

Clearly, these three schools have very different student bodies and very different contexts. Despite their apparent differences, the same issues that are covered in the following chapters apply to them all. What are their students' different needs and strengths? Are the schools in similar stages of readiness for change? What changes in content, characteristics, and supports of literacy instruction will best suit their students? And what will those changes cost them?

PART I

Principles for Improving Adolescent Literacy

CHAPTER 1

Adolescent Literacy: Myths and Realities

Gina Biancarosa, Annemarie Sullivan Palincsar, Donald D. Deshler,
& Marnie Nair

AS THE INTRODUCTION ILLUSTRATED, the United States is facing an adolescent literacy crisis. But understanding what adolescent literacy is and why so many adolescents struggle with literacy is not a simple task. For the layperson and experienced educator alike, all too often the idea of an adolescent literacy crisis connotes visions of teenagers who can't read at all. In fact, the crisis is not so clear-cut. An adolescent who struggles with literacy may struggle with one or many of a wide range of skills and content, and the reasons underlying those struggles can be equally diverse. In this chapter, we identify some of the most common erroneous ideas regarding adolescent literacy and attempt to provide you with an accurate picture of the nature of this complex situation.

Adolescent Literacy Myths

Our society embraces a number of erroneous ideas about adolescents in general, but of primary concern in this volume are misconceptions about the nature and roots of the adolescent literacy problem facing the United States. These myths are counterproductive to improving the literacy achievement of our youths. Although there are a number of such myths, we focus on debunking five of the most enduring:

1. Struggling adolescent readers can't read at all.
2. If an adolescent can read the words, comprehension naturally follows.
3. Adolescents today can't read like adolescents used to read.
4. Adolescents today can't read well because they spend too much time on TV, computers, video games, etc.
5. The adolescent literacy problem is primarily one of poverty, race, disability, and linguistic background.

Myth #1: Struggling Adolescent Readers Can't Read at All

Perhaps the greatest mistake that people make in thinking about adolescent literacy is thinking that adolescents who struggle cannot read at all. This myth arises in large part from how we talk about adolescent literacy achievement, particularly when referring to the National Assessment of Educational Progress (NAEP) and to state tests. Performance on these tests tends to be reported primarily in terms of achievement levels, significantly influencing our perceptions of the situation.

For instance, the NAEP reports three achievement levels: basic, proficient, and advanced (Perie, Grigg, et al., 2005). One problem is the terms themselves. *Basic* connotes some sort of fundamental skill set, and many tend to assume that what is basic is what should have been learned in earlier grades. In fact, basic achievement "denotes partial mastery of the knowledge and skills that are fundamental for proficient work at a given grade level" or below grade-level performance. *Below basic* is not an official NAEP achievement level but is also commonly discussed and represents the percentage of students scoring below the basic level. Essentially, the basic level is a moving target, which only makes sense if we wish to judge our students' ability to learn from grade-level texts. Thus, tasks that count as basic for 8th graders are more difficult than they are for 4th graders, and the expectations for 12th graders are higher again. Fourth graders at the basic level understand the general idea of what they read and can make "obvious connections" between what they read and what they already know (Perie, Grigg, et al., 2005, p. 27), whereas 8th graders can do all this but can also identify supporting details, "recognize and relate interpretations and connections among ideas in the text...and draw conclusions based on the text" (Perie, Grigg, et al., 2005, p. 29). As a result, 8th graders scoring "below basic" may be able to do most—but not all—of these things, or may be able to do so but only for easier texts.

> Perhaps the greatest mistake that people make in thinking about adolescent literacy is thinking that adolescents who struggle cannot read at all.

Another issue is how reading achievement levels get discussed. While the basic level signifies below grade-level performance, the *proficient* achievement level "represents solid academic performance" or grade-level performance, and the *advanced* achievement level "signifies superior performance" or above grade-level performance (Perie, Grigg, et al., 2005, p. 2). As a result, one of the most commonly cited NAEP statistics is the percentage of students scoring at or above the proficient level because adolescents who do not do so presumably struggle to some degree with grade-level literacy tasks. But the adolescents who score below proficient fall into two different levels: basic and below basic. For example, on the 2005 NAEP reading test 31% of eighth graders scored at or above the proficient level, 42% scored at the basic level, and 27% scored below the basic level (Perie, Grigg, et al., 2005). By and large, the adolescents who score at the basic level necessarily differ from the adolescents who score below basic. And even among those who fall into one or the other level, students may struggle with very different things. Most obviously, some percentage of those who fall into the below basic level doubtlessly do struggle with reading words, but the NAEP (and any state test) does not—and cannot—tell us what percentage of our students fits this description.

Consider how these terms get applied to Boston's Hampshire Middle School. The Hampshire Middle School seventh-grade students take their state's English language arts test each year. Just like the NAEP, this state characterizes students who meet grade-level expectations as *proficient* and those exceeding grade-level expectations as *advanced*. However, struggling students get labeled as *needs improvement* (most closely aligned to basic on the NAEP) or as *warning/failing* (or below basic on the NAEP). Although Hampshire has been judged as an underperforming school, 21% of the Hampshire seventh graders scored proficient in 2005. Of the 79% who did not reach grade-level expectations, 47% needed improvement and 32% of the seventh graders performed at the warning (or failing) level. Clearly the Hampshire students could be doing a better job, but just as clearly the majority of them can indeed read or they would not be able to reach even the "needs improvement" level. And at Hope Academy in New Orleans, many students had decent basic decoding skills but struggled with reading comprehension because of limited vocabulary and advanced decoding skills. Although not a single Hope student entering the seventh grade tested at higher than a third-grade reading level, the majority were in fact reading to some extent.

In short, students who score at the lowest levels may have substantial reading skills, but those skills may simply be well below grade-level expectations. Moreover, because of the way in which test scores are calculated and reported, the difference between scoring at one achievement level or the next can often be a matter of how a student responded to one or two questions. Achievement levels only tell us what proportion of students are or are not meeting certain standards, but they give us no information about why students score as they do.

Finally, the most recent National Education Longitudinal Study found that 89% of high school sophomores read with literal comprehension (Ingels, Burns, Chen, Cataldi, & Charleston, 2005, Figure 16). It was only when asked to make simple or complex inferences that we begin to see significant numbers of students demonstrating problems with reading; for example, while 46% were able to make relatively simple inferences, only 8% were able to make more complex inferences. Therefore, it is a mistake to interpret the percentage of students scoring at a particular achievement level as not being able to read at all. As the rest of this chapter illustrates, the reasons why adolescents struggle with literacy are quite diverse.

Myth #2: If an Adolescent Can Read the Words, Comprehension Naturally Follows

Another typical—but erroneous—assumption is that, if a student can read the words that appear in a text accurately and quickly, then comprehension will be the natural end product. This assumption is reflected in how comprehension gets taught, or too often does not get taught. Although a great deal of explicit modeling, instruction, and practice in word reading and spelling takes place in many U.S. elementary-grade classrooms, explicit instruction in comprehension is much less frequent (e.g., Pressley, Wharton-McDonald, Mistretta-Hampston, & Echevarria, 1998; Taylor, Pearson, Clark, & Walpole, 2000). Perpetuating this myth are the continuing debates over the existence of *word callers*, a term used to describe readers who appear to be fairly fluent in their reading but do not give evidence of understanding what they have read. Respected researchers still question whether readers can truly read quickly and accurately without comprehension (e.g., Hamilton & Shinn, 2003; Nathan & Stanovich, 1991). However, several recent studies have clearly demonstrated that such readers do indeed exist (e.g., Biancarosa, Mancilla-Martinez, Kieffer, Christodoulou, & Snow, 2006; Buly & Valencia, 2002; Catts, Hogan, & Adlof, 2005; Leach, Scarborough, & Rescorla, 2003; Lesaux, Lipka, & Siegel, 2006). Furthermore, the number of word callers can depend greatly on the school or district.

An analysis of a district in the northwest revealed that 18% of students were "automatic word callers": readers who were both fast and accurate but demonstrated poor comprehension (Buly & Valencia, 2005; Valencia & Buly, 2005). But as the Boston Higher Education Partnership Research Collaborative found in the Boston Public Schools, the proportion of such readers varied dramatically from school to school and from grade to grade. For example, in Boston's Fitzgerald School, where more than 90% of the K–8 students are Spanish–English bilinguals, more than half of the students demonstrated no problems with fluency or accuracy (Biancarosa et al., 2006). But at the Hampshire Middle School, almost 67% of the sixth-grade students and about 85% of the seventh-grade students were unable to read at their grade level with fluency and accuracy. Because so few of the Hampshire students were able to read accurately and fluently, the problem of word calling was small there compared with Fitzgerald. Thus, intervention at Hampshire would need to focus on both word reading and comprehension skills. Despite this variation of word calling across contexts, what these studies make apparent is that comprehension is not assured after accuracy and fluency have been achieved.

Myth #3: Adolescents Today Can't Read Like Adolescents Used to Read

One widely held misconception about adolescent literacy is the belief that adolescents are worse off today than they were 10, 20, or 30 years ago. In fact, adolescent literacy achievement has remained relatively stable. According to NAEP results, eighth-grade reading achievement has not changed dramatically in the last dozen years (Donahue et al., 1999; Lemke et al., 2001, 2004, 2005; Perie, Moran, et al., 2005). Nor have U.S. students changed much in their relative ranking in international comparisons (Martin, Mullis, Gonzalez, & Kennedy, 2003). What has changed are the demands that life after high school makes on students. This is discussed in more detail under Reality #1 in the next section.

On a more local level, single schools or districts often have histories of poor performance or good performance. Part of the impetus behind legislation like No Child Left Behind was the desire to stimulate improvement in such schools and districts. Of course, as anyone working in historically underperforming areas can tell you, the underlying reasons for poor performance are not easily or quickly remedied. Poor performance is often not the result of a lack of will but of a combination of factors. Lack of commensurate funding between poorer and richer districts is one reason, but community demographics also contribute to the numbers of students likely to struggle and to the ways they struggle. For instance, the Boston Public Schools have a long history of underperformance compared with wealthier districts in the state. Reform efforts there, as well as nationwide, have made small inroads resulting in small improvements in overall performance in the district. But these changes have largely come in kindergarten through fourth grade and not in the grades our adolescents attend. This ostensible intractability is one reason why the Boston Public Schools recently began collaborating with the Boston Higher Education Partnership and the Strategic Education Research Partnership with a request that research efforts initially focus on middle school literacy.

Myth #4: Adolescents Today Can't Read Well Because They Spend Too Much Time on TV, Computers, Video Games, etc.

Although it is tempting to point the finger at the increasingly multimedia landscape of adolescent diversions or the nature of home and community activities, the truth is that these factors do not determine whether an adolescent struggles with literacy or not. The claims are that because adolescents watch too much television, use computers too much, and play too many video games, they are poor readers and writers. In fact, these theories do not explain why so many youths struggle with literacy; indeed, there is evidence that some of these practices can foster literacy skills (Leander & Lovvorn, 2006; Plester, Bell, & Wood, 2006). Moreover, jobs and education after high school increasingly require adept use of various types of media to communicate (Lankshear & Knobel, 2002).

The most recent NAEP study of grades 4, 8, and 12 reveals that excessive television viewing (four or more hours daily) is indeed associated with lower reading achievement, but it also shows that students are watching less television than they were in the past (Donahue et al., 1999). About 35% of 4th graders, 38% of 8th graders, and 23% of 12th graders watch four or more hours of television per day, and these percentages do not align neatly with the percentage of students scoring below proficient in these grades. Moreover, the NAEP studies do not distinguish types of television programs viewed, which have been shown to influence whether the impact of viewing is positive or negative. More recent longitudinal studies have shown that watching educational or informational television is beneficial to student literacy performance. Watching such programs in preschool is associated with early literacy skills in elementary school (Wright et al., 2001) and with better achievement and more reading in high school (Anderson, Huston, Schmitt, Linebarger, & Wright, 2001; Gentzkow & Shapiro, 2006). Research has shown that both children and adults use the same comprehension skills and processes whether reading books or watching television programs (e.g., van den Broek, 2001; van den Broek, Lorch, & Thurlow, 1996).

As for computer use, the most recent National Education Longitudinal Study found that higher achieving high school sophomores reported using computers at home more frequently and in higher proportions than did their lower achieving peers (Ingels et al., 2005, Table 19a). Furthermore, higher achieving students used computers more often for both entertainment and educational purposes (Ingels et al., 2005, Table 20). Therefore, we cannot appeal to such easy explanations for why adolescents struggle with literacy.

Myth #5: The Adolescent Literacy Problem Is Primarily One of Poverty, Race, Disability, and Linguistic Background

One dangerous assumption often made is that the adolescents who struggle with literacy are predominantly one type of student. Whether that type is defined by family or neighborhood income levels, by student ethnicity or race, by disability, or by student language or immigrant status, simply falling into one or another group is no guarantee that an adolescent will or will not struggle with literacy. It is true that the literacy achievement gap between white students and their African American, Latino/a, and Native American peers is as real as it ever was and particularly stable among adolescents (Perie, Grigg, et al., 2005; Perie, Moran, et al., 2005). However, white students also have a high risk of struggling with adolescent literacy tasks. Although 85% or more of black and Hispanic students do not meet grade-level reading expectations, 61% of white eighth-grade students do not meet those expectations either (Perie, Grigg, et al., 2005). Similarly, although a higher percentage of low socioeconomic status (SES) students struggle with adolescent literacy, students from more privileged backgrounds also fall short of expectations at alarming rates. Whereas 85% of eighth-grade students eligible for free or reduced-cost lunch do not score proficient at reading, 61% of those not eligible do not score proficient (Perie, Grigg, et al., 2005). Likewise, being an English language learner (ELL), an immigrant, or both certainly raises an adolescent's chances of struggling with literacy. On the 2005 NAEP eighth-grade reading assessment, 93% of ELLs did not score proficient, but neither did 68% of non-ELL students. Given that ELLs are defined by their lack of proficiency with the English language, the disparity in this particular case is not terribly surprising. Similarly, large percentages of adolescents with disabilities struggle in acquiring literacy competencies (Hock et al., 2006).

Despite the alarming disparities among demographic groups, it is clear that white students, higher SES students, and monolingual English speakers also struggle with adolescent literacy in large numbers. Moreover, membership in one of the lower scoring groups does not ensure that a student will struggle with adolescent literacy. For example, monolingual English speakers in the United States often show lower signs of achievement and more signs of struggle than do students who were formerly ELLs (New York City Public Schools Division of Assessment and Accountability, 2000). However, recall the demographics of the students at Boston's Fitzgerald School; over 90% of the Fitzgerald students are Hispanic. In addition, over 90% qualify for free or reduced-cost lunches, and over 75% are considered ELLs. Yet 59% of the Fitzgerald seventh graders met state standards for reading and writing. On the other hand, Churchill Prep, a small urban middle and high school in the mid-Atlantic, serves predominantly white students with learning disabilities in grades 6 through 12. This private school costs approximately US$30,000 in tuition per year, and few students attend on scholarships. Considering only the demographics of the Churchill Prep student body might lead one to expect few problems with adolescent literacy, but in reality literacy is a source of considerable struggle for a majority of Churchill students; about 75% of the students have reading issues. In short, adolescents' group membership is neither protection against nor predictive of struggle with literacy. Having explored some of the myths pertaining to adolescent literacy achievement, we now turn to some of the realities.

Adolescent Literacy Realities

So how do we explain the adolescent literacy problem? How do we make sense of the alarming statistics regarding adolescent literacy achievement that dominate today's headlines? In the remainder of this chapter, we address some of the realities behind adolescent literacy.

Although the issue is complicated, there are four key ideas that will help us better understand the nature and roots of the problem:

1. Adolescent literacy demands have changed radically.
2. Instruction has not kept pace with demands.
3. The nature of adolescents' literacy struggles varies widely.

4. Variability in struggles means that intervention is complicated and assessment to guide instruction is critical.

Reality #1: Adolescent Literacy Demands Have Changed Radically

Although achievement appears not to have changed, expectations regarding literacy performance certainly have. What has been changing is the society in which our youths must live. Today's generation faces greater literacy demands when compared with prior generations. Demands for high-level reading and writing abilities are greater today in both higher education and the workplace than ever before (Achieve, 2005; ACT, 2005; American Diploma Project, 2004; National Commission on Writing, 2004, 2005).

Furthermore, the fastest growing professions have the greatest literacy demands, while those professions that are declining the fastest have lower than average literacy demands (Barton, 2000; Levy & Murnane, 2004). More telling still, as the demand for unskilled labor has decreased unemployment has increased, especially for those with low educational attainment (OECD, 2000). Even though the dropout rate in U.S. high schools has remained relatively stable since the 1990s (Greene & Winters, 2005; Laird, Lew, DeBell, & Chapman, 2006), between 1973 and 1998 the percentage of dropouts who are employed fell by two-thirds in skilled blue-collar and clerical professions and by nearly half in less skilled clerical and service professions (Carnevale, 2001). Meanwhile, the percentage of workers with at least some college or a college degree doubled in those same skilled professions and tripled in the less skilled professions (Carnevale, 2001). Although adolescents were once able to drop out and earn a decent living, those days are gone.

Unfortunately, it is not only our dropouts who struggle to make it in today's economy; high school graduates also struggle in both their work lives and their pursuit of further education. Recent reports by the National Commission on Writing (2004, 2005) reveal that the majority of both public and private employers say that writing proficiency has now become critical in the workplace and that it directly affects hiring and promotion decisions. Moreover, the demand for writing proficiency is not limited to professional jobs but extends to clerical and support positions in state government and construction, manufacturing, and service industries in the private sector. Yet employers and high school graduates themselves express dissatisfaction with how high school prepares youths for employers' writing demands (Achieve, 2005).

Furthermore, college instructors estimate fully half of high school graduates are not prepared for college-level writing (Achieve, 2005), while ACT estimates that 32% of college-bound high school students have little likelihood of earning good grades in college English courses because they do not meet readiness reading and writing benchmarks for college-level English composition courses (ACT, 2005). Indeed, the most recent research reveals that 42% of all postsecondary students take remedial courses (Adelman, 2004).

Reality #2: Instruction Has Not Kept Pace With Demands

Accompanying stagnant adolescent literacy and accelerating demands is another problem, one that we have some chance of affecting. Adolescent literacy instruction, especially comprehension instruction, has remained largely unchanged for years. As mentioned earlier, comprehension instruction does not receive much attention in U.S. elementary classrooms, but this problem is not a new one. The problem has been decried for the last three decades (Durkin, 1979, 1981; Pressley et al., 1998; Quirk, Trismen, Nalin, & Weinberg, 1975). This lack of explicit literacy instruction can be an enormous barrier for adolescents.

While in elementary school the literacy focus is on learning to read and write and reading and writing for fun, in middle and high school the focus shifts to using the written word to gather, learn, and express new information (Chall, 1996). Further complicating the situation is the fact that there is a wide range in the types of texts that middle and high school students are expected to read and write. For example, adolescents are expected to be able to read and comprehend not only literature—which in itself contains multiple genres, from poetry to novel to essay—but also scientific and technical writing, mathematical notation and equations, historical documents, Internet sources, encyclopedias and other reference material, to name just a few.

It would be a mistake to lay blame solely on teachers or on the education schools that prepare them. Several issues combine to make this instruction challenging for teachers. For one thing, as youths progress through the grades, the demands to read and write disciplinary and specialized texts increase; moreover, they are asked to do so for increasingly specialized purposes. Because of the changes in the literacy demands, the nature of literacy instruction needs to change after fourth grade and should become increasingly discipline-specific. Literacy becomes a requirement of content area learning and thus the responsibility of all teachers. Yet middle and high school teachers are generally required to take fewer courses in literacy instruction and development than are elementary teachers. What is more, any courses they are required to take tend to be overviews of literacy, rather than being embedded in the literacy practices integral and unique to particular content areas. Nor do these courses help middle and high school teachers develop the professional acumen needed to detect and appropriately address the needs of struggling students in their classes. These conditions are a reflection of licensure requirements and of current state standards, which provide little guidance about literacy in the content areas. Thus, today's adolescents do not necessarily receive quality reading and writing instruction linked to content and content area demands.

These problems cannot be solved simply by declaring every teacher a reading teacher or by adopting any one curriculum, no matter how powerful. Rather, they require a reconceptualization of adolescent literacy as the demanding and specialized practice that it is. For example, partnerships between literacy educators and subject matter teachers need to be promoted; literacy assessments need to reflect the domain-specific demands of literacy learning and use; and subject matter assessments and instruction need to reflect the reading, writing, and oral language skills that facilitate learning of the subject matter.

Reality #3: The Nature of Adolescents' Literacy Struggles Varies Widely

When teachers are asked what "typical" struggling adolescent readers look like, they usually emphasize that "typical" cannot describe the struggling adolescent reader. The Boston Higher Education Partnership Research Collaborative (BHEPRC) interviewed Boston middle school teachers about why adolescents struggle with literacy and found teachers' responses ranged widely. (Middle school teachers and administrators in Boston Public Schools have been sharing their perspectives on adolescent readers and writers with researchers from the BHEPRC since 2004. All quotes are from teacher interviews, and teacher and students names have been changed to protect anonymity.) One teacher explained, "One version of a poor reader is like Teresa. At the beginning of the year she had no understanding of what she read. A really poor reader is more like Jeremiah, who isn't reading at all unless you can get him completely focused. He is more of a worry than she is. His reading skills are better, but I worry about him more." Another emphasized the role of attitude in student performance: "Any given day a student could be in a great mood, and then another day they could totally be in a bad mood and that will totally affect your instruction in class." A different teacher highlighted how metacognitive strategies and prior experiences play interrelated roles in the struggles of adolescents: "The good readers and writers, they've learned...the metacognition...they've learned how to um, make up for any of their weaknesses.... The bad readers, either one of two things: either they don't know the strategies,...or they are just so frustrated from failure in the past." Other teachers point the finger at a lack of skills: "They lack so much...I am not going to say that elementary teachers don't work hard...but I don't know—the kids come with very few skills." As one teacher put it succinctly, "It depends on the kid...it really does."

The hard truth of the matter is that adolescents struggle with reading and writing in myriad ways and for myriad reasons. One of the difficulties in addressing the literacy needs of adolescents is the multiplicity of reading skills that older students are expected to have mastered. As students age, the set of expected reading skills grow; concurrently, the range of possible sources of reading difficulty grow as well. In fact, there is a wide array of skills and knowledge with which adolescents may struggle. Likewise, there are a multitude of social, cultural, and environmental factors that contribute to adolescents' struggles.

Skills and Knowledge as a Source of Struggle

The ability to determine the source of an individual student's reading difficulties begins by developing a clear understanding of the different components of reading that are necessary to successful reading comprehension—the building blocks supporting comprehension if you will. In order to paint a fuller picture, the following section includes a description of the major component skills of reading as well as anecdotal profiles of real adolescents who struggle with these skills.

DECODING. Many adolescent struggling readers—especially readers with learning disabilities—still struggle with sounding out words, a practice most commonly called decoding. Sad to say, however, struggles with decoding are not limited to adolescents faced with learning disabilities. But whenever adolescents struggle with decoding, they are likely to struggle in all areas of literacy. For instance, in one urban Midwestern district, eighth- and ninth-grade students who scored at the basic and unsatisfactory levels on state literacy assessments (akin to the basic and below basic levels on the NAEP) performed significantly below average in a wide range of reading component skills, including listening comprehension, letter–word identification, word attack, word reading efficiency, phonemic decoding efficiency, fluency, vocabulary, passage comprehension, and overall reading comprehension (Hock et al., 2006). Although the students assessed were not limited to those with learning disabilities, struggling adolescent readers in this district performed poorly on even basic decoding tasks. While such readers are not as atypical as we would necessarily prefer, they are not representative of all struggling adolescent readers.

Many struggling adolescent readers understand the rules of basic decoding but are not as familiar with the rules of decoding multisyllabic words. Recall the seventh graders at New Orleans's Hope Academy. Not one could read at higher than the third-grade level, yet most were able to decode at a basic level and struggled primarily with multisyllabic words. It would seem that the past several years' influx of money into early literacy programs emphasizing phonics instruction might reduce the number of students experiencing decoding difficulties in the near future. But multisyllabic decoding is not usually a focus of early literacy phonics instruction, and therefore many students are ill-prepared when they encounter texts that include an increasingly large proportion of previously unfamiliar multisyllabic words.

FLUENCY. Fluency is the ability to read with speed, accuracy, and phrasing so that the reader may focus on the act of making meaning of text. A failure to achieve reading fluency can be difficult to disentangle from other reading difficulties. Weaknesses in decoding and lack of reading practice can both lead to disfluent reading, and each weakness can cause readers to slow their reading to a point where comprehension is impeded. When decoding is not automatic, the reader's attention is on sounding out individual words rather than on making meaning of the whole. Often, even when slow decoders comprehend the beginnings of what they have read, they lose track of meaning as they progress through the text because their working memory becomes overwhelmed with the demands of both sounding out words and making sense of the text. It is not so surprising then that of the students at Boston's Hampshire Middle who evinced fluency problems, not a single Hampshire adolescent had fluency problems alone. Rather, struggles with fluency were always accompanied by struggles with comprehension and sometimes by struggles with accurate decoding.

Lack of reading practice also has an impact on fluency. Time spent reading not only helps to automatize decoding, it fosters familiarity—familiarity with different styles of writing, with words, and with knowledge of concepts that become the basis for understanding future reading material. As is frequently said, "practice makes perfect." And this familiarity increases the ease with which readers approach text and allows for fluent reading. This being the case, clearly students who read the least—most often economically poor students, ELLs, minority students, and special education students—are at a severe disadvantage in becoming strong readers (RAND Reading Study Group, 2002).

VOCABULARY AND BACKGROUND KNOWLEDGE. *Vocabulary* is defined as the knowledge of specific word meanings, whereas *background knowledge* is more often considered conceptual knowledge gained through familiarity or life experience. While the distinction is somewhat convoluted, consider the following example: Two students have lived in Southern Florida since birth. One has never left the state. The other has travelled to Vail, Colorado, to ski in winter. Neither student knows the meaning of the word *icicle*. The student who has travelled to Vail, however, has a much greater understanding of winter climate conditions and has seen an icicle without knowing what it was called. Both students must learn the meaning of the word *icicle*, but the student who has more conceptual or background knowledge related to the word—what an *icicle* looks like, how water freezes in nature, what cold feels like—is likely to have a much easier time attaching meaning to the word than the student with less conceptual knowledge or experience with cold climates. In spite of this distinction, vocabulary and background knowledge are inextricably linked and almost always co-occurring. In general, students with limited vocabularies usually have less background knowledge at their disposal and vice versa (Hirsch, 2003, 2006).

As hinted in the previous paragraph, limits to background and vocabulary knowledge can—but do not always—affect reading fluency (Perfetti, 1985; Perfetti & Bolger, 2004). This is because even the best of readers slow down when they encounter the unfamiliar and unknown. However, whether or not fluency is affected, weaknesses in background and vocabulary knowledge are almost certain to impede reading comprehension (Anderson, 2004; Hirsch, 2003, 2006; McNamara & Kintsch, 1996; Stahl, 2003; Wolfe et al., 1998).

It is well established that 90% to 95% of the total words in text must be known in order for students to adequately comprehend text (e.g., Carver, 1994; Chall, Jacobs, & Baldwin, 1990; Leslie & Caldwell, 1995; Na & Nation, 1985; Nagy & Scott, 2000). Furthermore, research is making it increasingly clear that limited vocabulary and background knowledge are most likely contributors to poor reading performance among a large subset of struggling adolescent readers (Biemiller, 2004; Chall & Jacobs, 2003; Chall et al., 1990; Nagy, 1988). In fact, problems with vocabulary were the strongest predictor of problems with comprehension for students at Boston's Fitzgerald School. In this predominantly Spanish–English bilingual school, half of the students performed below the 35th percentile rank on a standardized measure of reading vocabulary.

In a groundbreaking study, Hart and Risley (2003) found that there is a severe disparity in exposure to the spoken language when comparing middle class and poor children in the United States, with poor children hearing an estimated 30 million fewer words than their more affluent peers by third grade. Since repeated exposure is a requirement for learning new words and acquiring background knowledge, once again it is the economically disadvantaged adolescent who is most at risk for reading problems related to a lack of sufficient background and vocabulary knowledge.

While it is extremely hard to disentangle weaknesses in vocabulary and background knowledge in any practical sense, the following example may serve to clarify the distinction. The Fitzgerald students also illustrated differences between vocabulary and background knowledge. Although half of the students showed general vocabulary trouble on a standardized measure, their performance when they read expository texts aloud during an assessment of their reading fluency was strikingly different. As part of this measure, they read two different expository texts aloud: one about Mount Rainier and one about the Grand Canyon. Keep in mind that readability formulas and the assessment itself ranked the Grand Canyon passage as considerably more difficult than the Mount Rainier passage. Yet the Fitzgerald students performed much better on the Grand Canyon passage. Why? The Grand Canyon is a topic in the middle school curriculum at the Fitzgerald, one to which the seventh- and eighth-grade students had already been exposed, whereas Mount Rainier was a completely unfamiliar topic. Even though the vocabulary and syntax demands of the Mount Rainier text were less than the Grand Canyon text, most Fitzgerald students read the former text more slowly and with more errors than the latter text. It is important to note that, in spite of these examples, the two weaknesses are almost always co-occurring. In general, students with limited vocabularies usually have less background knowledge at their disposal and vice versa.

COMPREHENSION. Clearly, limitations in skills expected to be learned in elementary school—namely decoding, fluency, and vocabulary and background knowledge—all lead to reading comprehension difficulties for the adolescent reader. Students with weaknesses in any of these areas are in need of intervention in order to catch up with their peers. At the same time, many students who have mastered these skills still struggle with reading comprehension. For instance, among the students at Hampshire Middle in Boston nearly half struggled with comprehension alone, showing no problems with decoding or fluency.

Why is this? Repeatedly, research has shown that while some students have a natural inclination to "pick up" school-related skills by mere exposure, most students benefit from explicit instruction in almost every aspect of learning, including reading. Yet for many years schools have by and large neglected teaching students how to comprehend text and instead have expected students to acquire this ability without any direct instruction (Durkin, 1979, 1981; Pressley et al., 1998; Quirk et al., 1975; Taylor et al., 2000). This means that the challenges of older, struggling readers may reflect missed instructional opportunities accompanied by the ratcheting up of expectations regarding text comprehension, rather than an incapacity to comprehend (RAND Reading Study Group, 2002).

The students who are least likely to pick up school-related skills, like reading text to gain information without explicit instruction, are students with disabilities or those who come from less educated backgrounds and therefore homes where there is less familiarity with academic language and expectations. This means that a failure to provide this kind of instruction once again disadvantages the economically poor student, the ELL, the ethnic minority student, and the special education student.

But what are the particular practices with which these students struggle? They include basic comprehension skills, like simply getting the main idea or locating ideas in a text (Alvermann & Moore, 1991; Baker & Anderson, 1982; Garner & Reis, 1981; Johnston & Afflerbach, 1985; McKenna & Robinson, 1990; Moje, Young, Readance, & Moore, 2000; Stine-Morrow, Gagne, Morrow, & De Wall, 2004). They also include higher-level strategies, such as summarizing, making predictions, or questioning during and after reading as a means of fostering deeper comprehension (Alvermann & Moore, 1991; Brown & Day, 1983; Duffy, 1986; Garner, Wagoner, & Smith, 1983; McKoon & Ratcliff, 1986, 1989; Murray & Burke, 2003). Relatedly, they include metacognitive practices in which adolescents actively monitor the meaning they are making of texts and employ skills and strategies in an independent and problem-solving manner (Brown, Armbruster, & Baker, 1986; Cain, Oakhill, & Bryant, 2004; Cataldo & Cornoldi, 1998). Finally, they include the ability to be analytical about what has been read, often across multiple texts (Alvermann & Moore, 1991; Coiro, 2003; Goldman, 2004; Hartman, 1995; McKenna & Robinson, 1990; Moje et al., 2000). Adolescents may struggle with one or all of these areas of comprehension. So, for example, considering the Hampshire students who struggled with comprehension alone, most struggled with summarizing texts, but a smaller number struggled with making predictions. In particular, while they were relatively more able to make reasonable predictions about what they would learn after reading a page or two of an expository text, they were much weaker when it came to summarizing the entire text. Over half of the students gave especially poor summaries, which tended to focus on what they had read in the first page or two or to simply list a few facts they had gleaned, rather than synthesizing the information presented across the entire text.

Social, Cultural, and Educational Sources of Struggle

As the preceding section makes clear, adolescents have many skills and areas of knowledge that may underlie their struggles. However, the sources of their struggles do not always reside within their own skills or knowledge. Rather, they may have less easily defined—and measured—reasons for struggling. These reasons might be internal, such as their motivation for literacy or sense of hope for their own future. But the reasons are just as often external to an adolescent and include school structures, content area demands, discontinuities between home and school practices, and instructional histories.

MOTIVATION AND HOPE. In addition to the set of purely academic skills that are crucial to success in school, engagement and motivation take center stage in determining reading achievement for adolescent students (Guthrie, Alao, & Rinehart, 1997; Guthrie & Wigfield, 2000). The high dropout rate, an epidemic of chronic poor attendance, and the apathy exhibited by many older students who fail to participate in class or who fail to complete or even attempt to complete their school work (e.g., Eccles et al., 1993) point to the role of motivation in adolescent learning. A common complaint among teachers is that large numbers of bright-eyed and ambitious first graders who are mostly eager to participate and even willing to labor over independent reading all too often become bored and dispassionate by high school.

How and why do eager elementary students turn into increasingly disinterested adolescent students? It is true that adolescence is a time of both physical and emotional growth that can be distracting. However, even though motivation and hope are thought of as intrinsic to learners, they are influenced by school factors that too often contribute to a loss of engagement and motivation among adolescent students.

The demands placed on students grow—often dramatically—in middle school and continue to increase in high school. Students in secondary schools are expected to learn more—more information, more quickly, and more independently—than ever before. This results in an accompanying shift in how secondary students are taught. While elementary classrooms are often interactive in nature, with students learning from read-alouds, creative lessons, and even games, in too many secondary classrooms, there is an almost total emphasis on independent learning, with textbooks most often becoming the primary source for learning new material. When textbooks are the only reading material available to students, disengagement is a likely outcome, even for the brightest students.

For the able reader, this shift in expectations can be difficult enough and is best facilitated by explicit instruction and practice in how to learn from text. For weak readers, who are simply unable to read the materials that have now become their primary source for learning in school, making this shift is simply impossible and academic success appears unattainable. As one Boston middle school teacher noted, as repeated experiences of struggle and failure accumulate, students are less inclined to put forth effort. In such a case, loss of motivation and hope is an obvious outcome: How many of us make a voluntary choice to spend eight hours a day giving our all to something in which we are doomed to fail? Moreover, how many of us would retain any hope of ever succeeding?

These problems were illustrated in the assessment of Boston's Fitzgerald School students. In addition to assessing students' literacy skills, teachers opted to also assess their students' perceptions of themselves as readers using the Reader Self-Perception Survey (Henk & Melnick, 1995). This survey provides four self-perception scores: one for how students see themselves as making progress in reading, one for how they see themselves comparing with their peers in reading, one for how they believe others see them as readers, and one for how reading makes them feel. Judging from the numbers of students scoring below average by grade, teachers found that their students progressively saw themselves as comparing favorably with their peers in how well they read and in the progress they were making as readers. However, it was the individual students' results that shed the most light for teachers. The poorest readers were inevitably the ones who reported having negative feelings when reading, and for some reason a higher proportion of seventh graders reported negative feelings during reading. This information spurred the teachers to provide their students with more positive experiences, and not just with more directed instruction, in order to keep them motivated to read.

Unfortunately, it is precisely this sort of information that teachers seldom get from district and standardized assessments. Although the Fitzgerald teachers were interested in and adept at "reading" their students in many ways, even they were occasionally surprised by the survey of their students' self-perceptions. Most surprising of all to them was that a few high-achieving students reported low perceptions of themselves across the board. This was an especially poignant wake-up call for the teachers, as they came to realize that one cannot simply assume that the best readers are the most motivated or happiest readers.

SCHOOLING EXPERIENCES. Structural differences between elementary and secondary schools also contribute to adolescents' struggles with literacy. These differences are evident in everything from how the typical school day is structured to how many people—students and teachers—make up each school. Because of these differences, there are unique challenges to implementing a successful literacy program in middle and high schools.

First, the transition from the familiar to an entirely new environment and accompanying academic expectations presents difficulties for many students. The difficulties inherent in the typically abrupt transition from the elementary school to the middle school experience has led Boston to pilot several K–8 schools. Fitzgerald is one of these schools. This model has proven to provide a helpful continuity for students as they make the transition to the heightened demands of a middle school curriculum. For instance, instead of learning to navigate within a new and larger school, while at the same time adjusting to the different academic demands of a subject-divided school day, sixth-grade students at Fitzgerald have the luxury of tackling new academic demands while embedded in the small community that they have already been a part of for six years. Elementary-grade teachers keep an eye on their students long after they leave their classrooms. Middle-grade teachers also frequently make use of their easy access to their students' earlier teachers in planning and adapting their instruction. And it is the additional support provided by this continuity that is commonly cited by teachers at Fitzgerald as being a core reason for their success with students, especially those students in grades 6 through 8.

Time constraints are also a huge issue in middle and secondary schools. For instance, the heavy content learning and testing demands placed on students leave little time for targeted instruction in necessary literacy skills. Additionally, in middle and high schools the language arts classroom is commonly considered the only forum appropriate for literacy—and therefore reading comprehension—instruction. However, the language arts curriculum has its own heavy set of learning demands in terms of grammar, literary criticism, and writing, and covering these leaves little time for thorough instruction in reading comprehension, let alone time to remediate basic literacy skills. Finally, even if there were time in the language arts classroom for such instruction to occur, this would not be enough to prepare many secondary students to succeed, as the next section on reading in the content areas will make clear.

In addition to time constraints, implementing effective literacy instruction in middle and high schools is made difficult by a sheer increase in numbers. Middle and high schools are typically large, with more students and teachers than in elementary schools. And students no longer learn from the same teacher for a full school day. Instead, students move from class to class, typically in classes with a high student-to-teacher ratio.

For these reasons, implementing effective literacy instruction in middle and high schools is a time intensive effort, much more so than in elementary schools. Because middle and high school teachers typically see more students less often and for less time, it is more difficult for teachers to know their students' literacy learning needs. It is also more difficult for literacy instruction to be coherent across the curriculum. Time is needed for teachers to create that coherence. Schoolwide professional development time is required to allow *all* teachers to learn how to successfully include appropriate literacy instruction in their respective content area classes. Time is also required for teachers to retool their lessons and to do the collaborative work required to achieve schoolwide coherence in literacy instruction. But given the heavy demands placed on teachers who must prepare their students for increasingly rigorous high school graduation requirements and for college, finding this time can be a daunting task.

Administrators at the Hope Academy in New Orleans tackled these challenges by making schedule changes that built the necessary time into teachers' schedules. Three days a week, the school day began 40 minutes later for students than for teachers. This allowed the entire faculty to be available for collaborative work three mornings each week. One morning session each week was devoted to schoolwide professional development around literacy; one to grade level, cross-curricular discussion, and planning; and one to discipline-specific discussion and planning across grade levels. As a result, a shared vocabulary and understanding of literacy began to develop among teachers. This in turn, led to the emergence of a common set of literacy strategies being taught across classrooms and across grade levels that, in turn, allowed students enough practice to truly begin to "own" a toolkit of effective literacy strategies.

In addition to these more general issues, many students face structural challenges that are not shared by all. For instance, tracking is still a widely used practice. Although it makes a certain amount of sense for college-bound high school students to take rigorous courses that prepare them for the demands of college, too often the courses for students not bound for college include far less rigor, even though better literacy skills are required than ever before for success in the current society and economy. As a result, texts, instruction, and tasks vary in quality depending on students' tracks. Moreover, once students have been assigned to a track, it becomes difficult to break out of that track.

Furthermore, adolescent students who struggle the most spend much or all of their school time in remedial programs. These programs often concentrate on teaching remedial skills—phonics and the like—to the exclusion of teaching content that is on grade level. Yet, as discussed above, the students in these classes may or may not require decoding instruction. Even when decoding instruction is precisely what a students needs, these programs pose a problem. Since these students are typically cognitively capable of learning complex ideas, the outcome of spending day after day doing basic and often rote tasks is boredom, loss of interest, and little exposure to the knowledge and practices required for success outside school.

A final and particularly daunting structural challenge in secondary schools is the "ninth grade phenomenon" (Wheelock & Miao, 2005).The phenomenon refers to the rate at which students disappear between grades 9 and 10; a rate that has tripled over the last 30 years. For example, 440,000 students who were enrolled in grade 9 in 1998–1999 did not show up in grade 10 in 1999–2000 (11.4% of students). By the end of the century, the grade 9 to 10 transition was clearly the largest leak in the educational pipeline (Haney et al., 2004). A concomitant problem is that 57% of the students retained in grade 9 drop out by the end of four years, compared with 11% of their peer group (Neild, Stoner-Eby, & Furstenberg, 2001).

There have been a number of explanations proffered for the ninth-grade phenomenon, including the waves of academic reforms that introduced standards-based curriculum and high-stakes assessment. Other hypotheses concern the sense of anonymity that ninth graders may experience as they make the transition from middle to secondary school, the increase in academic demands, and the experience of greater differentiation by academic ability.

The higher a student progresses in the educational system without receiving appropriate intervention, the less and less likely it is that he or she will ever receive appropriate intervention. A common practice in high schools is for ninth graders who do not meet expectations to be retained in ninth grade. Thus, ninth-grade classes, especially those for the non–college-bound, tend to have more students facing more struggles with literacy, which in turn makes it even less likely that they will receive the help they need.

READING ACROSS THE CONTENT AREAS. There is an oft-spoken claim that "every teacher is a teacher of reading." We challenge this claim, arguing that it reduces reading and texts to mere tools for supporting knowledge building within and across domains. The alternative we wish to offer is that literacy skills, including reading, are shaped by the domain in which they are practiced. That is, reading in science is not equivalent to reading in language arts or in math. Although reading in each of the content areas depends on many of the same skills and knowledge, reading becomes more disciplinarily grounded in later grades. Reading is about coming to a deep understanding and appreciation of the nature of the subject matter and learning to read texts within content areas from the perspective of, say, an historian, a scientist, a mathematician, or an artist. Broadly speaking, it is about coming to understand the big ideas within domains, but it is also about learning how these big ideas were generated, evaluated, and eventually received by their respective communities. In essence, it is about *reading* the domain, and, in secondary school, *reading across* domains.

This is a critical issue in adolescent literacy precisely because reading, and writing, becomes the essence of content area learning. Yet, all too often, curricula and schools approach reading and writing as mere tools, when far more than instrumental use is demanded of students. In fact, content knowledge and strategy use are inextricably intertwined; students who know something about a topic are more likely to engage in productive activity to learn more about that topic (Alexander & Judy, 1988). Because the demands of text are often specific to each discipline, transfer of reading comprehension skills is not automatic. Instead, students need explicit instruction and guided practice specific to each discipline. When we fail to teach comprehension skills across the curriculum, many students' struggles with reading are likely to manifest as a failure in content area knowledge.

Understanding how this plays out for adolescents is difficult to imagine. Indeed, we tend to speak of a struggling reader as though the reader struggles equally with all things. In reality the struggling reader can struggle with one or more specific reading skills, or with a specific type of text. Consider, for example, the students at Fitzgerald. Although most of the fifth-grade students there who struggled with reading fluency struggled equally with narrative and expository texts, among the sixth- through eighth-grade students, very few showed any problems with narrative texts, but expository texts stood out as a source of difficulty. That is, middle school students who showed no signs of decoding or fluency problems when reading typical language arts types of text did have problems when reading other content area texts. Although it is tempting to attribute these differences to potential differences in vocabulary and background knowledge, these texts also clearly used different structures and made different demands than the narratives did.

For instance, reading science texts requires both domain-specific prior knowledge and reading strategies. Prior knowledge includes not only the domain of science (e.g., physics, chemistry, life science) or a specific topic within the domain (e.g., motion and energy within physics); it also includes knowledge of the nature of science and how the scientific community generates and evaluates received scientific knowledge. Specifically, scientists adhere to rules of evidence and argumentation (Duschl & Hamilton, 1998) that are different for most other domains. Students need to learn how to evaluate and generate scientific texts in terms of these rules. In addition, students need to learn to distinguish claims from evidence, conclusions from observations, and justifications from explanations (Norris & Phillips, 1994). The National Science Education Standards (National Research Council, 1996) actually delineate that scientific literacy includes the capacity to read and evaluate written information. The research of Norris and Phillips tells us that these interpretive skills are not developed without care and attention. Reading and interpretation skills need to be cultivated while a student is in school. In fact, the process of teaching science text from an inquiry stance (Hapgood, Magnusson, & Palincsar, 2004; Palincsar, Magnusson, Collins, & Cutter, 2001) can support students in assuming a critical stance toward text. Unfortunately, such teaching tends to be the exception rather than the rule.

In contrast to how reading and writing are practiced in science, reading and writing in each of the other content areas emphasize different purposes and strategies. Asking the question "What is the evidence for this claim?" is relevant whether one is studying historical documents, a science text, a mathematical proof, or an interpretation of literature; however, what counts as evidence differs across these domains. In history and the social sciences, readers and writers are expected to negotiate several texts, both historical and contemporary, to arrive at an objective as possible account of an event. As in science, this is not a practice that comes naturally or easily. Moreover, as in science, there are specific but different rules for what counts as evidence for a claim (Mosborg, 2002; Perfetti, Britt, & Georgi, 1995). In mathematics, the conventions of reading and writing mathematics texts differ from both science and history conventions. An area of particular challenge in math is both the sheer volume of unique vocabulary and the frequent reliance on unique mathematical understandings of words used in everyday English (e.g., *factor, product, rational, origin, mean, odd, face*). Furthermore, math word problems are a genre encountered nowhere else and an area of particular challenge to adolescents (Leong & Jerred, 2001). Finally, as noted in the preceding section, the language arts also have their own unique reading and writing demands that require specific practices for success. Learning to read, comprehend, and interpret a poem is not a skill that is relevant in other content area classrooms. Moreover, just as the other content areas have their own rules for evidence, the rules for evidence in language arts are unique, with literary analysis being particularly tolerant of disagreement and divergent interpretations of the same "evidence" (Applebee, Langer, Nystrand, & Gamoran, 2003).

CONTEXT DEPENDENCE OF ADOLESCENT LITERACY. Any discussion of adolescents' struggles with reading must acknowledge that although young people may struggle with in-school literacy practices, they usually have experience and expertise with literacy practices outside of school. Just as adolescents can exhibit problems with literacy in one content area but not another, many adolescents can exhibit proficiency in one context but not another. Reading is *not* reading no matter where or when or how it is done; reading is shaped by contexts, and contexts influence both practices and the meaning we draw from texts (RAND Reading Study Group, 2002).

In- and out-of-school literacy practices can be conceptualized as occurring in different "spaces" (Bhabha, 1994; Gutiérrez et al., 1999; Soja, 1996). The "first space" is informal and found in homes, communities, and peer networks, while the "second space" is more formal and encountered in work, school, and church. The integration of these two spaces is conceptualized as a "third space" because the work of bridging sometimes widely disparate worlds of home and school can be so challenging. But this third space is what is so often absent from adolescents' experiences in school. Instead, their out-of-school practices tend to be ignored or, worse, denigrated (Moje et al., 2004).

This attitude is perhaps most evident in the fourth myth discussed earlier. Society as a whole and even excellent teachers often place blame for students' struggles on the mismatch between home and school practices. One of the Fitzgerald teachers repeatedly bemoaned the fact that there was "so much these kids don't get at home" and that this was a primary reason for their struggles. Yet the same teacher argued that a key to helping the Fitzgerald adolescents perform well on state tests was allowing them to express their "voice" in their writing. This focus is something shared by all the middle school teachers at Fitzgerald and indeed may be one of the prime motivators in Fitzgerald writing performance. Interestingly, these conflicting opinions, discounting and valuing the students' out-of-school experiences, are appealed to as explanations for why the Fitzgerald students perform as they do on literacy assessments.

The situation at Fitzgerald is echoed in another predominantly Latino/a community and public school in Detroit (Moje et al., 2004). There, adolescents seldom brought out-of-school funds of knowledge to bear in the (science) classroom context even though these funds were sufficiently rich with possibilities not only to build bridges between in- and out-of-school contexts but also to expand and deepen understanding of the target content knowledge. In contrast to the language arts teachers at Fitzgerald, the Detroit teachers did not actively develop a "third space" for students.

One of the most obvious contrasts between in- and out-of-school contexts involves the reading and production of multimedia texts. Global popular media, including online cultures, have become integrally bound up with children's and youths' affiliations, identities, and pleasures (Hull, 2003; Lankshear & Knobel, 2002; Leander, 2003). The average child in the United States lives in a household with 2.9 televisions, 1.8 VCRs, 3.1 radios, 2.6 tape players, 2.1 CD players, 1.4 video game players, and 1 computer (Gitlin, 2001). Youths' participation in this media culture shapes the ways they communicate and the kinds of social identities they assume.

This kind of social participation is integral to the ways in which youths have come to make and contest meaning in their daily lives and, therefore, is of central import to educators. Technology modifies both expectations and strategies for meaning-making during reading, yet this aspect of adolescent literacy is largely ignored in language arts and other content area classrooms (Leander & Lovvorn, 2006).

At both the Fitzgerald and Hampshire schools, computer literacy is taught separately from reading and writing. Students attend this class, usually referred to as a "special," a few times a week. In some cases, other teachers collaborate with the computer teacher to link the computer-class activities to content area learning. But activities tend to focus on using programs like PowerPoint to create multimedia reports or represent information in graphs. They do not focus on how technology, especially the Internet, places new demands on the reader, including the necessity to critically evaluate the credibility and usefulness of information. Indeed, we have only begun to construct ways of teaching students to read on the Internet, helping them to coordinate, integrate, and evaluate information for its credibility and relevance to the questions guiding the user (Palincsar & Dalton, 2005; Palincsar & Ladewski, 2006).

EDUCATIONAL HISTORY. The final source of adolescent literacy struggles to consider is educational history. Although it is a deceptively simple idea, adolescents' prior education has a profound influence on whether and how they struggle with reading and writing.

The most obvious influence on adolescent literacy struggles is when elementary education emphasizes word-level skills at the expense of developing vocabulary, comprehension, and content knowledge. This lack of emphasis on meaning-making can lead to students getting the idea that reading is only about reading words as accurately and quickly as possible and may be one reason that we have so many word callers in our schools.

Even when instruction has been optimal in the elementary grades, many students begin to experience problems in their adolescent years because reading instruction, other than remedial instruction, largely stops after third grade. As noted earlier, comprehension instruction in particular is a real weak spot in U.S. classrooms (Durkin, 1979, 1981; Pressley et al., 1998; Quirk et al., 1975; Taylor et al., 2000). And even when instruction takes place, it tends to be located solely in the language arts classroom.

Instructional history is of particular importance for a subgroup of adolescents, namely English-language learners. Given the rapidly growing population of ELLs in American schools—an increase of 105% in that population over the last 10 years versus an increase of only 12% in the general school population (National Center for Education Statistics, 2006a)—developing these adolescents' linguistic knowledge and skill is particularly important. In general, research has shown that ELLs can develop word reading skills comparable to their native English-speaking peers (e.g., Lesaux & Siegel, 2003), but that they lag behind when it comes to comprehension (National Center for Education Statistics, 2006b). However, in some contexts, they perform equivalently to their monolingual peers (Lesaux et al., 2006) and can even outperform them after several years in an educational system (New York City Public Schools Division of Assessment and Accountability, 2000).

What is of more importance than whether students are ELLs or not is how the education system has dealt with them. For instance, ELLs who enter the system when they are young, appear to outperform those who enter when they are adolescents. This is in part because older students have more to learn; they must learn a new language as well as master challenging content in several classes. But it is also due to the fact that fiscal resources for supporting ELLs and struggling readers tend to be focused on kindergarten through third grade.

Even though younger ELLs have certain advantages, it is important to recognize that over half of adolescent ELLs have been in the U.S. educational system from the very beginning, yet they still qualify as having only limited English proficiency (Capps et al., 2005; Short & Fitzsimmons, 2007). Although the reasons behind this fact are too complicated to discuss in any detail here, there are a few reasons that are worth highlighting. For one, research has shown that switching instructional programs (e.g., from English immersion to bilingual support, or vice versa) has an adverse effect on English language and literacy mastery (New York City Public Schools Division of Assessment and Accountability, 2000). Poverty and high rates of family mobility are each a related reason, as is the likelihood of heavy out-of-school responsibilities. We know, for example, that the more a student moves from school to school, the more likely he or she is to struggle (Astone & McLanahan, 1994; Pribesh & Downey, 1999). Indeed, when students move across districts or states, it is highly likely that the instructional programs they experience will also change.

Finally, the educational experiences that immigrant ELLs have before they enter the United States are also extremely important. For instance, some immigrants arrive fully fluent in English and with a solid educational background. More likely, however, they enter with limited or no English knowledge and a great deal of variability in the education they experienced previously. Some adolescents enter U.S. schools illiterate in their own language, let alone English (Short & Boyson, 2004), because of lack of access to educational opportunities in their homelands due to military conflict, isolated locales that cannot attract full-time teachers, seasonal agricultural demands, or other reasons (Isserlis, 2000).

All of these factors come into play at Boston's Fitzgerald School, where over 90% of the students are Latino/a and 75% are ELLs. Located in a predominantly Latino community, the school has an influx of new students each year, many of whom are new to the United States and the American educational system. In 2005, a fifth-grade teacher welcomed a new student who turned out to be almost entirely deaf in addition to knowing very little English; months were wasted trying to get her appropriate supports. Due to space limitations, students who have not acquired fluency in English by the end of fifth grade switch to a different school for continued English-language support in their middle school years. Undoubtedly, the deaf student was one of these at the end of the year. Although Boston has a consistent policy for instructing ELLs, this change still puts the youths who switch schools at increased risk. Indeed, Fitzgerald's success with adolescent literacy may be due both to the loss of these students and to the consistency of the schooling experiences of those who remain. In fact, Boston is considering switching from a middle school organization to a K–8 organization citywide.

Reality #4: Variability in Struggles Means Intervention Is Complicated and Assessment Indispensable

Ultimately, every struggling adolescent reader has difficulty with reading comprehension. However, the variety of underlying causes for these reading comprehension difficulties makes helping struggling adolescent readers a difficult proposition. The variability in adolescents' literacy difficulties and the sources of those difficulties more or less guarantee that no single program or instructional method will solve every problem or every adolescent struggling with literacy.

Thus, it is critical that educators take into account the myriad instructional and structural supports that should also be in place to ensure adolescents improve their literacy. In addition, intervening with struggling adolescents is complicated by the fact that we have less time to make a difference. The further a student has progressed in the educational system, the more important it is that we intervene in targeted ways.

Therefore, it is a dangerous mistake to assume that a one-size-fits-all remedial program for struggling adolescent readers will suffice in the middle and high school classroom. Instead, middle and high schools will need to be prepared to address the needs of a diverse group. However, prior to addressing those needs, schools need to be able to discover and detail those needs. Unfortunately, the state literacy tests that adolescents take do not help schools very much in this process. Although they identify students who are not meeting standards, they yield little if any information about why they are not meeting standards. Thus, schools need to utilize more nuanced tests that provide rich information about students' reading and writing skills. These tests may include standardized, norm-referenced assessments of certain specific literacy skills rather than overall literacy achievement (for instance, a test that solely assesses student reading vocabulary), as such tests provide comparisons of students' abilities with those of a large group of their peers. But they will also need to include judicious use of diagnostic assessments, which permit close analysis of students' literacy strengths and weaknesses (for instance, tests that distinguish between word reading accuracy and word reading speed). Districts and schools that do not first somehow assess the nature of their students' literacy strengths and struggles inevitably set themselves up for failure, because without this information it is impossible to truly match adolescent literacy initiatives to student needs.

Conclusion

We hope that this chapter has clarified what the current state of adolescent literacy is in the United States, as well as what it is not. Although struggling adolescent readers have always existed, the changing face of American and global society means that it is more critical than ever before in history that we truly take on the challenge of addressing their needs. The challenge is not a small one, but the information we have presented here has hopefully conveyed that it is a manageable one.

In the following chapters, we address the content and characteristics of adolescent literacy instruction that help to address adolescents' myriad needs. Chapter 2 focuses on the content of adolescent literacy instruction: the skills, strategies, and behaviors that students need to learn. Chapter 3 focuses on the characteristics of adolescent literacy instruction: the ways and means of providing the most powerful instruction in adolescent literacy content. Chapters 4 and 5 then consider the costs and organizational issues involved in preparing to improve adolescent literacy instruction and intervention. As we discuss these topics, we continue to share some of the ways that schools, both those discussed earlier and others, have attempted to address the challenges their students face.

CHAPTER 2

The Content of Adolescent Literacy Instruction

*Marnie Nair, Donald D. Deshler, Gina Biancarosa,
& Annemarie Sullivan Palincsar*

B ECAUSE COMPREHENSION IS THE end-goal of reading in middle and high school, the reading difficulties of almost every struggling adolescent manifest as problems with comprehension. However, at best this is a limited assessment of the problem. As we discussed in Chapter 1, varying combinations of component skills (decoding, fluency, vocabulary and background knowledge, and comprehension), as well as social, cultural, and educational factors, can lie at the root of any one adolescent's struggles with literacy. Although some subset of these skills will form the basis of almost every strong adolescent literacy program, it is unlikely that any two programs will look exactly alike.

Before delving into these skills, it is critical for the educator looking to improve adolescent literacy in his or her district to note two things. First, there is need for precision in determining which skills are areas of weakness particular to each school and even within each school, as there is likely to be variation across students, highlighting the absolute necessity of ongoing accurate diagnostic literacy assessment. In addition to introducing some basic information as to what type of instruction has been proven to work, the examples throughout this chapter will illustrate how different schools have worked to build a literacy program specific to their needs.

Second, having the "correct" content is but one step in developing an effective adolescent literacy initiative. Educators who want to improve adolescent literacy also need to consider how instruction is delivered. We discuss this at length in Chapter 3, but suffice it to say here that effective literacy instruction for middle and high school students will and should in many respects look very different than effective instruction for elementary students.

Decoding (For Those Who Need It)

Decoding is fundamental to all reading, and certainly any decoding difficulties must be remediated *when they exist*. At the same time, it is critical that even in such cases decoding instruction not be construed as a "first" step. That is, instruction in other skills and inclusion in other literacy opportunities should not be held up while decoding difficulties are remediated. Rather, even adolescent students with poor basic decoding skills need to be supported in the acquisition of higher-level literacy skills and of grade-appropriate content in other subject areas. How this kind of integrated instruction gets accomplished is discussed in more depth in Chapter 3.

In addition, it is important to remember that while decoding can prove difficult for some secondary readers, studies indicate that there is considerable variability in the proportion of struggling adolescent readers whose difficulties include deficient decoding skills. For instance, while some have found relatively small percentages of students who demonstrated pervasive reading difficulties that included decoding problems (Biancarosa et al., 2006; Buly & Valencia, 2002; Lesaux et al., 2006), others have found that a third or more struggle with decoding as well as with a large number of other literacy skills (Catts et al., 2005; Hock et al., 2006; Leach et al., 2003). In spite of this, adolescent literacy programs commonly overrely on stressing basic decoding skills as the central remedy for adolescent literacy difficulties. Therefore, it is important to determine whether decoding is in fact an issue when adolescents struggle to read and thereby what role decoding instruction plays in potential adolescent literacy interventions.

For instance, at Hope Academy where few students read well, most students had enough exposure over the years to the most common single-syllable words that they had learned to recognize them, even without proper decoding instruction. Yet Hope students struggled to read unfamiliar and multisyllabic words. As discussed in Chapter 1, this weakness is often simply the outcome of a failure to offer necessary instruction to students. Because of changing curriculum and instructional trends, decoding—especially advanced decoding—weaknesses are too often found to be schoolwide or even systemwide. Such was the case in the Midwestern urban district that found that students who scored at basic or unsatisfactory levels on state literacy assessments *typically* had broad-based weaknesses in even the most basic literacy skills (Hock et al., 2006).

The good news is that the remedy for decoding weakness is straightforward. While students with learning difficulties typically need many more repetitions of new learning than do students who simply lack adequate instruction, remediating all decoding weakness requires phonics instruction that is sequential and systematic. It is also preferential that the instruction be time-intensive. This is not only because decoding is a prerequisite to all reading but also because of the role of motivation for adolescent learners. Learning phonics in middle or high school is an embarrassing proposition for most students and, therefore, the faster learned (and progressed beyond) the better. That said, mastering something so fundamental after many years of failure is also highly motivating for students who may have lost hope of ever being able to successfully participate in school; success with decoding instruction can provide a highly motivating early victory for readers who do struggle with decoding.

For instance, at Churchill Prep, a mid-Atlantic private secondary school for students with diagnosed learning disabilities, some students do still struggle with basic decoding. Many more struggle to read unfamiliar multisyllabic words. In order to determine the difference, a specialist administers an informal decoding assessment to each incoming student. Students who struggle with basic decoding are given daily one-on-one, sequential, and systematic phonics instruction until they have reached mastery of basic decoding. Since many more students struggle with multisyllabic decoding, all teachers are given training in syllabification, and in each content area class teachers and students work together to syllabify words that are previewed before reading the text. Providing teachers with such professional development can be a homegrown effort tailored to a school's or district's particular students, or it can center on one or more of the excellent professional books that provide guidance in this type of instruction (Bear, Invernizzi, Templeton, & Johnston, 2003; Beck, 2005; Ganske, 2000; Pinnell & Fountas, 1998). Or addressing decoding can rely on curricula such as those reviewed in the second half of this book. Note that many of these books and programs rightly emphasize the role that writing can play in enhancing metalinguistic awareness.

Fluency

Fluency is a common but often overlooked area of weakness for many adolescent readers. As discussed in Chapter 1, practice reading is the primary predictor of fluency. As logically follows, practice is also the cure for disfluent reading and, in keeping with this, a multitude of programs have been proposed that are designed to increase the time students spend reading. A number of excellent professional books provide teachers with guidance in fluency instruction (Rasinski, 2003; Rasinski, Blachowicz, & Lems, 2006; Samuels & Farstrup, 2006), but we highlight here some of the most pertinent issues for adolescents.

Many students spend little time reading independently because they do not have access to reading materials. For example, studies have repeatedly shown that children who live in poverty have substantially fewer—and often no—books in their homes or even in their communities (Neuman & Celano, 2001). A related problem (and perhaps just as serious) is that many schools lack an abundance of high-interest-leveled reading materials in an array of genres to provide students with the ample practice that they need (Worthy, Moorman, & Turner, 1999). Because struggling readers typically grow progressively less interested in participating in an activity at which they remain unsuccessful, it is also important to consider ways to motivate students to spend the necessary time reading independently (Guthrie et al., in press).

In addition to this, it is important to offer disfluent readers the opportunity to *hear* good reading. This can be accomplished through read-alouds or guided reading techniques that not only expose students to the rhythm and intonation of written text but also provide them with the opportunity to hear the proper pronunciation of new words (Carlisle & Rice, 2002).

At Hope Academy, very few students had been read to as young children. Fewer spent time reading books as adolescents. There were no books in a majority of their homes, and elementary schools in the area were notorious for the absence of even basic textbooks. Fluency rates were correspondingly low across the school. Two initiatives were implemented to build fluency among the students. First, a schoolwide DEAR (Drop Everything and Read) time was implemented. For 20 minutes following lunch each day, every person—both adults and students—in the building read a book. Sometimes teachers read aloud, but most days students read from a book they had checked out from the library and that was kept in their after-lunch classroom for this express purpose. In order to encourage participation, each student received a bookmark with space for the teacher to sign for each day that the student read quietly during DEAR. The student could redeem each full bookmark for pizza on a designated day.

However, DEAR time has been roundly criticized for ineffectiveness because students often choose books that are inappropriately challenging for them. Perhaps partly because of their recognition of the mixed evidence on simply having students read more, the second initiative at Hope Academy was to implement seventh-grade reading groups. For a week, teachers actively listened to and observed their students reading aloud. Based on this data and common training, teachers then grouped students of similar fluency levels into groups of four. Teachers then chose a book for each group. Because they knew the students well by this point, they were able to recommend books that were not only leveled appropriately but also would interest the group members.

As a final step in the drive to improve fluency at Hope Academy, volunteers and teachers were trained in guided reading techniques (Fountas & Pinnell, 2001, 2006; Rasinski et al., 2006; Samuels & Farstrup, 2006). Each group of four students, plus the adult leader, met twice weekly for 45 minutes for a group reading and book discussion. This intervention, coupled with DEAR time, substantially improved students' fluency levels. But perhaps most importantly, these initiatives began to cultivate a belief that reading is an enjoyable and positive activity.

Vocabulary and Background Knowledge

Research has repeatedly shown that vocabulary—and background knowledge—are robust predictors of reading comprehension (Anderson, 2004; Hirsch, 2003; Stahl, 2003). Fortunately, many guidelines exist for effective instruction (August, Carlo, Dressler, & Snow, 2005; Beck, McKeown, & Kucan, 2002; Hiebert &

Kamil, 2005; Nagy, 1988; Stahl & Nagy, 2005). The aim of such instruction is to offer "deep" vocabulary instruction, which not only builds the number of words that students know but also improves the depth of understanding of these words as well as the concepts that surround them. It is especially important for content area teachers to recognize that knowing words is more than recognizing them or being able to define them; knowing words includes a deep understanding of how words interrelate and can be used in multiple ways and have multiple meanings (Beck et al., 2002; Nagy & Scott, 2000). This is also a common area of weakness for English-language learners (ELLs) (Biancarosa et al., 2006; Umbel, Pearson, Fernandez, & Oller, 1992; Verhallen & Schoonen, 1993). Therefore, although vocabulary instruction is important for all adolescents, it has been recognized as especially important for ELLs (American Educational Research Association, 2004; Carlo et al., 2004; Genesee, Lindholm-Leary, Saunders, & Christian, 2005; Goldenberg, 2006).

> It is especially important for content area teachers to recognize that knowing words is more than recognizing them or being able to define them.

Sound principles of vocabulary instruction should guide teachers. One important principle advocated by many is pushing students to become active learners of words by providing them with opportunities and the motivation to talk about, compare, analyze, and use target words and by providing these opportunities on multiple occasions (August et al., 2005; Beck et al., 2002; Nagy & Scott, 2000).

One approach to vocabulary instruction designed specifically for ELLs is to help students recognize cognates: words that share similar spellings and definitions in their first and second languages (August et al., 2005; Carlo et al., 2004). An example of a Spanish cognate would be *atleta* (athlete). Exploiting cognates takes advantage of students' first-language knowledge and therefore ensures that ELLs, especially recent immigrants, understand basic words as well as the more sophisticated words that are typically targeted in vocabulary instruction (August et al., 2005).

At Boston's Fitzgerald School, assessments of the fifth- through eighth-grade students revealed vocabulary to be an area of common weakness. Nearly every student who scored more than a half standard deviation below the average on a standardized reading comprehension measure *also* scored below average on a standardized vocabulary measure. Consequently, Fitzgerald has partnered with researchers to implement new approaches to vocabulary instruction designed to take advantage of students' cognate knowledge and to expand their academic vocabulary, especially in the content areas. While the cognate-centered approach is targeted at fourth-grade students, the academic vocabulary curriculum, which is being piloted in several Boston middle schools including Hampshire, targets students in sixth through eighth grade. The latter curriculum attempts to emphasize high-utility academic words that are used across subject areas: words such as *invalidated*, *fundamentally*, *observe*, and *diverse*. New words are introduced by English language arts teachers each week but are reinforced throughout the week by teachers in the other content areas. In addition to providing students with the multiple, meaningful encounters with words that is so critical to learning vocabulary, the hope is that using the words across contexts will also encourage students to use the words and better understand their multiple uses and meanings.

As noted in Chapter 1, vocabulary is related to but different from background knowledge. Background knowledge is a reflection of a life experience and therefore is highly variable across students. Urban students may exhibit a lack of background knowledge about all things rural, while newly arrived immigrant ELL students may exhibit a lack of background knowledge about American culture. On the other hand, students who have a particular interest or hobby may suddenly surprise us with their vocabulary knowledge about a topic that they have spent independent time investigating. For students who have grown up in poverty and with little opportunity to explore the wider world, building background knowledge can be especially important. As might be expected, in addition to deep vocabulary instruction, background knowledge is also built by exposure to new concepts, places, and ideas.

Similar to the situation at Boston's Fitzgerald School, both vocabulary and background knowledge were areas of weakness for almost every student at New Orleans's Hope Academy. Consequently, the school targeted these areas across all grades and subject areas in several ways. First, a schoolwide vocabulary building program was introduced. Each week, a list of 10 words that were likely to occur across disciplines was posted on a word wall in the main hallway of the school. On this posting, each word was defined and was listed with its part of speech and an example sentence. Teachers were then asked to have repeated discussions about each word throughout the week, paying particular attention to each word's significance and possible uses in their particular discipline. In addition, an incentive program was introduced that recognized students when they used any of the words introduced to date. As an additional step to improving students' vocabulary and background knowledge, teachers were asked to identify and preteach vocabulary words important to their current unit of study and received professional development on how vocabulary instruction was best facilitated. Finally, monthly field trips—planned by content area teachers in rotation—were instituted at the school in order to supplement the acquisition of relevant conceptual and background knowledge. These trips were seen as opportunities to bring abstract concepts to life for students and provide them with experiences to bolster their understanding of knowledge gained at school.

Direct and Explicit Comprehension Instruction

Research proposes that direct and explicit comprehension instruction should be a part of all good adolescent literacy instruction (Biancarosa & Snow, 2004). This is especially true given that even strong elementary school readers often begin to struggle when they are faced with the advanced comprehension tasks required in middle and particularly high school. Once again, this is often simply due to lack of instruction because, while the challenge in learning to read well does not end when students learn how to decipher words on a page, reading instruction commonly ends there.

Research shows that instruction in comprehension strategies can be especially effective in improving students' ability to make meaning of text. In addition to teaching basic comprehension skills like summarizing, sequencing, and finding the main idea, it is important to explicitly teach students how to use cognitive strategies—such as using contextual cues (e.g., text features such as embedded questions) and text structure to support learning from text. Once introduced, students must also learn how to think metacognitively—or to determine which strategy is appropriate to apply to a given reading task. Altogether, these skills allow students to comprehend well enough to address critical thinking tasks. However, it is also important to recognize critical thinking as a skill in need of direct instruction (Alvermann & Moore, 1991; Dole, Duffy, Roehler, & Pearson, 1991; National Institute of Child Health and Human Development [NICHD], 2000; Pressley, 2000).

While all readers benefit from strategies for monitoring and repairing comprehension, these strategies seem to play a more important role for ELLs due to their more frequent encounters with unfamiliar vocabulary words. Successful ELL readers are able to marshal their reading strategies to compensate for the comprehension-inhibiting effect of unfamiliar vocabulary, implying the added importance of strategies for ELLs looking to build their vocabularies and comprehension (Genesee et al., 2005; Jimenez, Garcia, & Pearson, 1996).

It is especially important that all students receive instruction in comprehension strategies that is differentiated for each content area class because the demands of texts are often specific to each discipline and transfer of reading comprehension skills is not automatic. Therefore, students need explicit teaching and guided practice in comprehension as it relates to each discipline. When we fail to teach these comprehension skills across the curriculum, many students' struggles with reading are likely to manifest as a failure in content area knowledge (RAND Reading Study Group, 2002). In Chapter 3, we illustrate what comprehension instruction across the curriculum entails.

Writing

As noted previously, reading comes to dominate the later elementary and secondary school curriculum across the content areas. So, too, is writing increasingly used as both a measure of comprehension and a tool for learning across content areas. Thus, effective reading instruction for adolescents should be conducted in league with writing instruction and practice.

The link between writing and reading is multifaceted (Berninger, Abbott, Abbott, Graham, & Richards, 2002). For instance, when students use writing as a means to reflect about their use of comprehension strategies, their acquisition of those strategies improves (e.g., Commander & Smith, 1996; El-Hindi, 1997; McCrindle & Christensen, 1995). Similarly, writing in response to reading can foster improved thoughtfulness and critical thinking (e.g., Tierney & Shanahan, 1991; Tierney, Soter, O'Flahavan, & McGinley, 1989). For example, a common practice in middle and high school content area instruction is to have students read several texts and then demonstrate their learning through a written product that synthesizes those texts; yet research has shown that without instruction and practice, students do a poor job at this task (Britt & Aglinskas, 2002; Sandoval & Millwood, 2005).

Writing instruction seems particularly effective when it occurs in grades 6–8 and involves longer writing assignments (Bangert-Drowns, Hurley, & Wilkinson, 2004). Furthermore, according to one literacy expert, a full quarter of the time spent on literacy instruction across the content areas should be devoted to writing instruction that occurs across the content areas (Shanahan, 2004). The most recent meta-analysis of writing instruction focused on adolescents (Graham & Perin, 2006, 2007). It provided a list of 11 instructional practices found effective in improving the quality of adolescents' writing: (1) teaching students strategies for writing, (2) teaching approaches to writing summaries, (3) collaborative writing, (4) being specific about product goals, (5) word processing, (6) sentence-combining, (7) prewriting activities, (8) inquiry-centered activities, (9) the process writing approach to writing instruction, (10) the study of model writing, and (11) writing to learn. In addition, this meta-analysis noted a negative effect for traditional grammar instruction. However, the authors suggested that teaching grammar is still important and that alternative procedures, such as sentence combining, are more effective than traditional approaches for improving the quality of students' writing (Graham & Perin, 2007).

Effective writing instruction also involves students in daily writing, a wide range of composing tasks, a predictable routine that encourages reflection and revision, and teacher modeling of writing as a process and in the use of writing strategies (Graham & Harris, 2002; Troia & Graham, 2003). Quality writing instruction teaches students to use writing as a tool for thought across the content areas. And the more writing assignments require high levels of reasoning and engagement with academic content, the better the content of students' writing, regardless of student ability and school characteristics (Matsumura, Patthey-Chavez, Valdes, & Garnier, 2002).

Of course, much more detailed guidelines exist for excellent writing instruction than can be summarized here, and interested readers should refer to recent more comprehensive reviews for more information (e.g., Bangert-Drowns et al., 2004; Graham, 2005, 2006; Graham & Perin, 2006, 2007).

Writing is a facet of the literacy curriculum that takes on a special precedence in the middle grades at Boston's Fitzgerald School. Beginning in sixth grade, writing instruction and practice take up a large proportion of English language arts. Teachers at Fitzgerald emphasize developing students' voices as writers. It is this attention to student voice that teachers credit with their students' unusually good performance on state literacy assessments. The middle-grade teachers argue that when students come to see writing as the communication of their ideas they become more motivated to master the writing process. The teachers believe that it is this attention to voice and motivation in writing that allows their students to do so well on the state's seventh-grade language arts assessment, which includes a substantial writing portion.

Information and Communication Technologies Literacies

In today's world, the demands of technology must be addressed during adolescent reading instruction as well (Biancarosa & Snow, 2004). This is due in part to its growing presence in the daily work and play of Americans. However, hypertext and multimedia texts alter the reading and writing experience in important ways (Kamil, Intrator, & Kim, 2000; Labbo, Reinking, & McKenna, 1998; Leu, 2000). Although this is a new area of research, preliminary evidence demonstrates that multimedia and hypertext make greater demands on readers' attention and comprehension processing (Mayer & Moreno, 1998; Moreno & Mayer, 2002). Furthermore, readers' experiences with and preferences for these new text forms affect their comprehension (Dillon & Gabbard, 1998; Leu, 2000).

An important consideration in information and communication technologies (ICT) literacy use is that the amount of knowledge that students brings to a task significantly predicts their navigational strategies. One study found that high-knowledge readers used strategies that mirror those competent readers use when interacting with traditional text, while participants with low-domain knowledge engaged in random search and selection of resources and allocated more time to viewing special features (movies and sound effects) (Lawless & Brown, 2003). Whereas this study was conducted with college-age students, another study of sixth-grade students had similar results (Wallace, Kupperman, Krajcik, & Soloway, 2000). Without instruction students reduced the task to finding the "perfect source," which they regarded as a single page with the answer; this goal appeared to supersede the issue of coming to a deep understanding of the content. Students also had trouble engaging in a style of productive exploration that would ultimately yield useful questions to guide the ongoing search. And while the students had sufficient basic skills to use a Web browser and a search engine, they made relatively simplistic use of these tools in their navigation and search activity. Students infrequently used hyperlinks, failed to modify keywords when provided feedback, and often engaged in apparently random search behavior. Studies such as these suggest that teachers cannot make assumptions about their students' literacy skills on the Web. Students may be facile at locating and activating tools, but this does not mean that they are using them effectively to develop deeper understandings of content. And, much like every other aspect of reading, research has begun to demonstrate that students can benefit from experience with and instruction in the use of these technologies (Brinkerhoff, Klein, & Koroghlanian, 2001; Brush & Saye, 2001).

Perhaps due to the constantly and rapidly evolving world of ICT, schools rarely include ICT in literacy instruction. For instance, at both the Fitzgerald and Hampshire schools in Boston, computer skills are taught separately from language arts or other content areas. ICT literacy instruction can occur effectively in this manner; however, just as with reading and writing instruction, students would likely benefit from integration of at least some ICT literacy practices into their subject area classes. Although such integration is desirable, the highly specialized nature of ICT practices mandates at least some separate attention in the curriculum.

In one middle school in Michigan, the integration of ICT literacy and reading and writing was accomplished by having students engage in a semester-long program of study in which they learned how to use the Internet to conduct research. The unit began by helping the students generate questions that were open, deep, and interesting to guide their search. They then learned how to generate key words that would help them to focus their search and find information germane to their question(s). They soon knew how to distinguish and choose among the various search engines and how to judge the credibility of a site. They also learned how to document the history of their search so they did not intentionally or unwittingly plagiarize, and they learned how to synthesize the information they had located. This unit promoted both ICT literacy and critical literacy in the students.

Alternative Literacies

Today, global popular media culture, including online culture, is an important part of young people's lives and will continue to be so as they age (Hull, 2003; Lankshear & Knobel, 2003; Leander, 2003). The Pew Internet Survey (Fox, Anderson, & Rainie, 2005) indicates that 87% of youths between the ages of 8 and 18 in the United States have access to the Internet, prompting the director of the survey to suggest that youths today are "digital natives in a land of digital immigrants" (Rainie, 2006, p. 3).

What are the implications for those of us who are concerned about reading and literacy achievement? There is a lot of interest in ways that popular culture might be used to enfranchise youths who have been typically marginalized from—or at least disinterested in—school literacy activities. For example, "fan-fiction" is the raiding of mass culture by fans, who use media texts such as anime (Japanese animation) as starting points for their own writing (Chandler-Olcott & Mahar, 2003), and such tendencies could be harnessed in a school environment with a little creativity. One relatively recent attempt to tap the motivating and educating power of global media culture was Digitarts, an online multimedia project space (Lankshear & Knobel, 2002). Originally constructed by and for young women in Australia, the website eventually invited the participation of socially and culturally disadvantaged youths across genders and contexts. Digitarts provided youths with courses on webpage development and a venue for showcasing multimedia works and for gaining access to the knowledge and tools necessary to the development of art and cultural practice with new technologies. Similarly, Digital Underground Storytelling for Youth (DUSTY) aims at closing the digital divide and providing youths access to new technologies and a context in which they can write, represent themselves and their ideas, and learn the power of communication (Hull, 2003). These different forms of representation have yet to be fully tapped by educators for their potential to provide alternative learning spaces centered on youth culture, new media, and new ICT literacies, both in and out of school.

Unfortunately, research in a predominantly Latino/a community and public school in Detroit has shown that students seldom bring out-of-school funds of knowledge to bear in the classroom context, even though these funds are sufficiently rich with possibilities to not only build bridges between in- and out-of-school contexts but also to expand and deepen understanding of the target content knowledge (Moje et al., 2004). Clearly, students need guidance from teachers in order to bridge their in- and out-of-school literacy practices. Teachers should actively develop "third" spaces that merge the "first space" of students' home, community, and peer networks with the "second spaces," which are encountered in work, school, or church (Moje et al., 2004, p. 41). By engaging students in experiments, discussions, and reading and writing activities that focus on, or at least include, texts and experiences of different communities, educators can identify the funds of knowledge (Moll et al., 1989) and ways of using language (Gee, 1996) that students bring with them to school. This knowledge ultimately helps teachers to more positively influence students' interactions with the formalized discourses found in school and work.

Conclusion

As noted at the beginning of this chapter, an effective adolescent literacy program will not simply meld all of the types of content mentioned above. Rather, it will represent a careful combination of content designed both to aid adolescents where they struggle and to build upon their strengths and prepare them for life in the 21st century. In order to do so, schools and districts will need to closely consider the adolescents they serve. Moreover, while schoolwide approaches to instruction can be especially effective in improving adolescents' literacy achievement, struggling adolescents will naturally have a diverse array of literacy strengths and needs. Thus, adolescent literacy intervention will almost always need to be tailored on an individual basis. That is, establishing an effective approach to adolescent literacy means tailoring a program to address the reading skills needs of *all* students, which requires meticulously determining not only the needs of the student body as a whole but also those of individual struggling students. In addition to addressing the appropriate reading skills, an effective program will reflect research-based best practices in both the characteristics of and supports for adolescent literacy instruction. We turn to this discussion in Chapter 3.

CHAPTER 3

Characteristics and Supports of Adolescent Literacy Instruction

Annemarie Sullivan Palincsar, Marnie Nair, Donald D. Deshler,
& Gina Biancarosa

BASED ON RESEARCH, WE know that good reading instruction for adolescent readers—whether struggling or not—typically contains certain common elements. These consist of characteristics common to effective instruction, the ways in which the content of adolescent literacy instruction gets conveyed. They also include organizational and structural supports that allow for this instruction to take place. We begin with a discussion of the key characteristics of successful adolescent instruction.

Characteristics of Adolescent Literacy Instruction

Teaching for Transfer

It is simply not enough for literacy instruction to occur in English language arts (ELA) classes alone (Biancarosa & Snow, 2004). Instead, effective instructional principles should be embedded in content, both by incorporating content area texts in ELA classes and by incorporating good literacy instruction in content area classes. This is not the same as the traditional and popular call for "every teacher to become a teacher of reading." Rather, the emphasis is on the recognition that the reading and writing students do in later grades increasingly takes place in content area classes. Consequently, reading and writing demands also become increasingly specific to each discipline in their requirements.

It is this reality that makes it foolish to believe that ELA teachers can or should effectively teach all the literacy practices and strategies that students will need across all school subjects. Simply put, beyond mere recall and summary skills, the most effective strategies for reading a novel or short story with comprehension are not the same as the most effective strategies for reading a math word problem or historical documents. Research has found that teaching students strategies adapted or specific to a content area improves their ability to engage with and understand content areas texts (e.g., Carnine & Carnine, 2004; Lederer, 2000; Mastropieri, Scruggs, & Graetz, 2003; Palincsar, Magnusson, Collins, & Cutter, 2001; Schleppegrell & Achugar, 2003; van Garderen, 2004). It is crucial that adolescent literacy instruction take into account the discipline-specific aspects of reading. We illustrate this point drawing from history instruction.

Mosborg (2002) makes the point that historians are storytellers; but, in contrast to fictional narratives, the claims made in historical texts are subject to warrant. This means that students need to learn about the role of footnotes and references as a way of establishing these warrants. Mosborg also points out that teachers need to elicit students' own background narratives as a way of helping the students to contrast the past and present, as well as to contrast their own views with those of others. In Mosborg's research, these background narratives were activated by engaging students in conversations about contemporary newspaper articles.

> Powerful ways of approaching text in the teaching of history involve teaching students the tools that are integral to the conduct of history and engaging the students in the application and evaluation of those tools.

Another example, drawn from history, comes from the research of Bain (2006). Bain is a history teacher and history educator who has explored ways of helping students learn how to read and understand history texts, which are typically dry and fairly uninteresting. Bain encouraged his secondary students to assume a critical stance in their reading of their history texts. The key to this effort was to prepare his students as experts on a particular historical topic (the 14th-century pandemic of the bubonic plague) by providing them with a broad array and number of documents, including a majority of primary documents from the European record, along with some pieces from China and the Muslim world. The textbook was not among the documents students consulted. Whole-class and small-group presentations and discussions provided the contexts in which students were supported to read, weigh, and corroborate evidence regarding such issues as how 14th-century citizens made sense of the plague and how families and institutions responded to the plague. Following these rich experiences, the students were invited to consider the textbook's account of the plague. Examining letters written to the textbook's authors, Bain documented that these secondary students, as a collective, identified the same set of historiographic shortcomings identified by professional historians who critiqued this textbook.

In summary, powerful ways of approaching text in the teaching of history involve teaching students the tools that are integral to the conduct of history and engaging the students in the application and evaluation of those tools—a set of practices quite similar to the teaching of science text, the difference, of course, being the set of tools.

Diverse Texts

Giving students access to and experiences with diverse texts is another critical element of effective reading instruction for adolescents. Students who read more types of texts have been shown to be better readers (Campbell, Kapinus, & Beatty, 1995). And combining effective instruction with increased access to a wide variety of books in classrooms has been shown to improve achievement results (Guthrie, Schafer, et al., 2000). This diversity is important because adolescents need to learn to use reading comprehension strategies flexibly when reading a variety of texts for a variety of purposes. Therefore, in addition to diversity across the content areas, texts should be diverse in their style, genre, and topic. Moreover, access to texts with age-appropriate content but at a range of difficulty levels is especially important for struggling adolescent readers. Struggling readers need books that are interesting enough to motivate them to read and learn (for review, see Schiefele, 1999), but they also need texts that are neither so difficult that they become overly frustrated nor so easy that they are not challenged (O'Connor et al., 2002). Diverse school and classroom libraries provide the added benefit of an increased likelihood of representing a wide range of student interests, which can help to encourage wide and frequent reading (e.g., Dreher, 2003; Fink, 1995; Ivey & Broaddus, 2001). In sum, when school and classroom libraries incorporate books that vary not only in style, genre, topic, and content area but also in difficulty level, struggling adolescents will have increased opportunities to build both their reading skills and their motivation to read.

Among the more innovative practices we have seen is one of the simplest: The eighth-grade teacher at the Fitzgerald School in Boston decided one year to turn a large portion of her book-buying budget over to her students. The teacher was stunned by the enthusiasm with which her students greeted this idea and all the more so when she witnessed the great diversity of texts they chose. The students skillfully negotiated with one another to ensure they were able to buy a large number of books and multiple copies, while meeting the wide range of interests in the group. Needless to say, independent reading took place with an unaccustomed level of enthusiasm that year.

Self-Direction and Choice in Goal Setting and Reading

Good adolescent literacy instruction works to build and sustain students' motivation and ability to direct their own learning. In fact, reading instruction that promotes engagement and self-directed learning has been found to improve motivation, self-competency, reading comprehension, and strategy use (Guthrie & Alao, 1997; Guthrie, Anderson, Alao, & Rinehart, 1999; Guthrie & Humenick, 2004). One simple and effective way to improve students' motivation and ability to independently direct their own reading and learning is to provide them with choices in their reading and learning (Carbo, 1983; Cordova &

Lepper, 1996; Reynolds & Symons, 2001; Schraw, Flowerday, & Reisetter, 1998). But such choices should not be an afterthought or addendum to the curriculum. One effective model teaches students to set literacy and learning goals for themselves, which improves both student learning and motivation (for review, see Schunk, 2003).

Text-Based Collaborative Learning

Somewhat related to the issue of motivation is the importance of text-based collaborative learning. Although a common argument for collaborative learning is that it improves motivation, research has shown that when collaborative activities focus on shared text-based learning tasks, students' comprehension improves on both researcher-designed and standardized tests (NICHD, 2000). Collaborative learning is text-based when students' activities center on reading and writing. The text may be a novel or short story, or it may be content area specific, such as a math word problem, scientific report, or historical document. Grouping students and allowing them to read and complete focused activities with texts has been found to improve comprehension and learning across the content areas for upper elementary through high school students, as well as with English-language learners (ELLs) and students with learning disabilities in inclusive settings (e.g., Bryant, Vaughn, Linan-Thompson, Ugel, & Hamff, 2000; Fuchs, Fuchs, & Kazdan, 1999; Klingner, Vaughn, Arguelles, Hughes, & Leftwich, 2004; Langer, 2001; Vaughn, Klingner, & Bryant, 2001).

It has been suggested that this type of instructional activity is so effective at improving comprehension and learning because grouping students with different reading levels together allows struggling readers the benefit of peer models and helpers (e.g., Almasi, 1995; Klingner & Vaughn, 2000). Such groupings also expose more advanced readers to cognitive or conceptual confusions, which have been shown to improve learning and engagement (e.g., Almasi, 1995; Guzzetti, Snyder, Glass, & Gamas, 1993). Based on Piagetian theory (Piaget, 1977), cognitive conflict occurs when students are confronted with ideas that differ from their own. This creates conflict or disequilibrium in their thinking and forces them to work to assimilate these ideas and arrive again at a stable state of thought. For example, in science class, discussing what happens to a cube of sugar when it dissolves in water, one student in a group may believe the sugar crystals have joined irrevocably with the water molecules, another may believe the sugar has only temporarily joined to the water molecules, while a third may believe that the sugar is still entirely separate but has only changed from a solid to a liquid state. Learning and comprehension are enhanced when students discuss these ideas in small groups by appealing to texts they have all read in order to "articulate and support their views with evidence from texts" (Guzzetti, 2000, p. 93). Students can thus build, contemplate, and revise their thinking, and they can do this with any text from any subject area (e.g., they could just as easily be defending and debating interpretations of historical events or of fictional characters' actions).

Formative and Summative Assessment

As suggested in Chapter 2, an effective adolescent literacy program relies on effective adolescent literacy assessment. While formative assessment is designed to inform instructional decisions, summative assessment is designed to gauge the efficacy of a program and to summarize the learning of students.

Formative assessments enable teachers to adapt their instruction to student learning and needs on an ongoing basis. They differ from summative assessments, which relate students' overall progress to benchmarks or to other students, in that a formative assessment provides detailed information about students' specific strengths and weaknesses (Fuchs, Fuchs, & Hamlett, 1989). Although linking formative assessment to clear criteria or goals can improve its usefulness (Fuchs, Deno, & Mirkin, 1984), what is critical is an explicit focus among teachers on gaining information about students' progress in order to improve instruction (Boston, 2002). Good formative assessment can improve student learning and achievement (Black & Wiliam, 1998; Wiliam, Lee, Harrison, & Black, 2004). Frequent formative assessment helps teachers measure student progress toward curricular goals and determine student responsiveness to instruction and intervention (Fuchs & Fuchs, 2002). And research has shown that formative assessment is especially useful to teachers in inclusive classrooms (Calhoon & Fuchs, 2003; Fuchs, Fuchs, Hamlett, Phillips, & Bentz, 1994).

While formative assessment is meant to guide teachers' instructional decisions, summative assessment is designed to appraise how instruction has affected student skills and achievement (Wiliam & Black, 1996). Good summative assessment investigates effects on both individual student outcomes and class- and school-level outcomes. Summative assessments may be either criterion- or norm-referenced. In other words, they may compare student performance to predetermined benchmarks and goals or to a population of similar students. This type of assessment allows teachers and administrators to evaluate how well instruction is helping students to improve their literacy and determine whether additional or alternative methods are required for some or all students. Simply put, summative assessment can help to determine how well an instructional approach is working for each individual student, for each class, and for a school as a whole.

Scaffolds for Struggling Students in Content Areas

All adolescents who struggle with reading for one reason or another need scaffolds for acquiring critical content knowledge while they are still mastering English literacy skills. This instruction can be similar for students no matter the source of their difficulty. For instance, the strategies that work to support students with learning difficulties also work for ELLs. In addition to tutoring strategies, such as classwide peer tutoring (Fuchs, Fuchs, Bentz, Phillips, & Hamlett, 1994) and strategic tutoring (Hock, Pulvers, Deshler, & Schumaker, 2001), which have proven effective in supporting these students, all content area teachers must be able to modify and enhance their instruction so that all students have access to the curriculum. Research has shown that teachers can learn to make these modifications and find them easy to implement (Bulgren, Deshler, Schumaker, & Lenz, 2000; Bulgren, Lenz, Schumaker, Deshler, & Marquis, 2002) and that such modifications improve student learning (Bos, Anders, Filip, & Jaffe, 1989; Bulgren, Deshler, & Schumaker, 1997; Bulgren et al., 2000, 2002; Bulgren, Schumaker, & Deshler, 1988, 1994b; Horton, Lovitt, & Bergerud, 1990).

For example, a science teacher analyzing her curriculum might decide she has dual purposes for a particular unit of study: to impart critical core knowledge of the classes of the animal kingdom (e.g., reptile, amphibian, bird, mammal) and to educate students in the process of scientific comparison. Therefore, in the initial phases of instruction, she explicitly models the identification of salient characteristics of one class (e.g., reptile) and elicits comparisons to the other class (e.g., amphibian) by asking her students questions. Initially, this activity is teacher-centered, but in subsequent comparisons she deliberately shifts more and more of the responsibility for identification and comparison of traits to her students. Her ultimate goal is to convey not only the defining characteristics of each class of animal but also the process by which scientists determine these defining characteristics. Students are scaffolded in their acquisition of this critical content knowledge, which thereby supports their ability to read and write about science.

Technology as Tool

Technology has been lauded for its promise for improving education. Specifically, technology is often seen as a tool for managing instructional time because it can provide students with additional individualized instructional supports and practice opportunities, and even opportunities for additional exposure to new ideas. In keeping with this, research has found that many technological applications designed to support students with literacy problems have a positive impact on adolescent students' reading and writing (Graham & Perin, 2007; Leu, 2000; MacArthur, Ferretti, Okolo, & Cavalier, 2001; NICHD, 2000; Palincsar & Dalton, 2005; Palincsar & Ladewski, 2006). And as might be expected, the promise of technology coupled with its potential efficiency has resulted in a number of computer-based literacy curricula.

In fact, there has been a recent explosion of interest in using technology as a support for improving students' reading comprehension, in addition to the more traditional approaches designed to support decoding and spelling growth. Early forerunners include programs that target basic reading skills like decoding and spelling (e.g., Failure Free Reading, Lexia, Phonograpix) or target many reading skills (e.g., Accelerated Reader, Autoskill Academy of Reading, PLATO Learning, READ 180), while more recent programs have targeted higher-level reading skills like comprehension strategies and metacognition (e.g., Achieve3000, Thinking Reader). Several projects funded by the Institute of Education Sciences investigate the effectiveness of technology for supporting growth in comprehension (e.g., iSTART, TICA, and several projects by CAST; see Appendix).

The outcomes of embedding learning supports designed to improve comprehension have generally shown that while there are positive effects on comprehension within the supported environment, only some transfer to improvement with reading print (Palincsar & Dalton, 2005; Strangman & Dalton, 2005). Moreover, the findings are mediated by student characteristics and by a number of contextual variables, such as the teachers' views on literacy and experience with technology integration and level of technology access (Palincsar & Dalton, 2005; Strangman & Dalton, 2005). These limitations highlight the need for a more comprehensive model of reading and the learner to guide the design of more effective, customized learning environments. At the same time, one of the older technological supports for literacy is the word processor, and word processing has relatively consistently been found to support higher quality writing by adolescents (Graham & Perin, 2006, 2007).

Supports of Adolescent Literacy Instruction

It is critical to remember that instructional change must be accompanied by structural and organizational supports to be most effective. In order to capitalize on the benefits reaped from efforts to improve instruction via curricular changes, the structures and conditions that foster improved instruction must also be considered. Attention to both supportive school environments and quality literacy instruction has the most promise for improving adolescent literacy.

Increased Time for Literacy

One critical support is increased time for literacy during the school day. If literacy instruction is limited to a single, brief period each day, teachers will be unable to incorporate all the instructional elements detailed above. Extending literacy instructional time can be accomplished not only be extending the ELA period but also by bringing an explicit focus on literacy practices to content area classes. As noted above, this does not necessarily mean that every content area teacher needs to become an ELA teacher but rather that teachers need to be supported in considering the unique role that literacy plays within their content areas, as well as the instructional practices and strategies that cut across content areas. Research has shown repeatedly that time devoted to instruction and practice is a strong predictor of achievement (Gettinger, 1984, 1985; Guthrie et al.,

2001; Kane, 1994; National Education Commission on Time and Learning, 1994; Rosenshine, 1978; Rosenshine & Stevens, 1984). Researchers have recommended that students should spend at least two and as many as four hours per day actively engaged with reading and writing texts (Biancarosa & Snow, 2004).

High-Quality Professional Development

Without high-quality and sustained professional development the instructional elements above are unlikely to be implemented well or at all. Research has shown that teacher professional development affects student achievement (Garet, Porter, Desimone, Birman, & Yoon, 2001). However, not all professional development reaps the same benefits. Specifically, long-term, ongoing professional development is more effective at improving teacher practice and student outcomes than is short-term professional development (Darling-Hammond, 1998; Garet et al., 2001). The effects of professional development in research-based instructional approaches are best sustained when a collegial atmosphere of inquiry is created (Burbank & Kauchak, 2003; Darling-Hammond, 1999; Frey, 2002; Gersten, Chard, & Baker, 2000; Gersten & Dimino, 2001; Supovitz, Mayer, & Kahle, 2000). It is especially critical that teachers are supported in their efforts by school and district administration and are able to hold regular, extended, and reflective discussions about students and their attempts to implement instructional innovations (Cutter, Palincsar, & Magnusson, 2002; Englert & Tarrant, 1995; Hamilton & Richardson, 1995; Vaughn, Klingner, & Hughes, 2000). Additional important factors in providing effective professional development include adapting instructional approaches to local contexts; embedding opportunities for teachers to build a thorough understanding of methods and the theories behind them; and establishing deliberate, detailed, and realistic plans for sustained change (Gersten et al., 2000).

Teacher Teams

Another important structural support for improving adolescent literacy is the creation of teacher teams. Literacy instruction becomes more consistent and cohesive across classrooms when teachers are able to meet regularly in consistent groups not only to plan instruction but also to discuss current research and the theories underlying their instruction (Englert & Tarrant, 1995). Therefore, effective teaming requires school scheduling that allows for ample meeting time and consistent team membership, support in the principles and processes of teaming, adjusting team size for maximum efficacy, and a schoolwide vision for teaming (Spraker, 2003). Interdisciplinary teams may take longer to get acclimated, but given consistent meeting time they come to coordinate their curricula and instructional strategies, as well as design support systems for the neediest students (Erb, 1997). A critical factor in effective teacher teaming is that teachers plan their instruction together to ensure they choose and present the most important content in a consistent way and that the modifications and accommodations they make for difficult content and struggling students are both appropriate and consistent (Ermeling, 2005; Lenz & Adams, 2006).

Schools that create a collaborative and communal environment for teachers through interdisciplinary teaming have a positive effect on student engagement and achievement, and improve the equity of educational achievement among students (Flowers, Mertens, & Mulhall, 1999; Frey, 2002; Lee & Smith, 1993, 1996). Additionally, teachers who participate in team meetings end up more satisfied with the teaching experience and more confident in both their own ability and the ability of teachers in general to affect their students' lives positively (Erb, 1997; Flowers et al., 1999; Lee, Dedrick, & Smith, 1991; Raudenbush, Rowan, & Cheong, 1992). Hence, since teacher retention is an issue for many schools—especially those with the poorest student performance—teaming certainly holds great promise for improving literacy outcomes in low-performing schools.

Coordination Across Content Areas

When schools develop a comprehensive and coordinated literacy plan, they amplify their chances for successfully improving adolescent literacy. A comprehensive plan does not mean a cookie-cutter plan. In fact, research on middle school reform has suggested that "idea-driven" changes in school structures and practices are more effective than "checklist-based" approaches because

> being able to "check off" these practices often becomes an end unto itself, with little regard as to why these practices should be implemented or in what forms and at what levels they need to be present to contribute to a more effective teaching and learning process. (Felner et al., 1997, p. 547)

Although a comprehensive literacy plan should be deliberate and include clear-cut objectives, it should also be coordinated across content areas, which requires a great deal of common understanding and a true sense of collective responsibility amongst teachers and administrators beyond that developed within teacher teams. Communal school organization and a collective approach to reforming school structures are related to both higher levels of teacher satisfaction and efficacy (Lee et al., 1991) and higher levels of student engagement and achievement (Frey, 2002; Lee & Smith, 1993, 1996). Furthermore, the more collaborative and cooperative the school structure, the more the students benefit (Lee & Smith, 1996).

Strategic Tutoring

Individualized instruction via tutoring has been found to be particularly effective in grades 4 and above (e.g., Bessai & Cozac, 1980; Cohen, Kulik, & Kulik,

1982; Hock, Pulvers, et al., 2001; Hock, Schumaker, & Deshler, 2001; O'Connor et al., 2002). What makes tutoring effective is not simply the one-on-one attention, but a strategic approach to tutoring (Babbitt & Byrne, 1999; Gaffney, Methven, & Bagdasarian, 2002; Staub & Lenz, 2000). Strategic tutoring is tutoring that is directed by student needs and provided on an "as needed" basis. A critical focus of strategic tutoring is on instilling independence by giving students support not only in completing specific tasks but also in strategic practices that will allow them to read, write, and learn independently. Strategic tutoring is a particularly effective way to meet the needs of students who would benefit from intense intervention.

Literacy Coaches

Some states and districts have turned to literacy coaches as a form of support for classroom teachers seeking to meet the literacy needs of their students. As this volume goes to press, there is little systematic research on the efficacy of literacy coaches, particularly at the secondary level. Research at the elementary level (e.g., Scott, 2006) reveals that schools are adopting a broad range of models for using literacy coaches. Some of them engage the coach in assessing students, while others engage coaches in demonstration teaching or leading teacher teams in planning activities.

Given our earlier discussion, we offer one caution about the use of literacy coaches at the secondary level. If they come from the ranks of reading specialists who have taught at the elementary level, they may not be sensitive to, or knowledgeable about, the domain-specific demands for reading and writing at the secondary level. Furthermore, they may not have the content knowledge to work in powerful ways with subject matter teachers. Given this limitation, districts may wish to consider recruiting and preparing literacy coaches from the ranks of subject matter teachers. However, if a coach comes from the ranks of subject matter teachers, it will be important to ensure that the coach has the necessary pedagogical and instructional skills and literacy knowledge to share with classroom teachers. In short, effective literacy coaches need to have knowledge of subject matter demands and literacy instructional procedures, as well as the ability to share and model such procedures that will promote successful learning and implementation by teachers.

This three-part expertise makes it critical that schools and districts have a protocol for identifying and evaluating potential literacy coaches. One resource for developing such a protocol is the *Standards for Middle and High School Literacy Coaches* published with support from Carnegie Corporation of New York by the International Reading Association (IRA, 2006) in collaboration with the National Council of Teachers of English, the National Council of Teachers of Math, the National Science Teachers Association, and the National Council for the Social Studies. Taking things one step beyond standards, San Diego State

University (SDSU) has developed a performance-based assessment that they use to select educators to become literacy coaches (Ivey & Fisher, 2006). The evaluation includes rating the content of a professional development plan drafted by the candidate, as well as the candidate's presentation skills, oral communication skills, interpersonal skills, and knowledge base. Of particular note is that the SDSU assessment acknowledges the importance of communication and interpersonal skills when working with adult learners.

To date, the evidence of the efficacy of coaching is scanty. However, simply judging what success is can be challenging. In some places, coaching is intended as a form of professional development rather than as a direct aid to struggling students; in others, the situation is the opposite; and in still others, coaches are seen as more administrative in their functions, overseeing the implementation of initiatives and curricula. Which of these models a school or district adheres to has tremendous implications for how they should be evaluated.

For instance, the Boston Public Schools use the professional development model. In Boston's case, it is more suitable to judge success by teachers' professional growth and satisfaction than to look for immediate effects on student achievement. The problem with looking for student effects is that the intervention is not directly delivered to students but rather to teachers, whose practice is expected to change over a period of time. Thus some delay should be expected before student effects are seen. Judging by teacher support and enthusiasm alone, literacy coaches have been used with mixed success in Boston. One critical factor in both coach and teacher satisfaction with coaching appears to be whether a coach is assigned full time to a school or must split time between two or more schools. Teachers in schools with full-time coaches tend to speak more positively about their coaching experiences. But other factors affect coaching success as well. One of the more successful Boston examples of coaching is at Turner Middle School. Turner is fairly similar to Hampshire in that both serve high proportions of struggling students and both have full-time coaches. Turner is distinguished by its teachers' unanimous support of their coach, whom they liberally credit with their professional growth. In contrast, the Hampshire coach evokes more mixed responses among the teaching staff. As with any literacy intervention—be it professional development, a curriculum, or other type of reform—success depends on more than the model implemented. Some of the factors behind the mixed success can be implementation, leadership, and readiness for the model, which are discussed in detail in Chapters 4 and 5.

Conclusion

Clearly, improving literacy outcomes for adolescents is not a task for the faint of heart. In addition to ensuring that the content of adolescent literacy instruction is appropriate and matched to student needs, several characteristics and supports of instruction also need to be in place. While we could hardly recommend that any single school or district attempt to implement all of the content and characteristics of adolescent literacy instruction discussed in this chapter and Chapter 2, we do recommend that serious thought go into the choices you make. It is crucial that educators realize that the right content offered in a developmentally inappropriate or inadequately supported way is as doomed to failure as inappropriate content delivered in fully developmentally appropriate and supported ways.

Effecting change in adolescent literacy is a demanding task, requiring strategic planning, careful consideration, and an ongoing effort of the highest caliber. In addition to these demands, there is an obvious fiscal cost involved as well. In the following chapter, we weigh the financial costs of implementing literacy change and, using real cases, investigate how differences in program implementation can be reflected in very different costs for the same program. Chapter 5 then considers the organizational traits that signal readiness for change, for without such readiness both the smallest and largest of investments can come to naught.

CHAPTER 4

Costs of Implementing Adolescent Literacy Programs

Henry M. Levin, Doran Catlin, & Alex Elson

THE CHALLENGE OF ADDRESSING inadequate literacy among adolescents goes beyond identifying the magnitude of the literacy problem and its solutions. Progress in addressing adolescent literacy challenges also depends heavily on schools choosing appropriate programs and implementing them well. This is a central focus of this book, as well as other recent reports on the subject (Biancarosa & Snow, 2004; McCombs, Kirby, Barney, Darilek, & Magee, 2005).

Sadly, the history of school reform is replete with repeated attempts to adopt reforms that are subsequently abandoned on the basis that they were ineffective. Clearly, schools need to choose reforms that have promise, and this volume provides a catalogue of approaches. But we would be remiss in not pointing out that the challenge of getting reforms to "work" is as much a responsibility of the schools as it is of the developers of the reforms.

Too often reforms are adopted by schools in a mechanical fashion as if a perfunctory acceptance of the reform and its training requirements are sufficient to routinely yield educational success. Very often such adoptions are not accompanied by the appropriate leadership, resources, and commitment to succeed. The result is that considerable time and resources are wasted as schools and school districts recycle through reform after reform with little long-term progress.

This chapter highlights issues of implementation and the costs of program choices, while Chapter 5 details issues of school and district leadership and readiness for change as integral elements for improving adolescent literacy outcomes. After reviewing the literature on implementation of educational reforms, this chapter proceeds to a study of differences in implementation and costs among a sample of schools that have adopted the same adolescent literacy program for three very different programs (READ 180, Questioning the Author [QtA], and Reading Apprenticeship [RA]), which are also listed in Part

II of this book. We conclude the chapter with some recommendations for procedures that will improve the chances for a successful implementation.

Importance of Implementation

The traditional view of educational reform at the school district or school site is that it begins with the identification of an educational challenge that needs to be resolved. Typical challenges are low student achievement or inappropriate student behavior in terms of disruptions or absenteeism. The decisionmakers consider a number of alternatives such as new textbooks, curriculum packages, software, and staff development and choose from among the alternatives. New materials are purchased, professional development follows, and the reform is considered to be in place. Within a few months the decisionmakers begin to look for results. When the expected improvements are not forthcoming in a year or two, it is assumed that the reform did not work and there is a search for a new reform. This behavior is so typical that anyone who has worked in a particular school or school district for a decade or so will have experienced as many as three or four different reforms dedicated to the same problem and dozens of different reforms addressing the myriad issues facing their schools.

What is notable about this approach is that it is part of standard school procedure in that it is the most common approach to seeking school improvement. School reforms are adopted in a perfunctory manner that implicitly assumes that the adoption of new materials and professional development will automatically transform the school and alleviate the problem. But this is almost never the case, so the search for solutions continues to follow this repetitive pattern as previous efforts fail and are replaced by something new. Why do schools seem to be perpetually adopting reforms to address persistent problems without the reforms succeeding?

Two reasons are given for this. The first is that schools are unique institutions rather than ones that can be altered effectively by a cookie-cutter approach. Change strategies must take account of the unique features of the school situation, including previous school experience with reforms, school leadership, commitment to change, staff capacity, student characteristics, and available resources. Schools with habitual adoption and turnover of reforms may see reform as a ritual rather than a reality to be taken seriously. School administrators often lack a full understanding of the needs of a reform and how to create productive roles that will support the reform. School staff may not believe that change is needed and may attribute problems to factors such as teacher turnover, inadequate resources, and student limitations. Furthermore, schools often undertake interventions without a clear idea of what resources are required and where they will be obtained, and school districts may encourage or mandate adoptions of reforms without providing the supportive conditions for success.

Any strategy for reform must build on not only the theory and details of the reform but also the concrete features and realities of the school in which the reform is being enacted (Evans, 1996).

The second reason is related to the first. Not only does each school differ as a context for change, but even an understanding of these differences may not be fully adequate for developing a strategy for change. The reason is that schools are not quiescent or inert organizations waiting to follow instructions from outside experts on how to alter themselves. They respond to outside interventions, molding them in ways that are often unpredictable and even unrecognizable. In a famous set of studies by the RAND Corporation, it was found that although adopted reforms are designed to change the school, the school has the agency and wherewithal to reshape the reform, even to neuter it completely. In fact, the failure of school reforms has been largely attributed to the capacity of the schools to swallow external interventions without allowing the reforms to fundamentally change school directions. (The literature on resistance to school change and on how schools shape reforms, rather than reforms shaping schools, is substantial. On the former, see Evans [1996]. On the latter, see the summary in McLaughlin [1990] of the RAND Change-Agent studies.)

Although the literature on the importance of paying attention to the details of implementation is voluminous (c.f., Berends, Kirby, Naftel, & McKelvey, 2001), the complexities of school organizations and operations typically neglect implementation planning. The RAND multiyear evaluations of the New American Schools concluded that, "Throughout the history of research on program initiatives, one finding has emerged again and again: Implementation dominates outcomes" (Berends et al., 2001, p. 23; see also Fullan, 1991; Pressman & Wildavsky, 1973). The conclusions drawn from the literature are that schools need to plan in depth the details for implementing reforms, beginning with the specification of the types of resources that will be needed and their costs—as well as how they will be deployed.

This chapter shows how such resources can be identified and their costs determined. This attention to resource needs and uses in adopting a reform shifts attention to the details of the intervention from what is often viewed as a mechanical adoption of a program that should automatically ensure success by virtue of its adoption.

Resources and Implementation

Although there may be many reasons for poor implementation, two of them are failure to account for the resources that will be needed to promise success and failure to procure the appropriate resources. An example of the first is that effective reform requires concrete efforts to ascertain the precise resources that are needed. One cannot simply assume that they will be available when needed.

For example, reduction of class size has specific resource consequences in that more teachers must be hired and more classrooms must be provided. Often schools simply assume that sufficient accommodations can be made without adequately anticipating the specifics. Then, at a late hour, they find themselves searching for the additional space and qualified personnel, an oversight that is unlikely to solve the logistical shortcomings.

Provisions for time commitments of personnel are often overlooked or not properly scheduled. For example, longer instructional periods for literacy activities also mean that provisions for teacher assignments and scheduling must be changed. If the school day remains fixed, resources and time must be reallocated with obvious consequences for the overall scheduling of classes and assignments. In an extended day additional teaching resources must be provided. Time for professional development includes not only the time allocated to formal workshops and professional development but also the time required for instructional planning among faculty and consultation and evaluation by coaches with classroom teachers. Often no formal arrangement is made to capture the time that these activities necessitate. Rather, it is just assumed that the time will be "found." Leadership of school principals for the reform means that time must be found in the schedule of principals and other school-site administrators to engage in training, teacher meetings, classroom observations and feedback, modeling good practices, and so on. Yet many reforms simply assume that administrative staff will find the time for all of these activities by rearranging their daily schedules, even though no provision has been made to reduce other responsibilities. In some cases, schools are expected to have a full-time or part-time coach. In too many cases a Title I coordinator or department head is just given an additional assignment without provision to shed other responsibilities or otherwise free up time for their new roles.

Fortunately, there are relatively simple tools for schools to identify the resources that are needed to implement reforms. These tools are easy to use because they build on the resources and activities that are integral to the intervention. The basic model used to evaluate the resources that will be needed and their cost is what is known as the "ingredients method" (Levin & McEwan, 2001). This method requires that planners follow a number of relatively simple steps in planning implementation.

The first step is to identify the "ingredients" or resources that will be required to effect a reform (Levin & McEwan, 2001, Chapter 3). This must be done in a systematic way and entails participation by both school and district staff. School leadership and teachers need to understand what it takes to implement the reform, and district staff need to become cognizant of program requirements and funding needs. Most of this type of analysis can be done by using a financial spreadsheet such as Excel. Personnel positions are listed according to their qualifications and the portion of time that will be needed. If the principal is expected to allocate one-quarter of her time to the reform, that requirement is identified in a formal way rather than entrusted to "whether and when she has time." The same is true of other personnel positions. At the same time it is important to begin to identify where these personnel will come from. Will extra teachers be needed to free up time for professional development and teacher discussions and deliberations? If so, how many positions will be needed and with what qualifications? Clearly this will have implications for hiring or reassignment.

Facilities needs and specific furnishing and equipment are also identified. If additional classroom space is needed for reductions in class size, that space should be specified. If computers, software, instructional materials, and other equipment are required, these also need to be denoted. Ultimately, all of the ingredients will be listed with sufficient detail on qualities and characteristics. Compilation of the needed ingredients is not only important for developing a complete list of resources associated with the intervention, it also gives school and district personnel a better understanding of the needs and purposes of the overall reform and enlists joint support in obtaining the resources. Specific sources of information in identifying ingredients include the descriptive materials on the reform and interviews with the sponsor or developer of the intervention, articles and reports on experiences of other schools in adopting the intervention, and observations and interviews (often by e-mail or telephone) with personnel in other schools or districts that have adopted the intervention.

> ...the adoption of a promising reform, in itself, is not sufficient to ensure that the reform has predictable costs and effectiveness.

The second stage in using the ingredients method to identify resources and implementation needs is to associate each ingredient with its cost. Methods of setting out the cost for each have been well developed in the literature (Levin & McEwan, 2001, Chapter 4). A complete listing of the ingredients and their costs will provide an estimate of the overall cost of the intervention. It also clarifies the resources that must be in place to promise success so that the school year begins with the necessary personnel and adjustments in schedule and group size that are integral to the specific reform.

The third stage is to ascertain where the resources will come from. In some cases, reallocation of the budget will be necessary, assigning existing resources to the intervention in place of using them for activities of a lower priority. In other cases, new resources will be required with implications for school budgets or for obtaining volunteer support. At this stage the details of financing the intervention must be in place in order to move forward with the reform.

Each of the interventions listed in this book has been formulated and applied to improving adolescent literacy. Although the developers of each reform have made considerable investments in constructing and testing their models, this is no assurance that when the intervention is adopted in a specific setting it will produce results. The foregoing discussion asserts that the adoption of a promising reform, in itself, is not sufficient to ensure that the reform has predictable costs and effectiveness. How the reform is implemented will contribute heavily to its probability of success or failure and its cost.

Implementation is a joint responsibility of the model developer and the school and school district. The model developer must provide clear guidelines with respect to how the reform works and what modifications it requires to usual school practices as well as the ingredients required to make it succeed. The school and school district must set out a blueprint in advance that allows for identification, funding, and acquisition of the required resources and planning activities that the reform comprises. This will vary from site to site, depending upon the initial alignment of programs and personnel. In some schools the challenge of any specific reform will require greater modifications of resources and be more costly than in others. For example, as we will show below, a reform that requires a small class size will obviously be easier to implement in a district that already has smaller classes than in one with larger classes. Moreover, a large reduction in class size will be more expensive as will be the search for additional classrooms to accommodate the smaller classes.

In what follows, we illustrate dramatically different costs and methods of implementing the same reforms. The purpose of this effort is to assist school decisionmakers and schools in selecting from among these—or other interventions to improve literacy among their students—on the basis of their students' needs and the careful consideration of the costs of implementation. In some of the cases discussed below, the reasons for wide divergence in costs are due to the need to make larger departures from existing practices at some sites than at others. In other cases, the site decisionmakers have decided to make modifications in the models. In yet others, there are idiosyncratic factors that seem to enter into implementation decisions. In all cases, we suggest that careful planning and analysis in advance of the launch of the reform is likely to provide better implementation and cost management.

We should also note that there is nothing nefarious about the differences in implementation patterns and costs that will be presented. Our purpose is more descriptive than analytical. Although we are illustrating the variability in implementation among a small sample of adolescent literacy reforms, the overall findings should not be viewed as unique. Virtually all reforms show this type of variability, even ones that are largely implemented by "formula." For example, one of the most widely used reading reforms at the elementary school level, Success for All (SFA), shows similar variability despite its relatively rigid requirements in materials, organization, and instructional practices. Using the ingredients method of estimating costs, King (1994) found that Success for All had an implementation cost ranging from about US$500 per child to about US$1,300 per child, even though it appears to have a cost of only about US$150 per child for materials and training (about US$75,000 for a school with 500 students). The difference is that SFA requires schools to provide extended class periods for reading, smaller class sizes, and additional personnel in the school for supporting the reform. Whether large differences in cost from site to site are associated with differences in effectiveness among sites is beyond the scope of this study, but that is certainly a possibility.

Three Adolescent Literacy Programs

To demonstrate the variability in implementation and subsequent variability in costs, we have selected three highly regarded reforms for improving adolescent literacy:

- READ 180
- Questioning the Author
- Reading Apprenticeship

These programs are also reviewed in Part II of this book. We obtained information on implementation of these programs at different sites. In particular, we collected data on the logistics of the implementation as well as the resources used to carry out the intervention at a number of different sites. Bear in mind that each developer provided the same description of the intervention and its implementation requirements to the different sites. From the perspective of the developer, success requires that the nature of the professional development and the provisions necessary for the reform have similarities to ensure quality control from site to site. We describe the three interventions and explore differences in their implementation and costs among sites to see how much variance exists.

READ 180

READ 180 is a reading intervention designed for struggling readers in late elementary, middle, and high school (see Part II, page 186). Its goal is to improve students' decoding, fluency, and comprehensions skills. The program was developed through collaborative research between Vanderbilt University and the Orange County Public School System in Florida. It was piloted with more than 10,000 students between 1994 and 1999 (Scholastic Research and Evaluation Department, 2006). Scholastic began publishing READ 180 in 1999 and currently markets the program to school districts across the United States.

READ 180 lessons consist of whole-group, small-group, and individualized literacy instruction. During whole-group instruction teachers read aloud, engage students in shared and choral reading, and model fluent reading and the use of reading strategies. The class is then divided into three groups that rotate through three reading stations: small-group instruction, computerized instruction, and independent reading. In small-group instruction, the teacher gives more personalized reading instruction to a small group of students. At the computer station, students receive individualized instruction via a program that advances to new text only after students demonstrate mastery in fluency, word recognition, spelling, and comprehension. The program provides support for readers, including a video to enhance background knowledge, pronunciation, translation, and definitions for difficult words in the text; decoding tips; and a summary of the student's reading accomplishments. During independent reading, students self-select texts from the READ 180 library and listen to audiobooks, which model fluent reading and comprehension strategies. The READ 180 lesson ends with another short period of whole-group instruction (Florida Center for Reading Research, 2006).

Scholastic recommends that READ 180 be delivered to students in daily 90-minute instructional blocks. Using this model, students get 20 minutes of whole-group instruction and three 20-minute rotations through the stations, followed by a 10-minute wrap-up. Scholastic also suggests limiting enrollment in READ 180 classes to 15 students. While many school districts follow these recommendations closely, others do not have either the resources or flexibility to modify the school day or to drastically reduce class size to fit Scholastic's recommendations. When this is the case, schools mold the program to fit their specific circumstances. Some schools use the READ 180 program with average or only slightly reduced class sizes. Others split the 90-minute instructional block into two 45-minute periods within the same day, or even into two 45-minute periods on consecutive days. The intervention has also been used as an after-school program, administered as infrequently as two times a week.

Questioning the Author

QtA is an instructional technique rather than a complete literacy program or curriculum (see Part II, page 183). It is designed to engage late elementary through high school students in critical reading, thinking, and discussion. The goal is for students to improve comprehension and retention of the information presented in texts (Beck, McKeown, Hamilton, & Kucan, 1997). As such, it has been used primarily with content area texts, particularly in the social sciences, but is intended to be appropriate for interactions with any type of text. The technique was developed by researchers at the University of Pittsburg and Bethany College in cooperation with the Pittsburgh Public Schools.

Using this approach to literacy instruction, teachers model their own reading processes for students (Beck, McKeown, Sandora, Kucan, & Worthy, 1996). In addition, they make use of a carefully constructed set of questions, referred to as queries. The queries are posed at planned intervals during the reading of the text and are designed to assist students in constructing meaning. Students are encouraged to see authors as fallible human beings who do not always express information and ideas clearly. Through student-to-student interaction, the group works collaboratively to demystify the text and uncover its more subtle meanings. Teachers use discussion moves such as "marking" (drawing attention to an idea) and "revoicing" (using other words) to enhance student discussion and comprehension (Florida Center for Reading Research, 2006).

QtA requires few resources outside of professional development costs. However, the training time varies widely, ranging from approximately 4 to 12 days per teacher in the first year. Because teacher preparation is an integral part of this program, developers believe that new practitioners will need 1.5 hours to prepare for each lesson. This is because appropriate queries must be planned out by teachers for each new text. However, most schools are unable or unwilling to give teachers the additional planning time needed for this preparation; as a result, teachers must either implement the technique without the suggested preparation time or spend many hours outside of school preparing texts and developing queries. The developers also recommend rearranging the classroom furniture into a U shape so that students can see one another's faces during the discussion. Some teachers choose to follow this suggestion, and others do not.

Reading Apprenticeship

RA is an approach to literacy that seeks to demystify academic reading for middle and high school students who struggle with text comprehension (see Part II, page 191). Similar to QtA, it is not a complete curriculum so much as a pedagogical approach. In contrast to QtA, RA aims to root literacy instruction and practice in the subject areas by attending to the unique demands and practices within each discipline. Developed by the Strategic Literacy Initiative (SLI) at WestEd, it is based on the premise that remedial, basic-skills programs result in a "literacy ceiling" that can limit academic and other opportunities (Greenleaf, Schoenbach, Cziko, & Mueller, 2001, p. 86). To surpass these limitations, RA prepares educators from all content areas to embrace new and complex conceptions of reading as well as new ways to develop students' academic reading skills. In RA classrooms, teachers and students act as partners in a collaborative inquiry into reading as they engage with texts in their specific subject area.

In order to create classrooms where students are active and effective readers and learners, RA trains teachers to reframe reading and writing in their subject areas by planning along four dimensions: social, personal, cognitive, and knowledge building. The social dimension focuses on creating and maintaining a supportive learning environment where students are comfortable making mistakes and asking questions. The personal dimension seeks to improve students' identities and attitudes as readers. The cognitive dimension provides students with strategies and tools to aid comprehension, with an emphasis on group discussion of when and why certain tools are useful. The knowledge-building dimension involves recognition and expansion of the knowledge students bring to a text. These four dimensions are linked in the classroom through "metacognitive conversation," a practice that makes the invisible aspects of each dimension visible and open for discussion (for detailed discussion of dimensions, see Schoenbach, Braunger, Greenleaf, & Litman, 2003).

While it is possible for RA to be implemented by a single teacher, SLI emphasizes the importance of cross-curricular implementation. In an ideal implementation, all teachers in a school will implement RA, meeting regularly to discuss progress and strategies. It is important that "full implementation" schools make time for such meetings to occur.

SLI trains educators in RA through a variety of professional development opportunities, ranging from an eight-day SLI series of sessions to one-day sessions provided by local "teacher experts." Nevertheless, across all professional development, educators are trained to see reading differently through examining their own reading process and that of adult peers and students. Because RA focuses on retraining content area teachers, program implementation does not require structural change to the school schedule, purchase of new equipment, or additional personnel.

Data and Analysis

It is important to note that this project was constrained to three months during the summer of 2005. This meant that both time limitations and vacations at school sites limited the more refined collection and analysis of data that would be required in a precise cost accounting. However, we believe that differences in the resource patterns among sites and the overall cost magnitudes are representative.

A five-step method was used to gather and organize data for this study; this approach is part of the "ingredients method" described in Levin and McEwan (2001, Chapters 3 and 4).

First, we reviewed published program documents for each intervention. These documents included general program descriptions, implementation guidelines, reports by previous program evaluators, district and program websites, implementation videos, journal articles, and various other sources of information. This review of published materials familiarized us with the programs and alerted us to potential costs and pitfalls of implementation.

Second, we contacted program developers by telephone and, where possible, met with them in-person. Developers explained both the minimal and ideal resources required for successful implementation of their intervention. They described the primary obstacles to implementation as well as the resources and actions that schools and districts commonly used to overcome those obstacles. Each of the three program developers provided a wide range of program literature and contact information for successful program implementers around the United States.

Third, we conducted telephone interviews with school and district personnel—teachers, principals, technology specialists, district literacy coordinators, and superintendents—to learn how programs were being implemented at the local level. Our goal was to document and understand the various ways that a single model took on different operational features at the sites of implementation. Respondents at each site were asked not only to describe the pattern of implementation but also to identify the characteristics of personnel required for successful program implementation. For example, one district noted the necessity of a full-time district literacy coordinator, while another had no such position. In addition, respondents described the nature of the professional development offered to teachers, administrators, and technicians. Finally, they described the materials and the facilities required to implement the program. Some of the interventions required the purchase of additional technology and the procurement of additional classrooms, while others did not. At each of these stages, local staff described problems they encountered as well as the resources and actions they used (or tried to use) to overcome them. In some cases, it was difficult to schedule interviews because school personnel were out of the office for the summer. We note the number of sites contacted at the beginning of each program's results section. The time frame also made conducting observations of the interventions impractical.

Fourth, we used the above sources of information to construct ingredients lists for each site's implementation. This list outlined the personnel, materials, and facilities used at each implementation site and could be compared with the developers' recommended ingredients. The purpose of this method was not to highlight inconsistencies between implementer approaches and developer models, but rather to show future schools and districts the real range of resources required to implement a given intervention. By identifying the ingredients that are actually used in an intervention, we hope to inspire schools to think more deeply about the resources, time requirements, and personnel needs that contribute to program success.

Fifth, we created Excel spreadsheets detailing the ingredients and relative costs for each intervention across different sites. Costs were assigned to the ingredients using national averages, developer costs, and individual estimates. Total program costs were determined as well as program costs per student. Although major cost components such as program licenses, professional development, and computers are purchased in the first year, they continue to provide services over a number of years; using proper costing techniques, these costs were annualized where appropriate. That is, only that portion of the cost of such ingredients that should be charged to a single year of use is included in these estimates. To annualize costs, we assumed five years of program implementation at a 5% discount rate. Five years is also a number recommended by Scholastic, although the program has been implemented beyond five years in some sites. Exceptions to the five-year expected lifespan are noted in Tables 4.1–4.3. (For further information on how to annualize costs, see Levin and McEwan [2001, pp. 67–70].)

Findings

The following presentation describes the findings from analysis of site implementation of each of the reforms. Since this work was performed over the summer, we were limited in both time and access to school personnel in obtaining data. Accordingly, what follows should be viewed not for its precise cost analysis as much as for its patterns of resource use and the magnitudes of cost. Also, our purpose is not to compare the cost of different intervention models, because some are more modest than others, a factor that may be reflected in both their scope and effectiveness, and because they have distinctively different goals. Results for each program are summarized separately in the following sections and in Tables 4.1–4.3. Each of the tables reports for a given program the costs of that program's ingredients, the costs at an "idealized" site described by its developer, and the costs at one or more actual implementation sites. We close the chapter by offering our readers some conclusions and insights gained through this study.

READ 180: Ingredients and Costs

The list of ingredients for READ 180 was derived from telephone conversations and e-mails with numerous sites suggested by Scholastic, the sponsor of READ 180. Three of these sites, chosen for their diversity in geographic region and school size, are included in Table 4.1. In addition, we obtained details on the intervention from meetings, phone conversations, and correspondence with Scholastic representatives. The main categories of cost ingredients include personnel, professional development, facilities, equipment and materials, and licenses purchased. Table 4.1 provides a listing of ingredients with the additional quantities of each for three READ 180 school sites and the recommended model of Scholastic.

Personnel costs were divided into five categories: school administrators, school technicians, district coordinators, district technicians, and additional teachers required for program implementation. Additional teachers are required for READ 180 when schools cut class sizes for the program and/or alter their schedules to accommodate the recommended 90-minute class period. Therefore, we calculated the number of additional teachers needed for READ 180 where the READ 180 requirements deviated from existing class sizes and period lengths.

Clearly, the simple purchase of READ 180 courseware in itself is inadequate to ensure increased student literacy achievement without appropriate staffing, professional development, and use of the courseware. One purpose of this report is to make the less conspicuous costs of adolescent literacy programs visible to future implementers. All sites reported that district leadership and support are required to initiate and sustain an effective implementation of READ 180. For example, a teacher from a large urban district reported that in

TABLE 4.1. READ 180 Implementation Models

INGREDIENTS LIST	INGREDIENT Costs (US$)	INGREDIENT Annual Costs (US$)	SCHOLASTIC Inputs[a]	SCHOLASTIC Annual Costs (US$)	READ 180 SITE ONE Inputs	READ 180 SITE ONE Annual Costs (US$)	READ 180 SITE TWO Inputs	READ 180 SITE TWO Annual Costs (US$)	READ 180 SITE THREE Inputs	READ 180 SITE THREE Annual Costs (US$)
LICENSES (Packs of 60)	$32,000.00	$7,392.00[b]	1	$7,392.00	186	$1,372,472.64	18	$133,056.00	40	$295,680.00
PERSONNEL (FTE)										
Additional teachers[c]	$57,355.00[d]	$57,355.00	1	$57,125.58	36.86	$2,114,105.30	17.93	$1,028,375.15	3.12	$178,947.60
READ 180 teacher:student ratio			1:15		1:30		1:15		1:24	
Percentage reduction from 30-student class size[e]			50%		0%		50%		20%	
School-level administration	$105,282.50	$105,282.50	no rec.		n.r.		n.r.		0.02[f]	$2,105.65
In-school technician	$57,355.00[g]	$57,355.00			2.36	$135,357.80	.45	$25,809.75	0.83	$47,604.65
READ 180 district technician	$95,385.00	$95,385.00			1.13	$107,308.13	4	$381,540.00	0.40	$38,154.00
READ 180 district coordinator	$85,892.50	$85,892.50	no rec.		0.90	$77,303.25	0.33	$28,344.53	0.80	$68,714.00
PROFESSIONAL DEVELOPMENT										
First-year teachers trained[h]			1		270		58		37	
First-day implementation training	included		yes		yes		yes		yes	
Second-day implementation training	included		yes		no		no		no	
Read online course	two included		yes		limited		no		no	
Seminar series	$2,500.00	$577.50	two optimal		no		no		no	
Independent district training							7 days		3 days	
Noncontract training	$120.00	$27.72			270	$7,484.40	348	$9,646.56	185	$5,128.20
Substitute days					270		464		185	$5,994.00
Total teacher training days			2		270		464		185	
Administrator training	$105,282.50	$24,320.26	0	$315.85[i]	0	$72.96	0	$0.00	0	$33.78
Technician training	$57,355.00	$13,249.01	.01	$66.25	0.24	$3,219.51	0.13	$1,748.87	0.07	$883.18
Half-day implementation training	included				81		no		no	

(continued)

TABLE 4.1. READ 180 Implementation Models (continued)

INGREDIENTS LIST	INGREDIENT Costs (US$)	INGREDIENT Annual Costs (US$)	SCHOLASTIC Inputs[a]	SCHOLASTIC Annual Costs (US$)	READ 180 SITE ONE Inputs	READ 180 SITE ONE Annual Costs (US$)	READ 180 SITE TWO Inputs	READ 180 SITE TWO Annual Costs (US$)	READ 180 SITE THREE Inputs	READ 180 SITE THREE Annual Costs (US$)
One-day implementation training	included		yes		no		no		no	
One-day technical training	$9,000.00	$2,079.00			no		22	$2,079.00	no	
Two-day technical training	$12,000.00	$2,772.00			no		no		1	$2,772.00
FACILITIES										
Classrooms			no rec.		166		18[j]		20	
EQUIPMENT AND MATERIALS										
Student computers	$600.00	$138.60	5	$693.00	1,660	$230,076.00	108	$14,968.80	144	$19,958.40
Application server	$2,000.00	$462.00	1	$462.00	85	$39,270.00	18	$8,316.00	20	$9,240.00
Printers	$120.00	$27.72	1	$27.72	166	$4,601.52	18	$498.96	20	$554.40
Cassette players	$4.00	$4.00	5	$20.00	n.r.		n.r.		144	$576.00
Headphones	$10.00	$10.00	5	$50.00	n.r.		n.r.		144	$1,440.00
Additional books for classroom	$499.00	$183.23[k]			n.r.		n.r.		18	$3,298.19
Project achievement reading kits	$169.00	$62.06[k]			n.r.		yes	$1,117.02	50	$3,102.84
Total cost				$66,152.39		$4,019,271.50		$1,635,500.64		$684,186.89
Students served				60		6,701		1,080		2,400
Cost per student				$1,102.54		$610.55		$1,514.35		$285.08

FTE = full-time employees

no rec. = no specific recommendation; depends on size of implementation and district resources

n.r. = not reported

a Reported by Scholastic READ 180 National Implementation Manager.

b All one-time costs are annualized over five years using a 5% discount rate unless otherwise noted.

c Additional teacher formula, for each 100 students, assuming a class size of 30 and six-period day: 100 / (READ 180 class size × READ 180 periods per day) = X; 100 / (30 × 6 periods per day) = .56 ; (X students enrolled in school − .56) / 100 = new teachers per READ 180 student × number of READ 180 students served = number of additional READ 180 teachers.

d All personnel costs were calculated using national averages for the 2004–2005 school year (source: Educational Research Service) plus 25% estimated fringe benefits, unless otherwise noted.

e We assumed an original class size of 30 at all sites, although many districts reported higher class sizes in non-READ 180 middle and high school language arts classes.

f Number of additional hours divided by 1,440 (work hours per year). This formula for personnel is used throughout the study.

g No national salary information was available. Teacher salary information was used as an estimate of in-school technician costs.

h The cost of the teacher time is calculated as part of teacher salaries. It also affects substitute time.

i Formula used to derive opportunity cost of training: Hours of training / 1,440 = % FTE. FTE × # trained = total training FTE. Total training FTE × annualized salary = opportunity cost of training. This calculation was used for all personnel opportunity costs.

j This district uses only "oversized" classrooms for READ 180.

k Annualized over three years based on reports from sites.

its first four years of READ 180 instruction his school had four different principals—none of whom were committed to READ 180. As a result, there was vast inconsistency in implementation, with children constantly shifting in and out of READ 180 classes. In the fifth year of implementation, the school hired a principal who was supportive of READ 180 and, for the first time, the teacher had the same students from September to June. In addition, support for program challenges was readily available, as were resources for program essentials such as headphones and technical support. In this case, both additional principal time and school resources were needed to maximize the success of the program. The above description of essential support systems was echoed by Scholastic as well as teachers, principals, and district personnel at all sites.

While some districts reported few technology problems, others described technology as a primary obstacle to program implementation. In all cases, technology-related personnel provided essential support to READ 180 teachers. Many schools employ on-site technology specialists to resolve problems quickly, and all districts in our sample use a district-level technology expert who travels from school to school, resolving hardware and software problems.

To determine program costs for school administrators, school technicians, district coordinators, and district technicians, we convert the amount of time spent on READ 180 per school year into a percentage of a position (assuming 1,440 work hours per year) and divide that number by the average national salary for that position. All personnel costs were calculated using national averages for the 2004–2005 school year (Educational Research Service, 2005) plus 25% estimated fringe benefits.

Scholastic provides numerous options for READ 180 professional development, some of which are included in the cost of the program licensing. For teachers, Scholastic states that two days of implementation training as well as participation in its online course—both provided with the purchase of READ 180—are necessary in the first year of implementation. Optimally, Scholastic recommends that districts purchase a selection of additional half-day seminars and/or additional online reading courses. For school- and district-level administrators, Scholastic recommends participation in a half-day leadership development course, included in the price of the program. Finally, for technicians, Scholastic provides a READ 180 Technical Training Program at an additional cost of US$9,000 for one day or US$12,000 for two days. The training prepares technicians to provide program support within their school environment.

Additional professional development costs that are not included with the purchase of READ 180, but are important for schools to consider, include substitute teacher costs (where required), additional teacher training, and the opportunity costs associated with time spent on READ 180 training. Because professional development is intended to exert an impact beyond the year that it is provided, the costs are annualized.

Additional classrooms make up the primary facility requirement for READ 180 to accommodate reduced class size. (The annualized value of additional classrooms is not included here on the assumption that if only a small proportion of students were enrolled in READ 180, space might be found for 90 minutes a day. However, if larger numbers were enrolled and schools were fully utilized, our assumption will understate the costs.) While Scholastic provides no recommendation for facilities, it is important to note that READ 180 classrooms must be large enough to house computers for one-third of the students as well as provide sufficient space for the small, independent reading and computerized instruction groups.

Because READ 180 is a technology-based intervention, equipment and materials are vital to program implementation. Student computers and application servers constitute the largest equipment cost. However, this cost varies depending on the existing technological infrastructure of a school. For example, a school without adequate models or numbers of computers for READ 180 will incur greater first-year technology costs than will a school with the proper infrastructure already in place. Scholastic recommends a specific arrangement of system requirements for the best performance of READ 180; however, it acknowledges local differences in technology infrastructure and makes recommendations to schools and districts on the basis of the technology they already have.

While computers and servers constitute the largest equipment costs, full implementation also requires a printer, headphones, and cassette/CD players. Districts can also purchase additional classroom books and project reading kits. Costs for equipment and materials were annualized based on their average lifespan.

In order to determine the costs of implementing Scholastic's recommendations for READ 180, one must know the situation of the school prior to implementation. Much of the cost depends on preexisting local conditions such as class size, technology infrastructure, length of class periods, and personnel characteristics. Using information from three districts, all of which enthusiastically endorse READ 180, we were able to calculate the range of approximate costs associated with implementing this program. These results are found in Table 4.1.

READ 180 Site One

Site One is a large urban/suburban school district with an enrollment of close to 300,000 students. During the 2004–2005 school year, this district used the READ 180 program to instruct approximately 6,700 students. Initially, Site One adopted an "early bird" schedule in which students arrived at school prior to the beginning of the regular school day. Attendance was a serious problem, so Site One modified its schedule to allow students to receive READ 180 instruction daily, in 90-minute blocks during the school day. In addition, READ 180 classes are capped at 30 students, a significant reduction from the 38 students per class average reported by the district. (In both this case and that of Site Three we questioned the large class sizes reported to us. Respondents replied that in both cases the districts were growing so rapidly that school construction could not keep up with the expansion of enrollments, resulting in very large classes at certain grade levels. However, because we could not confirm that the class size was initially this large, we have used a class size of 30 as the initial level. Bear in mind that Scholastic recommends a maximum class size of 15 for READ 180.)

At Site One, the Coordinator of Instructional Programs coordinates READ 180. She spends approximately 90% of her time on READ 180–related activities, which includes meeting with Scholastic and district personnel, observing teachers, and reporting READ 180 results to interested parties. Each of the 81 schools that are using READ 180 has its own Educational Computer Strategist (ECS), who spends approximately one hour per week on READ 180, usually resolving problems with computer hardware. A technical field manager trains the ECSs and provides specialized knowledge on the READ 180 software as needed. All of the district's 210 READ 180 teachers attended one day of professional development prior to implementing the program in their classrooms.

Site One purchased 185 stages of 60 READ 180 licenses in 2004, giving it the capacity to serve 11,110 students with the intervention; however, during the last school year only 6,701 students received READ 180 instruction. The reasons for this underutilization varied from school to school and included lack of administrator support, the inability of teachers to manage the small-group structure of a READ 180 classroom, and a lack of school funds for READ 180 materials. These implementation problems and the resulting idle licenses greatly increased the per-student cost of READ 180 for Site One. An additional 37 teachers are needed to accommodate the time requirement for READ 180 extended class periods. (Because class size remained at 30—double the READ 180 recommendation—there was no additional need for teachers to reduce class size.) The salaries and benefits for these teachers constituted the other major expense in implementing READ 180 at Site One. The cost per student at Site One for 2004–2005 was estimated to be about US$600.

READ 180 Site Two

Site Two is significantly smaller than Site One, serving an enrollment of almost 48,000 students, with 1,080 in READ 180 classrooms during the 2004–2005 school year. Site Two adheres closely to the Scholastic model. READ 180 classes are limited to 15 students, half the size of the reported average middle school language arts class. In addition, class periods for READ 180 are 90 minutes long, which is twice the average class period length in the district. With these two modifications the school district would need to hire approximately 18 additional teachers, without reducing other school programs. The additional personnel cost is by far the largest resource burden for Site Two.

In this district, the Secondary Reading Supervisor is responsible for overseeing READ 180. Managing the program occupies about one-third of her time. While Scholastic provides one day of training to teachers, the Secondary

Reading Supervisor provides seven additional days of training to READ 180 teachers throughout the school year. This extra professional development necessitates substitutes for the 58 teachers who use READ 180.

Four district-level computer technicians work exclusively on READ 180. (Scholastic views these costs as discretionary on the part of the district. The new version of READ 180 will provide for a centralized data processing and analysis system.) Their job entails providing hardware and software support to schools, updating computer programs, and running the district's unique centralized computer system, which enables the district coordinator to see and manage student data from the district office. Computer technicians stationed at each school deal with simple hardware problems related to READ 180 in addition to non–READ 180 technology issues at the school.

In addition to the classroom stations suggested by Scholastic, this school district has a "computers down" station in each classroom. This area contains skills cards and other noncomputerized reading activities and allows teachers to continue using the READ 180 small-group instructional model, even when the computers are not working.

The cost of implementing READ 180 at Site Two is about US$1,500 per student, the highest in our study. Reducing class size by 50% for READ 180, doubling the instructional periods, and hiring four district technology experts contribute heavily to this cost. Additionally, Site Two's higher costs may be attributable to the relatively small size of its implementation and the attempt to centralize the data.

READ 180 Site Three

This school district is a suburban district that enrolled about 420,000 students in 2004–2005. READ 180 is used to remediate literacy instruction for about 2,400 students. As was true for Sites One and Two, Site Three substantially reduced class size in READ 180 classes from a reported average of 38 to 24 students per class. However, because we could not confirm officially the initial class size, we calculate the costs based upon an average class size of 30. Unlike the other sites, Site Three does not modify the school schedule for READ 180, so students receive 45–55 minutes of instruction daily instead of the recommended 90 minutes.

The implementation of READ 180 at Site Three is facilitated by the Program Specialist for Literacy in Secondary Education. She spends about 80% of her time overseeing READ 180. Part of her job is augmenting the two-day implementation training offered by Scholastic with 2–4 additional training days for teachers. All of the training takes place during the school year, so substitute teachers are hired to cover the READ 180 classes. READ 180 teachers are also asked to participate in monthly meetings outside of their contract time, for which they are paid an hourly wage.

School-level microcomputer specialists, employed by most high schools and some middle schools spend about two hours a week per READ 180 classroom.

They perform routine maintenance on READ 180 computers and programs. When schools cannot afford a microcomputer specialist the teachers and district technician spend more time on the technological aspects of the program. One district-level READ 180 technician works with all of the schools and trains the microcomputer specialists (the district initially purchased a two-day technology training from Scholastic). READ 180 maintenance, upgrades, and trainings occupy about 40% of his time.

Currently, Site Three spends about US$285 per READ 180 student. The cost is significantly lower than those of the other sites because this district uses 45- to 55-minute periods as opposed to the 90-minute suggested class periods. While we cannot comment on the effectiveness of this approach, the students at Site Three receive half as much READ 180 instruction as those at the other two sites, allowing the teachers to instruct twice as many students.

READ 180 Summary

Table 4.1 compares the ingredients and costs of implementation at the three READ 180 sites and for the Scholastic recommended model. Bear in mind that the overall numbers are sensitive to the scale of implementation, but the per-student cost provides a reasonable picture of the difference in magnitude of the costs at each site and the Scholastic recommendation. What is most remarkable is the variability in implementation logistics and the consequent differences in costs. For example, the recommended Scholastic model for implementation would entail about US$1,100 in costs if followed faithfully in a district with a class size of 30. (The cost estimates in Table 4.1 are on the conservative side because we did not include several areas of potential cost, including the annualized costs of extra classrooms, where needed.) But in Site Three the cost is only one-quarter of this amount because there was only a small reduction in class size (30 to 24 students) and no increase in instructional time. This comparison also illustrates the substantial impact on costs of changes in class size and length of instructional period. For example, the costs imputed for the additional teacher resources in the Scholastic Model are about US$950 a student, far in excess of the relatively modest charges for licensing the program and the equipment that is required. Clearly when class size is kept constant or reduced only slightly or instructional time is maintained or increased only a small amount, the costs of READ 180 are also reduced. However, these deviations from Scholastic's recommended implementation model might have a serious impact on effectiveness.

Questioning the Author: Costs and Ingredients

The ingredients needed to successfully implement QtA were determined through extensive oral and written contact with the developers at the University of Pittsburgh, and with one implementation site. Although we contacted other sites repeatedly, we were unable to conduct interviews due to the timeframe of this study.

QtA is a professional development program that aims to equip teachers with new tools for engaging students in text and curriculum. It does not require additional materials or modifications to the school day. Because there are very broad guidelines for class size and no recommendations for period length, it is extremely unlikely that schools will hire additional staff for the express purpose of implementing QtA; however, it is suggested by the developers that a minimum of two teachers per school should be prepared so that they can plan lessons and provide support to each other.

Costing results for QtA are found in Table 4.2. The main costs of this program are incurred for professional development. In addition to the materials for teachers and the initial training, schools are expected to hire consultants to observe each teacher eight times during their first year of implementing QtA. Each observation costs US$187.50, meaning that the observation bill for one teacher is US$1,500. Like other one-time professional development expenses, this cost is annualized over the expected life of the program, making it about US$350 per year. (We have used a five-year expected lifespan consistently throughout this study.) Alternatively, districts can hire a full-time facilitator to train teachers and do the observations. The developers estimate that someone in this position would need to spend about three hours per month with each teacher-implementer.

The developers suggest that administrators attend the one-day training and do about three observations of each teacher, so that they understand and are able to support the teacher-implementers. Both of these activities have opportunity costs, which are calculated by multiplying the administrator's salary and benefits by the percentage of time that person spends on the program. Using national averages for administrator salaries, we calculated this cost to be about US$1,300 annually.

A hypothetical high school or middle school that trained two teachers in QtA following the developer's guidelines would spend only a very modest amount of about US$11 per student annually. The emphasis is on incorporating in the existing curriculum and teachers' repertoires the capacity to ask questions in a manner that elicits thinking and articulate responses from students. The very low cost reflects the fact that modifications are not required in class size, scheduling, personnel augmentation, or additional facilities and materials.

Questioning the Author Site One

QtA Site One is a district with a total enrollment of 3,200 students. In this district, QtA has been implemented in language arts classes in grades 3 through 8. Because most of the teachers who adopted the approach work in elementary schools, they only teach one group of students per day.

In addition to a two-day initial training provided by the developers, 25 teachers and three administrators received QtA-related professional development

TABLE 4.2. Questioning the Author (QtA) Implementation Models

INGREDIENTS LIST	INGREDIENT		UNIVERSITY OF PITTSBURGH			QtA SITE ONE[a]		
	Costs (US$)	Annual Costs (US$)	Inputs[c]	Costs (US$)	Annual Costs (US$)	Inputs[b]	Costs (US$)	Annual Costs (US$)
PERSONNEL (FTE)								
Additional teachers required[d]	$57,355.00[e]	$57,355.00	0	$0.00	$0.00	0	$0.00	$0.00
QtA teacher:student ratio			1:20[f]			01:22.5[g]		
District teacher:student ratio			1:20			01:22.5		
Students per teacher trained			120[h]			22.5[i]		
School-level administration	$105,282.50	$105,282.50	0.01[j]	$1,052.83	$1,052.83	0	$0.00	$0.00
District-level administration	$85,892.50	$85,892.50	0	$0.00	$0.00	0.03	$2,576.78	$2,576.78
PROFESSIONAL DEVELOPMENT								
Teacher training	$55.00[k]	$12.71	2	$110.00	$25.41	25	$1,375.00	$317.63
Day 1 workshop	$2,500.00[l]	$577.50	1	$2,500.00	$577.50	1	$2,500.00	$577.50
Day 2 workshop			0			1		
Demonstration lesson—45 minutes	included		yes			no		
Observations—eight per teacher	$187.50	$43.31	16	$3,000.00	$693.00	200	$37,500.00	$8,662.50
or District facilitator	$85,892.50	$19,841.17	0.04[m]			not used		
Monthly meetings, annually	included		18 hours[n]			1,800 hours[o]		
Total training days per teacher			4.25			12		
Substitute days first year[p]	$120.00[q]	$27.72	0			225	$27,000.00	$6,237.00
Planning time first year			1.5 hours per lesson			45 minutes[r]		
Planning time after first year			45 minutes per lesson			45 minutes[r]		

(continued)

TABLE 4.2. Questioning the Author (QtA) Implementation Models (continued)

INGREDIENTS LIST	INGREDIENT		UNIVERSITY OF PITTSBURGH			QtA SITE ONE[a]		
	Costs (US$)	Annual Costs (US$)	Inputs[c]	Costs (US$)	Annual Costs (US$)	Inputs[b]	Costs (US$)	Annual Costs (US$)
School administrator training	$105,282.50	$24,320.26	0.01	$526.41	$121.60	0	$0.00	$0.00
District administrator training	$85,892.50	$19,841.17	0.01	$429.46	$99.21	0.18	$15,718.33	$3,630.93
FACILITIES								
Classrooms			2			25		
EQUIPMENT/MATERIALS			standard			standard		
Total cost				$7,618.70	$2,569.54		$86,670.10	$22,002.33
Students served[s]				240	240		625	625
Cost per student				$31.74	$10.71		$138.67	$35.20

FTE = full-time employees
a School district with 3,200 total enrollment.
b Provided by the Director of Curriculum and Instruction.
c Provided by Dr. Margaret McKeown, University of Pittsburgh.
d Costs for teacher time were only calculated above and beyond inputs before the implementation of QtA.
e All personnel costs are calculated using national averages for the 2004–2005 school year plus 25% for fringe benefits unless otherwise noted.
f Average of suggested class size of 12–28.
g Average of reported class size of 20–25.
h Twenty students per period, six periods per day.
i These teachers were multisubject classroom teachers who stayed with the same students all day.
j Calculated by dividing the number of hours spent on QtA by the estimated total number of hours worked, 1,440. Similar calculations are made using the same method throughout the table.
k Cost of teacher materials for professional development provided by Dr. Margaret McKeown, University of Pittsburgh.
l Flat rate for training provided by Dr. Margaret McKeown, University of Pittsburgh.
m About three hours per month per QtA teacher.
n One hour per teacher per month.
o One full day (eight hours) per teacher per month.
p The substitute days may differ from total training days because some training took place over the summer.
q This is an estimate that we used throughout the study. Substitute costs vary substantially by region.
r Standard for the district.
s Students per class × class periods per day = students served per year × 5 = students served over the five-year implementation period.

one day per month throughout the year. Removing the teachers from class-rooms for nine days incurred US$27,000 in substitute teacher costs. (Substitute teacher costs are estimated assuming that a substitute teacher costs US$120 per day.) The other large cost for QtA Site One was for teacher observations. At eight observations per teacher, the district paid an estimated US$37,500 to the University of Pittsburgh for consultants to do observations. Annualized, this cost becomes US$8,662.50 per year over five years.

The cost of implementing QtA at Site One is estimated to be about US$35 per student per year. This cost estimate may be low because teacher-training time was not included in the analysis. The higher per-student cost at QtA Site One is attributable to a one-day-a-month professional development session for all teachers, which is not required by the developer of the model. Still, the cost per student is very modest.

An interesting note is that this district reported very little teacher turnover. The director of Elementary Curriculum and Instruction described it as a place where "Teachers get a job and stay for their career." From this perspective, it makes sense to invest heavily in professional development because teachers may use the technique to benefit students in that district long after the professional development period is over, clearly an important consideration for model choice and implementation.

Reading Apprenticeship Ingredients and Costs

The list of ingredients for RA was obtained through reviews of program literature and from telephone conversations with the developer, Strategic Literacy Initiative (SLI) at WestEd, and implementers from multiple sites, two of which are represented in Table 4.3. The primary ingredient categories for RA are personnel and professional development. Because RA is a professional development process that trains teachers to think and teach in a new way, there are no facilities or equipment costs associated with implementation.

Schools and school districts need not hire additional teachers to implement RA because the program is delivered by content area teachers in their content area classes. While the personnel costs for teachers do not change with RA, the program does incur opportunity costs for school- and district-level administrators' time. To determine these costs, we converted the amount of time spent on RA per school year into a percentage of a full-time position and divided that number by the average national salary for that position.

Rather than endorse a specific model of implementation, SLI provides schools and school districts with a range of professional development options to choose from. The National Institute in Reading Apprenticeship (NIRA) is an eight-day "training-of-trainers" program designed to prepare school, district, or department leaders to train teachers in local professional development sessions or implement RA in their own classrooms. Site-based trainings, provided

TABLE 4.3. Reading Apprenticeship (RA) Implementation Models

INGREDIENTS LIST	INGREDIENT		RA SITE ONE			RA SITE TWO		
	Costs (US$)[a]	Annual Costs (US$)[b]	Inputs[c]	Costs (US$)	Annual Costs (US$)	Inputs[d]	Costs (US$)	Annual Costs (US$)
PERSONNEL								
Additional teachers for RA	$57,355.00	$57,355.00	0	$0.00	$0.00	0	$0.00	$0.00
RA teacher:student ratio			1:22			1:26		
District teacher:student ratio			1:22			1:26		
School-level administration	$105,282.50	$105,282.50	0.01[e]	$1,052.83	$1,052.83	0.01	$1,052.83	$1,052.83
District-level administration	$85,892.50	$85,892.50	0.05[f]	$4,294.63	$4,294.63	0.07[g]	$5,964.76	$5,964.76
PROFESSIONAL DEVELOPMENT								
First year teachers trained								
NIRA[h]	$4,000.00	$924.00	8	$33,000.00[i]	$7,623.00	no		
West Ed Site–based training[j] from						no		
One day	$7,500.00	$1,732.50						
Seven days	$50,000.00	$11,550.00						
District-customized			42	$60,000.00	$13,860.00	4[k]	$4,000.00	$924.00
Bay Area Network Series	$1,000.00	$231.00	no					
Paid collaboration time[l]			yes	$6,000.00	$6,000.00	n.r.		
Training after first year								
Site-based training	included		yes	included		no		
Continuing Network Series	included		no			4	included	
Substitute days	$120.00	$27.72	234[m]	$28,080.00	$5,897.00	28[n]	$3,360.00	$776.16
School administrator training	$105,282.50	$24,320.26	0.00[o]	$421.13	$97.28	0.04[p]	$4,211.30	$972.81
District administrator training	$85,892.50	$19,841.17	0.01[q]	$773.03	$178.56	0.04[r]	$3,340.26	$771.60

(continued)

TABLE 4.3. Reading Apprenticeship (RA) Implementation Models (*continued*)

INGREDIENTS LIST	INGREDIENT		RA SITE ONE			RA SITE TWO		
	Costs (US$)a	Annual Costs (US$)b	Inputsc	Costs (US$)	Annual Costs (US$)	Inputsd	Costs (US$)	Annual Costs (US$)
Total cost				$133,621.62	$39,003.30		$21,929.15	$10,462.16
Students served in 2004–2005				1,271	1,271		1,150	1,150
Cost per student				$105.13	$30.69		$19.07	$9.10

n.r. = not reported

a All personnel costs were calculated using national averages for the 2004–2005 school year (source: Educational Research Service) plus 25% estimated fringe benefits. All program costs are provided by WestEd.

b To annualize costs, this table assumes a five-year lifespan and a 5% discount rate unless otherwise noted.

c Provided by assistant district superintendent.

d Provided by assistant district superintendent and school principal.

e Twenty hours per year.

f Seventy hours per year.

g One hundred hours per year: includes 6 hours of staff training meetings per month and 40 hours of marketing, securing resources, presenting, organizing, etc.

h National Institute in Reading Apprenticeship. See www.wested.org/cs/sli for more information.

i $4,125 per teacher. This number includes travel expenses.

j For a complete description of these options, see www.wested.org/cs/sli/print/docs/sli/services.htm.

k Twenty teachers have been trained over five years at approximately 4 per year.

l District pays teacher leaders for collaborative monthly meetings.

m Five days per teacher for the site-based training and three days per teacher for 8 teachers for NIRA training.

n Seven days per teacher for 4 teachers.

o Six hours total: four hours half-day training and two hours end-of-year meeting.

p Fifty-six hours per administrator. One administrator participates in the seven-day training each year.

q Participation in school administrator half-day training.

r District administrator participates in half-day training.

by SLI staff or certified RA consultants, range in length from one to seven days of training. Finally, the Bay Area Network Series is a seven-day program, similar to NIRA but designed for educators in the Bay Area. (For full descriptions of RA professional development options, see www.wested.org/cs/sli/view/serv.) Following the first year of implementation, SLI offers continued training that is included with the purchase of the program. Other significant costs associated with professional development include substitute costs and opportunity costs for school and administrator training time.

In evaluating the data below, it is essential to remember that both sites from which we obtained information were recommended by SLI, and both enthusiastically endorsed RA. Thus, it is possible that our data do not account for (a) the full range of variety in RA implementation and (b) implementation obstacles experienced by less successful districts. Despite the fact that both sites have experienced success with RA, we found a wide difference in implementation between the two sites that had a large impact on costs. Because this is not a cost-effective analysis, however, we cannot comment on the relative effectiveness of the two approaches.

Reading Apprenticeship Sites One and Two

RA Site One and Site Two are both rural districts in the same state. During the 2004–2005 school year, Site One, a district comprising five high schools, trained 42 teachers and served approximately 1,270 students. In the same year Site Two, implementing RA in one large high school, trained 57 teachers and served approximately 1,150 students. While both sites trained similar numbers of teachers who served similar numbers of students, the costs per student were significantly different with Site One spending just over three times more per student annually. These differences are due to different methods of implementation, but the overall cost at both sites is relatively modest because no additional personnel, materials, or facilities are needed.

The primary costs for Site One were in professional development. The district customized the site-based training to provide 42 teachers with five days of training by SLI experts for US$60,000. In addition, it sent eight teacher-leaders to participate in NIRA for the cost of US$33,000. These teachers returned to their schools as leaders of program implementation. The total substitute costs for these trainings were around US$28,000.

While Site One paid SLI around US$90,000 for professional development, Site Two paid only US$4,000 because it trained its teachers "in house." Site Two sent four teacher-leaders (including one administrator) to the Bay Area Network Series. These teachers, rather than SLI experts, provided training to the site's 53 remaining teachers during monthly professional development meetings, one-third of which were set aside by the principal for exclusive focus on RA. (The teacher-leaders trained in 2004–2005 joined other teacher-leaders trained by SLI in previous years.) The substitute costs for the Bay Area trainings were around US$3,360. It is important to remember that in both models the professional development costs are low estimates because we do not account for teacher training time.

Outside of professional development, the primary cost to both sites was for school and district administrator time. While the costs do not seem high, it is essential that this category not be overlooked by future implementers. In Site One the assistant superintendent spent approximately 70 hours per year on RA, whereas in Site Two the assistant superintendent spent about 100 hours per year. These are significant numbers, considering the numerous responsibilities and obligations of top district administrators. In both sites, this time was spent in staff training meetings, working with program developers and school administrators, securing program resources, organizing logistics, and so forth. While such time commitments are clearly not required for program implementation—both site administrators emphasized that they went above and beyond the requirements for successful RA implementation—both sites emphasized that without such strong district involvement and organization, it would be difficult to consistently implement the intervention at a high level.

In addition to the large time investment by district administrators, there are three other similarities that are important to note. First, school administrators at each site attended the vast majority of teacher-related professional development sessions. At Site Two, for example, the three top administrators attended the Bay Area Network training over the course of three years, along with most in-school collaborative meetings and trainings. Second, both sites adhere closely to SLI's recommendation that RA be "embedded in subject-area instruction across the curriculum, rather than becoming the sole purview of the English department" (Greenleaf et al., 2001, p. 89). Taken together, these two factors advanced implementation by creating collaborative cultures of literacy with extensive administrative support.

Third, both sites reported few problems with teacher turnover. Because RA is an approach to the professional development of teachers, the risks associated with turnover are high. For example, a teacher who is trained in his second year and leaves by his fifth will raise the annualized cost of RA implementation by reducing its lifespan. Thus, local retention rates should be considered when generalizing RA data across districts. That being said, high-turnover schools can minimize this risk by selecting the teacher-leaders who are most likely to remain at the school over time.

Recommendations for Successful Implementation

An important finding from this study is that implementation costs may vary considerably from setting to setting because of differences in implementation.

Some of the variation in costs may be due to different prices for resources among areas, such as differences in teacher salaries and benefits among places with low costs of living and high costs of living. These are not reflected in our data because we used an average of "national" prices in estimating the costs. Other reasons may be due to students with a greater incidence of special needs, such as immigrants and English-language learners (ELLs), or a greater incidence of poverty that requires more intensive services. However, we believe that most of the difference is simply due to differences in implementation among school sites, with some using more resources than others for the same intervention. Whether these differences are merited by differences in outcomes is unknown and requires careful and rigorous evaluations that are beyond the focus of this chapter. However, on the basis of work we have done on school district reform, we suspect that a significant amount of the differences are not related to either the nature of the students or differences in effectiveness, but simply to differences in implementation.

We believe that if schools were to pursue the following recommendations, they could provide more effective implementation and better monitoring of costs.

Selection of Intervention

The selection of an intervention ought to entail sufficient time to gather appropriate information and to include discussions and input by teachers and other staff who will be involved in implementation. Considerable experience affirms that staff agreement on goals and knowledge of and commitment to reforms provides greater promise of success. Datnow (2000) has emphasized that the process of participation of teachers and other staff in becoming informed about the issues leading to new interventions and the choice of interventions is key to their cooperation. However, she found that often this process of school "buy-in" has been carried out in a perfunctory manner, culminating in a ritual vote that reaffirms the obvious and declared preference of key administrators. An authentic process of informing staff and obtaining their input is more likely to enhance their understanding of the need for change and their willingness to get involved in both the choice of an intervention and its effective implementation.

Given the presence of many reforms dedicated to improving adolescent literacy, it is crucial to attempt to match potential choices of reforms to student needs and the capacity of a school to implement the intervention. A review of the various alternatives will reveal that different reforms have been developed for different groups of students (e.g., ELLs) or students with different learning needs. Evaluations of results will also emphasize where these reforms have shown success. Furthermore, the descriptions of the interventions will suggest strengths that schools might build on such as experience with the use of educational technologies or particular approaches to student grouping or scheduling that match up well with specific reforms. Obviously, it is better to choose potential reforms that match school strengths than to require the schools to develop major new ones in order for a reform to succeed.

Implementation Requirements

The adoption of a reform that matches the needs and strengths of a school is based upon the overall features of the school and reform. However, such a decision does not address the details of implementation and their costs. The ingredients method allows for both planning the intervention and ascertaining its costs. This method calls for decisionmakers to identify and specify all of the resources and conditions that will be required to make the reform a success. Details on identification of ingredients, personnel, facilities, equipment, supplies, and other resources can be found in Levin and McEwan (2001). The goal of this activity is to be clear about what will be needed with special attention to the qualitative dimensions of the resource, such as the qualifications of appropriate personnel. Information on required ingredients can be obtained from three sources. First, developers can provide descriptive materials and information as well as reference other sites that have adopted the reform. Second, these other sites can be contacted, and visited if close by, to observe the program. Third, practitioners at these sites can be interviewed on details of their implementation as well as lessons learned from their experience. All of this information can be integrated into a plan for implementation and the resources necessary for the plan to succeed.

Costs and Resource Availability

Two key questions on which good implementation rests are "Has adequate funding been put aside to cover the cost of the reform?" and "Are the appropriate resources available?" The way to ascertain the answer to the first question is to know the cost of the reform by placing a cost on all of the ingredients (Levin & McEwan, 2001). Not all of the ingredients require additional funding if some of them can be obtained through reallocation of existing resources from less productive uses. Many reforms stumble because available personnel in the school such as administrators, coordinators, and coaches do not have the skills or experiences that are necessary to provide support for the reform. This may place the school in a difficult situation where personnel must be marshaled from those internally available in the school or district, but where those who are readily available are inappropriate.

From the analyses of cost and resource availability, it is possible to ascertain both the obstacles to implementation success as well as possible solutions for overcoming those obstacles. If the costs exceed the resources that are available, it is important to seek additional resources or to decide how to accommodate reform within available resources. For example, the cost of additional personnel and space for reducing class size to some prescribed level may exceed the funding and space that are available. Schools will need to confer with developers on how to address this shortcoming or whether successful implementation can take place despite this shortfall. A similar analysis must be done in terms of ensuring that appropriate personnel are in place. At the point of implementation planning, the specific personnel who will work with the reform should be noted. This is important for two reasons. First, the particular personnel should be familiarizing themselves with the reform and their roles well in advance of the actual implementation. Second, those who are planning the implementation need to size up required qualifications against those of the potential appointees. If available personnel are inappropriate, the organizers of the reform will need to seek alternatives or confer with the developers on what might be done.

Implementation Plan

All of this taken together contributes to the formation of an implementation plan. All resource requirements are identified, and provision is made for their availability for the reform. Funding is adequate to cover their costs or to provide appropriate resources from within the school organization. Plans are made to acquire materials, software, and equipment in sufficient time to launch the reform. A timeline and calendar for professional development and other activities such as monitoring, classroom observations, feedback, and evaluation of results must be set out. If the school site lacks the funding and available resources to implement the reform along the lines recommended by the developer, discrepancies will become obvious and there will be time to enable a search for alternatives. Minimally, this approach to costing and implementation planning will establish whether the reform is feasible in the sense of the school's having the operational and financial capacity to undertake it. More promising is the possibility that such planning will provide a blueprint for implementation—avoiding many of the unpleasant surprises and unintentional compromises that many schools have had to face, leading to underperformance of the reform.

Conclusion

As noted earlier, our work in school district reform suggests that much or most of the differences in program costs, both between programs and between sites implementing the same program, are related simply to differences in implementation. We do not believe these differences to be reflections of either the nature of the students at different sites or differences between programs in their effectiveness. Rather, they reflect conscious decisions made by administrators. What is unclear is the extent to which these choices alter the effects programs have on students.

An underlying assumption of program developers and of too many implementation models is that teachers and administrators are in agreement about the nature of the adolescent literacy problem and its solution at a particular site. The next chapter addresses this assumption head-on and provides you with a framework for understanding your own school's or district's readiness for implementing any adolescent literacy program.

CHAPTER 5

School and District Change to Improve Adolescent Literacy

Reed T. Deshler, Donald D. Deshler, & Gina Biancarosa

ALTHOUGH THIS BOOK AS a whole is intended as a guide through the process of identifying and addressing adolescent literacy challenges in schools and districts, this chapter and the previous one focus on helping administrators think through the issues that influence program choices and, ultimately, effectiveness. Chapter 4 laid bare the influence that implementation choices have on program costs. It is beyond the scope of this book to explore how those same choices influence program effects. However, this chapter builds on these ideas by exploring in more detail the organizational issues that lie behind a successful implementation: readiness for, widespread engagement in, and assessment of adolescent literacy improvement. Furthermore, it underscores the idea that improving adolescent literacy is a far more complicated undertaking than finding a magic bullet. This chapter also highlights that, as complicated as the undertaking may be, careful, coordinated, and successful action is possible.

We begin by considering one principal who tried to improve adolescent literacy in his school. (We chose one example rather than several because the issues involved are intricate and require deep consideration. For additional examples of the school change process that center on adolescent literacy, we suggest one of several helpful school and district portraits in existing adolescent literacy publications [Berman & Biancarosa, 2005; National Association of Secondary School Principals, 2005; Short & Fitzsimmons, 2007].) After describing his journey, we connect this principal's experiences to guiding principles for effective organizational change. We hope that this chapter, together with Chapter 4, will give school and district administrators some concrete guidance to ensuring the effective implementation of any adolescent literacy program(s).

A Midwestern High School Case Study

When Wayne Sumner (pseudonym) was hired to be the new principal of Bernadine High School (BHS) in the summer of 2000, the superintendent told him he had to "turn the school around." The previous spring the district leadership had received the results from the North Central Evaluation process. The picture painted by this evaluation made it painfully clear that major changes had to be made to alter the school's literacy performance. Wayne had been a very successful principal in two other high schools in another district during his 16 years as a school leader. In light of his past record, the superintendent and school board explicitly hired him to provide the leadership that would change the literacy achievement of BHS students.

BHS draws 1,200 students from rural areas in its Midwest community. The student population is 59% Caucasian, 33% Hispanic, and 8% African American. Almost half of the students qualify for free and reduced-cost lunches, and an increased number of English-language learners, who have come to the area with their migrant-worker families, have enrolled at BHS. Assessment tests indicated that half of the school's 390 ninth graders read below grade level, with one-third of them performing two or more years below grade level. Moreover, the graduation rate had fallen to 82%.

In studying the history of BHS, Wayne learned that in the 1970s and 1980s the school had one of the best academic records of comparable schools in the state. With rapidly shifting demographics, however, academic performance began to fall rapidly in the early 1990s. In an attempt to address the declining test scores, one change after another was implemented over 10 years. School leaders tried to address a broad array of problems simultaneously, ranging from increasing the number of graduating students receiving postsecondary scholarships to raising sagging reading and math scores. While each change was well-intentioned, many of the BHS staff thought that these changes were often hastily adopted and initiated through a top-down approach with little input from teachers and staff. In the wake of one reform after another, it was clear to Wayne that BHS staff members were weary from their engagement in constant change initiatives and leery of what the new principal might ask them to do next.

Wayne knew from his previous experiences in improving literacy outcomes in high schools that it would be important to approach his assignment by following two guiding principles. First, rather than trying to do everything at once, he should target the high-priority areas for change determined through staff input. Second, to secure significant improvement in literacy outcomes, a comprehensive array of factors needed to be implemented in a coordinated way over a sustained period (at least four to five years). Additionally, Wayne pledged to himself that he wouldn't try to force solutions that had worked in his other schools onto the BHS staff because "one size does not fit all."

Consequently, to determine which areas should be prioritized, Wayne spent a lot of time listening to individual staff members regarding their perceptions of the most pressing literacy challenges facing BHS students. He heard a great deal of willingness and readiness to support a literacy initiative, but he also heard a great deal of frustration over past initiatives. With a deeper understanding of the feelings, perceptions, and readiness of the staff in hand, Wayne began making the case that BHS administrators and teachers must find a way to raise the literacy performance of those students who were low performers. His message was not only one of urgency but also one of sensitivity. He explained to the staff that he was sensitive to the large number of reforms and change efforts they were asked to engage in during the past decade. As a result, he pledged to them that, for the next four to five years, improving the literacy performance of BHS students would be the school's top priority, and that he would shield the staff from outside pressures to take on other change initiatives. He went out of his way to respond to questions and concerns and always ended any presentation on adolescent literacy with a "Yeah, but..." segment in which teachers were encouraged to raise their doubts and concerns.

When Wayne finally convened a School Improvement Team, the members were prepared for the charge that he gave to them: to establish a prioritized plan of action to markedly improve literacy achievement for those students in BHS performing more than two years below grade level. Furthermore, he reminded the team that all members of BHS had an important, but unique, role to play in improving literacy achievement. Therefore, the plan of action should carefully consider the unique skill sets and contributions that various members of the staff should be expected to assume. In other words, Wayne wasn't willing to accept any solution that assigned a limited number of staff (e.g., the school's two literacy coaches) full responsibility for addressing the problem. In addition, he indicated that any solution that involved putting all of the low-achieving students in the same subject matter classes would be unacceptable because it would be tantamount to tracking. Finally, he made it clear to the team that he would fully support their work and assist them in fulfilling their charge.

To guide their work in building literacy services to improve student outcomes, the School Improvement Team adopted the Content Literacy Continuum (CLC; see Figure 5.1) as a framework (Lenz, Ehren, & Deshler, 2005). The continuum depicts five increasingly intensive levels of instructional support that should be available to all struggling adolescent learners, ranging from incorporating inclusive teaching methods in general education classrooms to providing one-on-one or small-group services of speech–language pathologists and other specialists. The CLC framework was seen as a good match for BHS because it is grounded in three notions for improving literacy outcomes for all adolescents. Moreover, the CLC framework emphasized Wayne's and his School Improvement Team's belief that the entire school must take on the challenge of improving literacy achievement. The CLC highlights that (a) there are unique (but very important) roles for each

FIGURE 5.1. Content Literacy Continuum

Level 1: Enhance content instruction (mastery of critical content for all, regardless of literacy skills)

Level 2: Embedded strategy instruction (routinely weave strategies within and across classes using large-group instructional methods)

Level 3: Intensive strategy instruction (mastery of specific strategies using intensive–explicit instructional sequences)

Level 4: Intensive basic skill instruction (mastery of entry-level literacy skills at the fourth-grade level)

Level 5: Therapeutic intervention (mastery of language underpinnings of curriculum content and learning strategies)

Originally published in Lenz, B.K., Ehren, B.J., & Deshler, D.D. (2005). The content literacy continuum: A school reform framework for improving adolescent literacy for all students. *Teaching Exceptional Children, 37*(6), 60–63.

member of a secondary staff relative to literacy instruction; (b) some students require more intensive, systematic, explicit instruction of content, strategies, and skills; and (c) literacy coaches may be a necessary part of an overall solution, but they aren't sufficient in and of themselves.

To guide their work, Wayne suggested that the School Improvement Team address the five levels of the CLC by conceptualizing them as questions and address them incrementally over several years rather than all at once. The latter was important to ensure that neither they nor the staff would get overextended and burned out on the change process.

Year 1: Enhancing Content Instruction (CLC Level 1)

The first question that the team went about answering was aligned to Level 1 in the CLC and emphasized the role that every member of the teaching staff would have in the initiative: What should we do across our school staff to ensure that students will get the 'critical' content in spite of their literacy skills? To address this question, the team adopted a plan of action that involved inviting the 32 general education teachers who taught core academic classes (e.g., science, history, English, math) to participate in intensive staff development to learn how to implement Content Enhancement Routines from the Strategic Instruction Model (see Part II, page 208) in classes that contained students with academically diverse skills, including several who lacked sufficient literacy skills to fluently read and understand class texts. Content Enhancement Routines (Lenz & Deshler, 2004) are instructional practices designed to help teachers organize and present critical information in such a way that students can more easily understand and remember it. These routines included an Anchoring Table (Bulgren et al., 1994a) and the Comparison Routine (Bulgren, Lenz, Deshler, & Schumaker, 1995). Over time, teachers across core content areas began to incorporate these practices, or routines, into their day-to-day instruction. Through these routines, students engaged in lively debates that led to greater understanding of the concepts they were discussing and the potential to increase their literacy skills as they improved their ability to understand, analyze, and apply what they read in class. Three years after the first introduction of content enhancement, about 90% of content teachers actively used the routines in their classrooms.

Year 2: Embedding Strategy Instruction (CLC Level 2)

During the second year, the School Improvement Team focused its energies in answering a second major question: What steps should we take to ensure that powerful learning strategies are embedded across the curriculum? This question aligned to Level 2 of the CLC framework. While staff were encouraged with the success experienced through the use of Content Enhancement Routines (Level 1 of CLC), it was clear that these interventions alone were not sufficiently powerful to enable all struggling readers to succeed in their content classes. Although the teaching routines supported students' learning of content, the students needed strategies they could wield independently. Therefore, the School Improvement Team chose to adopt Reciprocal Teaching (RT; see Part II, page 197) as a schoolwide approach. They would use RT to teach students how to effectively interact with their subject matter texts by reading strategically for comprehension. The primary students targeted by RT are those reading at or below the 35th percentile. It involves explicit instruction in and modeling of critical comprehension strategies, including summarizing, generating questions, clarifying, and predicting. To provide sufficient opportunities for practice and feedback and to optimize the effects of RT, teachers were taught how to arrange students in groups of 10 or fewer so students would have numerous opportunities to interact with one another and their teachers around texts. Hence, subject matter teachers received staff development on how to integrate these strategies within the context of their classes. By learning how to incorporate RT within some of their classes, subject matter teachers were prepared to model and teach some critical reading strategies.

Year 3: Intensive Strategy and Basic Skill Instruction (CLC Levels 3 and 4)

Evaluation data taken at the end of the second year indicated that encouraging progress was being made by a significant number of subject matter teachers in successfully implementing interventions at the first two levels of the CLC (i.e., Content Enhancement Routines and Reciprocal Teaching). Hence, with a growing sense of momentum around the initiative, the School Improvement Team decided to answer two questions related to Levels 3 and 4 of the CLC in their third year: (1) What should we do for those students who need more learning strategies instruction than can be offered within the context of the general education classroom because of the constraints of that setting? (2) What should we do for those students who are reading below the fourth-grade level?

To address the first of these questions, the School Improvement Team recommended the formation of a literacy class that would meet daily. Students who were reading between two and four levels below grade level were eligible for enrollment in this class; it also included some of the students who continued to struggle in spite of instruction provided through Level 1 and Level 2 interventions. The teacher–student ratio in these classes was, at most, 1 to 15. The teachers for these classes received in-depth professional development in how to teach an array of literacy strategies to struggling adolescent learners. They then taught students task-specific learning strategies using more intensive, explicit, and direct instructional methodologies than were used in RT. Care was taken to use highly engaging, leveled reading selections and to provide intensive instruction in all literacy areas, including writing. Moreover, instruction was accompanied and driven by ongoing formative assessments to help guide the instructional process, so that ongoing and rapid changes could be made in students' instructional programs for optimal response to their learning needs. Finally, teachers deliberately taught students how to generalize what they learned in these classes to the demands they encountered in their subject matter classes. In short, through these classes, students received instruction that was intensive and extensive in terms of added time for specific literacy instruction to close the broad achievement gap these students were trying to overcome.

In answer to their fourth question regarding students who were reading at or below the fourth-grade level, the School Improvement Team chose to continue a program that had been used at the school for several years, Corrective Reading (CR; see Part II, page 149). The team noted, however, that there were some students who were not responding to the CR program. These seemed to be students with specific language problems. For them, the team chose to add a program used successfully in a neighboring district: the Wilson Reading System (see Part II, page 224). This program was designed for use with secondary students with severe decoding and spelling difficulties. Students are placed in the program on the basis of their performance on an individualized assessment, which is part of the program and lessons. The program consists of systematic, sequential, and intensive phonics instruction, which takes place individually or in very small groups of students with similar levels of reading performance.

Years 4 and 5: Therapeutic Intervention (CLC Level 5)

As the School Improvement Team continued to study student performance data on struggling learners, they realized that there was a relatively small yet significant number of students for whom the existing interventions were not enough.

These appeared to be students with underlying cognitive, metalinguistic, and metacognitive problems. Thus, as a final step in its work to implement a comprehensive array of literacy services, the team addressed the final level of the CLC with this question: What should we do for those students who have underlying language disorders? To help formulate appropriate programs for these students, the team recommended that some of the speech–language pathologists in the school district be reassigned to BHS to capitalize on their knowledge and expertise. This was an unusual request because generally speech–language pathologists spend little time working with adolescents in secondary schools. It took considerable advocacy from Wayne to have district leaders support this resource allocation, but Wayne and his team eventually got what they wanted.

Three Core Principles to Drive Successful Adolescent Literacy Initiatives

With the pressures to increase student outcomes in light of No Child Left Behind expectations, numerous attempts have been made to change how secondary schools are organized and operate. While such efforts have been well-intentioned, often they have been hastily adopted and initiated through a top-down approach thus ignoring many important principles of organizational change (e.g., Fullan, 2001a). In the wake of one reform effort after another, educators gradually acquire what Morgan (2001) refers to as "change fatigue." Those who are continually targeted by change efforts soon tire of trying yet another magical solution, and thus their motivation to engage in such efforts may wane. This reaction against school-improvement efforts underscores the importance of carefully tending to known principles of organizational change.

As we stand back and evaluate what transpired at BHS, several lessons can be learned concerning how schools and districts can best prepare for and implement measures to improve adolescent literacy outcomes. Most prominent perhaps is the sheer magnitude of the School Improvement Team's undertaking to implement a broad array of changes at BHS. Both Wayne and his School Improvement Team understood that to effect lasting change in their students' literacy achievement, change had to be comprehensive and coordinated. It was not enough to adopt a new curriculum because no single curriculum addressed the breadth of their students' needs. Instead, they adopted a framework that helped them think about the variety of students at their school and how their specific struggles might be alleviated.

In addition to this important mindset, those familiar with theories of organizational change will recognize that principles for effective organizational change seem to be at the root of the success at BHS. We highlight three of these principles and illustrate how school and district leaders can use them to build a foundation for success in choosing and implementing adolescent literacy reforms:

1. Organizations and people must be ready to make change.
2. Key stakeholders must be engaged in making decisions about changes to be made.
3. Self-assessments that measure progress toward key goals must be used to define success.

Organizational Change Versus Individual Transition

The term *change* is often used interchangeably for *transition*, but in this chapter we use these terms for distinct purposes. Thus, before we unpack the three principles of effective organizational change for improving adolescent literacy, we review our use of the terms *change* and *transition*.

Although both change and transition deal with the idea of going from one state to another, organizational change is an event that occurs in an organization and as such is largely external to those involved. In contrast, an individual transition is largely psychological and experiential in nature. Whereas organizational change generally happens quickly (e.g., often in the form of an announcement from central or building administrators), individual transitions are usually gradual. Moreover, organizational change is generally initiated with a much clearer focus on desired outcomes.

However, organizational change does not occur in a vacuum but, rather, involves individual transitions as well. While organizational change refers to specific organizational events, such as the adoption of an adolescent literacy intervention program, it also generates individual transitions, as individuals are required to adapt to change. Consequently, much of what follows will cover both organizational change and individual transition issues. Indeed, successful school change inevitably involves individual transitions and organizational changes; one without the other can lead to incomplete or unsustainable transformation, which is not an acceptable outcome given demands for meeting average yearly progress (AYP) targets and pressures to close other achievement gaps.

Principle #1: Organizations and People Must Be Ready to Make Change

In his efforts to improve adolescent literacy at BHS, Wayne spent a lot of time up front preparing himself and his teachers for change. Wayne knew that his success in leading BHS to adopt new ways of addressing the school's literacy challenges would be directly correlated to the degree to which those involved were ready for the change. He knew that attention must be given to the readiness of the organization and its people to plan, organize, and develop the capabilities needed to implement the planned change. He also recognized that underlying organizational readiness is the notion that the individuals affected understand, accept, and are willing to modify their behaviors to make the change happen. The major categories of readiness that were at work at BHS are a compelling need, understanding of the need, leadership commitment, individual capabilities, organizational capabilities, stakeholder response, and competing events and resources.

Table 5.1 delineates these major categories and offers some high-level indicators that may suggest a school's or district's readiness in each area. Note that the items listed in the table are intended to provide a few of the high-level signs or considerations that may be assessed when determining readiness; however, to really answer these questions or address these considerations additional probing through other, more specific questions or via a survey may be required. In other words, Table 5.1 does not constitute a complete readiness assessment tool.

A Compelling Need

Any change effort should start by establishing the case: a compelling need for the change initiative. Doing so provides the justification for the effort and the investments that will be required. If a compelling need doesn't exist, then even the efforts of a charismatic leader or teacher may fall short of getting the initiative started or sustaining it once started. However, it is this compelling need for change that engages the hearts and minds of those affected (Fullan, 2001b). Teachers, staff, and students can do remarkable things when motivated and inspired to embrace the proposed intervention.

In the case of BHS, the need had clearly been identified by the district. Wayne was hired with the charge of turning the school's literacy achievement around. But Wayne went a step further by talking to his teachers to be sure they saw the same need that district leadership did. At BHS, although they were weary of a consistent stream of reforms, the teachers indeed recognized their school's flagging literacy achievement and wanted to address the problem.

Understanding of the Need

The next category of readiness is enhancing the understanding of the need. This means that stakeholders need to recognize more than the existence of a problem; they need to understand the gap between current and future performance in order to be able to specify clear objectives. When teachers and administrators have a clear understanding of the rationales underlying the proposed change, they can begin to explore the implications, possibilities, and challenges associated with it. Failure to achieve a basic level of understanding leads almost immediately to resistance. Before district and building stakeholders invest time and energy into adopting a new literacy intervention, they need opportunity to have their major questions and concerns addressed. Those promoting the new literacy program should provide answers to these questions for all stakeholders.

TABLE 5.1. Categories of Change Readiness Considerations

Compelling Need	The desired future state is obvious and necessary.
	Relevant information exists that supports the need for change.
	An accurate picture of the organization's current condition (e.g., student outcome data, ranking with comparable schools) is available.
	The need for change is greater than the resistance to the change.
Understanding	The gap between current state and desired future state is clear to all stakeholders.
	People believe that the change is good, reasonable, and appropriate.
	People have access to information that profiles the school's strengths and weaknesses relative to the proposed literacy program
	The objectives of the change have been clearly communicated to all key stakeholders.
Leadership Commitment	Leaders are committed (words and actions) to making this change happen.
	Behavioral and performance expectations have been articulated.
	The priorities that will guide decision making during implementation have been communicated.
Individual Capabilities (Tools/Skills)	People feel prepared to address the disruption (personal and professional) caused by this change.
	People have the necessary resources, knowledge, information, and skills to support and participate in the change.
	New roles and responsibilities (if applicable) have been established.
	People understand and accept the new roles they are being asked to play.
Organization Capabilities (Processes/Systems/ Structures)	Information and feedback are available to inform the organization about how well the change is going.
	The organization has the capabilities and processes to implement/execute the change(s).
	Processes, systems, and structures exist or are being developed that are needed to support the change.
Stakeholder Response	Feedback from key stakeholders (e.g., teachers, students, parents, administrators, staff) has been incorporated into the literacy program plan.
	Key people who must support and be involved with the change have been identified.
	Key external stakeholders and their influence are known and are being managed.
	There is no significant resistance to the change.
	Individuals are being given the support and time needed to learn about and accept the change.
	The readiness for change has been regularly measured and monitored throughout the change process.
Resources and Competing Events	The action items and responsibilities required to implement the change have been defined.
	There are no other events or projects competing for resources and attention.
	This change is congruent/consistent with other initiatives in the organization.

Adapted from Deshler, R., & Smith, K. (2006). *Organization change and individual transition tool book.* Manuscript submitted for publication.

Wayne made sure that his teachers had time to air their concerns both privately and publicly. Even as momentum for the BHS adolescent literacy initiative built, Wayne continued to actively solicit doubts with his "Yeah, but..." closings to staff meetings. This invitation to fully consider the ramifications of the initiative made it much more likely that Wayne understood his teachers and that his teachers understood him.

Leadership Commitment

The next readiness category, leadership commitment, is central to effective transformation. Leaders can exercise considerable influence in setting the tone for the behaviors and performance targets expected by key stakeholders. Because leaders' behaviors are scrutinized in public and in private, the fidelity between a leader's public words and private actions is critical. Often leaders set the conditions for successful change by modeling desired behaviors, making it safe to experiment and give feedback, and providing coaching to those expected to conform or modify behaviors—such as teachers, staff, and specialists. When necessary, leaders must candidly confront those who fail to perform or those who engage in counterproductive behaviors.

In his efforts to understand his staff and to communicate honestly with them about the adolescent literacy challenge they were taking on, Wayne was indeed modeling desired behaviors and providing a safe arena for hashing out the details of change. Moreover, by establishing the School Improvement Team at BHS, Wayne provided for leadership beyond his own office. Enlisting multiple stakeholders on the team led to a sense of unity and commitment to actions that have been reasoned out collectively. Moreover, it offered those on the team support for elaborating and challenging their own ideas.

Individual Capabilities

Determining the individual capabilities of key stakeholders is an important part of readiness; it provides an indication of the necessary technical skills (e.g., proficiency with specific instructional practices) as well as emotional and intellectual capabilities required for effective change. Some districts (or schools) that have undertaken significant literacy initiatives find that they don't have the bench strength in their teacher or administrative ranks to deliver the level of instruction required for the literacy program to achieve the desired results. Two things occur if teachers or administrators are unable to exhibit the needed behaviors: (1) Results do not come as hoped for or predicted, and (2) resistance and disbelief that the change will really work grow.

Organizational Capabilities

In addition to individual capabilities, schools and districts must have the organization capabilities, infrastructure, and resources needed to support new literacy initiatives. Thus, schools and districts pursuing literacy reforms must develop systems, processes, professional development, and structures needed to support and implement the planned interventions. Leaders who announce a new literacy program and assume the necessary organizational capabilities and supports are in place have a high risk of failure. One of the most critical supports is the ability to measure baseline performance and monitor performance in closing achievement gaps. Providing feedback is essential to informing the school/district and its stakeholders of what is happening and what is being accomplished. When progress is off track, this feedback should trigger needed corrective actions.

Wayne and the BHS School Improvement Team both evaluated the individual and organizational capabilities at BHS and responded to perceived needs. This was most evident in their providing targeted professional development for teachers across the subject areas. They clearly recognized that subject matter teachers infrequently have the background knowledge and experience to effectively implement literacy reforms. In the initial stages, this meant training in Content Enhancement Routines and in RT. Moreover, they did not stop after the initial evaluation of capabilities; but as new goals were enumerated and each new stage of the initiative began, they reevaluated. As a consequence, they were able to recruit training, or in the final stage new personnel, that provided the needed expertise for success.

Stakeholder Response

The next key readiness category is that of stakeholder response. Eliciting and managing the responses of stakeholders (e.g., teachers, administrators, parents) is important in getting them to embrace the changes rather than resist them. Resistance can be overt, ranging from vocal criticism against the program in staff meetings to refusal to genuinely participate in professional development activities, and even to organized resistance to changes by members of a department or informal group of colleagues. Resistance can also be covert, such as using a new instructional technique in classroom instruction only when being observed or failing to volunteer for special assignments related to the roll-out of a part of the literacy program. Whether the resistance is overt or covert, its impact on literacy reform can be damaging. There are numerous strategies for addressing the issue of resistance and helping stakeholders embrace change; some of these are one-on-one feedback sessions, mentoring with change advocates, special assignments, joint planning, and vision/purpose development.

At BHS, Wayne went a long way toward avoiding resistance by ensuring his staff's understanding through individual conversations and group meetings about the initiative. His "Yeah, but..." closings to meetings also provided his teachers with a publicly sanctioned way to express doubts and concerns. As a result, Wayne had a good sense of his staff's worries and potential objections, but more importantly, his staff members came to understand that he valued their input and that he saw them as active partners in the adolescent literacy initiative at BHS.

Resources and Competing Events

The final readiness category is resources and competing events. Readiness for change is increased by understanding the competing events and resource demands that can present conflicts to the planned change. With so much happening in schools and districts due to AYP pressures, new initiatives or programs risk falling on deaf ears, thus not being able to deliver the promised results. Highlighting or exposing the connections between and among various initiatives (e.g., Why is such-and-such new literacy program important *and* how does it relate to or fit in with the other initiatives to which we've been dedicated?) is one way to make a new program not seem like a competing event but, rather, a logical next step in the reform journey. A process for establishing the connection among initiatives in a school or district can embody the following steps:

1. Identify all current initiatives.
2. Highlight the key objectives of each.
3. Overlay the new initiative being implemented with its key objectives.
4. Note overlaps in objectives covered by the identified initiatives.
5. Acknowledge gaps filled by the new initiative.
6. Develop talking points that can be used to explain connections to key players.

In addition, leaders of literacy reform initiatives must not only provide the skills and tools teachers and staff need to change but also take things off people's plates, so that they can focus unencumbered on the new skills and behaviors that must be mastered and integrated.

Wayne was particularly sensitive to this category of readiness in his efforts at BHS. In talking to his staff he learned that there was already a great deal of weariness at the seemingly endless stream of reforms at the school. Thus, he made a point of pledging to the BHS community that the adolescent literacy initiative would be the school's primary reform. Moreover, he stayed true to his word and protected them for several years from an influx of other innovations.

Although Wayne and the BHS School Improvement Team did not necessarily address every readiness category consideration listed in Table 5.1 (see page 101), they clearly addressed each category. Their efforts to ensure readiness for change at BHS inevitably contributed to the success they experienced.

Principle #2: Key Stakeholders Must Be Engaged in Making Decisions About Changes to Be Made

One of the best ways to engage people is to form teams that have a solid charter and a set of objectives toward which to work. Well-designed and well-run teams involve people in creating solutions and making decisions related to the change being contemplated and/or implemented. When stakeholders are involved in making certain types of decisions, they gain some ownership in the program and find a stake that helps them individually through the transition they must make. Convening a School Improvement Team was one of the early steps taken by Wayne at BHS.

Some of the types of decisions that teams or committees can participate in making include the following: what interventions to implement and in what sequence, whether a pilot is needed and if so with whom, how progress can be monitored and assessed, how success should be measured, what professional development is needed, and how to understand and support people as they experience the impacts of the change. Teams may use such tools as interviews, focus groups, surveys, observations, or faculty meetings to gather needed data for informing decision making. The BHS School Improvement Team played an active role in each of these decision areas and used a wide array of tools to do so.

While the use of teams and committees may be appropriate for many tasks, there are some decisions that should not or cannot be delegated to a team or committee. When a decision must be made quickly due to time-sensitive matters, a team or committee is not the best choice to make the decision. Likewise, teams or committees should not be involved in making personnel decisions (e.g., work assignments or performance feedback or evaluations). Leaders should consider which decisions can effectively be assigned to teams or committees and structure decision-making processes and principles accordingly. This is precisely what Wayne did when he gave the BHS School Improvement Team its charge to improve BHS students' literacy achievement. By deciding to focus wholly on improving adolescent literacy at BHS, Wayne limited his team's scope, but within that scope he gave the team wide-reaching control in achieving its goal.

> Effective leaders of change understand the work that needs to be accomplished.

Many formal school or district structures lack the flexibility and participation needed to effectively plan, design, and implement a complex change initiative like a literacy program. Effective leaders of change understand the work that needs to be accomplished and are able to assemble a structure for how the change can be planned, organized, designed, communicated, and eventually implemented. At BHS, the School Improvement Team decided that the CLC framework offered them the structure they wanted. Using the framework, the team chose to sequentially deal with specific aspects of adolescent literacy with which their students struggled—from content area literacy and learning to basic language skills. This enabled them to choose purposefully from the wide array of existing adolescent literacy programs and interventions, without feeling compelled to find the one program that would address all their needs.

Effective leaders also recognize that special change structures may be needed; these structures might include advisory committees, working committees, teams/subteams, and steering committees. At BHS, Wayne created the School

Improvement Team. However, each school or district may assemble a unique change structure depending on its organization capabilities, the capabilities of the individuals involved, and time and resources available to implement the chosen literacy program. As an additional illustration, another school that is implementing some new literacy initiatives might assemble a more detailed change structure that includes the following (see also Figure 5.2):

- Leadership Team—Comprises the top administrator, the project leader, and an instructional coach and is responsible for setting direction, establishing timelines, ensuring adequate funding, and monitoring performance throughout implementation.

- Advisory Committee—Comprises representatives of affected stakeholders (e.g., parents, students, teachers, or staff) and is asked to provide suggestions and input to the change program. Advice of the committee may be used to help the planning team know the minds/hearts of the stakeholders affected by the planned change.

- School Improvement Team—Comprises six to eight representatives from Implementation Subteams, is chaired by an assistant principal, and is responsible to meet twice a month to answer questions that surface during implementation and to provide direction on issues/conflicts identified by subteams.

- Implementation Subteams—Comprise teachers and staff from the school who are responsible for carrying out important aspects of the literacy

FIGURE 5.2. Illustration of Sample School Literacy Reform Change Structure

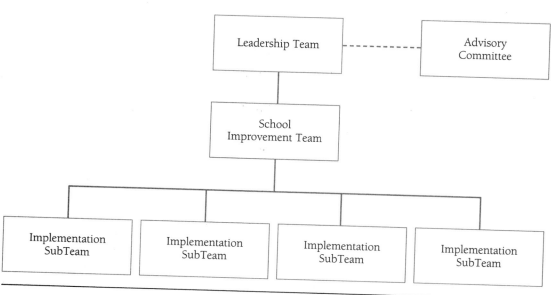

program's implementation; they are formed around topics or issues such as communications, instructional techniques, professional development, and/or measurement.

Whatever structure is assembled, a charter with role definitions should be developed along with an articulation of the connections to the other teams in the structure. Additionally, the linkages between the teams and roles in the change structure should be articulated as they relate to the formal structure of the school or district. For example, who makes budget allocation decisions for the literacy program—the project leader or a school administrator? Finally, because change structures are temporary they are generally dissolved when key milestones are achieved.

The teams and committees of the program's change structure facilitate two important things. As noted earlier, they provide a means of engaging stakeholders in the planning, design, and implementation of change. Second, they create the mechanism through which work is done, people are mobilized, and the program is actually implemented.

Principle #3: Self-Assessments That Measure Progress Toward Key Goals Must Be Used to Define Success

The literature on change and improvement, whether at the organizational or personal level, is replete with data underscoring the fact that improvement is accelerated when specific feedback is provided in a timely fashion. The powerful role that feedback plays in school improvement efforts has been underscored by a host of school reform efforts including Goldenberg, Saunders, and Gallimore's (2004) research on Getting Results schools; Horner, Sugai, and Horner's (2000) research on the application of positive behavioral supports to improve school-wide discipline; and Murphy and Lick's (2001) work on whole-faculty study groups. Central to each of these efforts is the establishment of teams of teachers and administrators who work together to address issues/problems deemed to be critical to improving student outcomes. In each case, problems are identified, solutions are proposed and implemented, and data are collected. It is the data that serve as the basis of teams making decisions, evaluating performance, and ultimately providing feedback to team members and other members of the school staff. Feedback that is grounded in data and specific and timely in nature is vital to moving a team toward accomplishing its stated goals relative to the reform initiative. Throughout the years of reform at BHS, the School Leadership Team monitored staff responses to and implementation of each new part of the adolescent literacy initiative. It was through this data gathering that Wayne and his team knew it was safe to expand their efforts from year to year. Indeed, it was the high rate of satisfaction and implementation that gave them the confidence to take on two reforms at once in year 3 of their initiative.

Another advantage to having regular feedback is that it provides both teachers and administrators with information they can use during coaching. Some people respond to change because they recognize the power or influence someone has, and thus they may try to please the person by conforming their behaviors to the feedback given. While motivation of this sort is less sustainable over time, it may be appropriate in the short term to provide the impetus people need to try new behaviors. The hope is that as they experiment with the new, desired behaviors, they will experience success. Given this success, some people may become converted to the new behaviors, skills, or approaches and be able to self-assess and self-improve going forward. This was particularly the case in the early stages of the initiative at BHS. As subject area teachers began to see the Content Enhancement Routines and RT work for their students, they became more and more enthusiastic as supporters and users of these instructional techniques.

Motivation and individual behavior modification are one thing, but action planning based on feedback and measurements is another. Schools and districts that are diligent in identifying performance gaps, formulating corrective actions, and assigning and following up on action items seem to find that they make progress. Action planning is a basic skill that is often overlooked or only partially done by leaders. Quite simply, action planning is the discipline of addressing the following questions thoroughly:

- What? (What must be done?)
- When? (When does it need to be done?)
- Who? (Who is responsible to carry out the task and ensure its completion?)

Table 5.2 provides a sample action-planning template. A tool like this used in staff meetings or subteam meetings can help drive accountability, focus on results, and make progress toward advancement of the literacy initiative. Generating such specificity at each stage of the BHS initiative contributed to the success experienced there. Some action-planning templates incorporate additional categories that add detail and focus; some of the additional categories might include date assigned, person responsible for follow-up, deliverable description, impact rating, dependencies/interdependencies, status, and so on.

Ideally, each meeting, team work session, or individual coaching session should involve the use of some type of action plan. At the start of each session, open action items should be reviewed to update status and to identify any barriers or issues preventing progress. When an issue or barrier surfaces, time should be spent understanding the issue and working with the person assigned to address it. Those responsible must be careful not to abdicate responsibility for the action item to the team, the leader, or the coach but to come with options or alternatives that can be considered. If someone responsible for an action item that has run into a barrier does not offer alternative solutions, that person should be coached on his or her responsibility to come with options. Doing so

TABLE 5.2. Action-Planning Template

Number	Action Item	Due Date	Person(s) Responsible
#	What needs to be done? (Sufficient detail should be provided to describe the action item. Doing so will allow for clarity at the time of follow-up.)	When does the task need to be completed? (Some action items will be urgent, and others may be completed when time permits.)	Who has been assigned to work on this action item? Who will be asked later if it has been done? (The person assigned should have the capabilities and means to effectively complete the action.)
1	Order high-interest reading materials for independent book study	Prior to end of fiscal year (June 30)	Barbara Jensen
2	Arrange for staff development session on strategies for enhancing vocabulary	August 15 (preparation week prior to school starting)	Jennifer Thompson
3			
4			

reinforces accountability and, more practically, prevents a meeting or work session from derailing as people try to solve the problem.

Project and team leaders should spend time in between meetings and work sessions checking to see how people are progressing on their action items. In this way, many issues can be resolved and barriers removed if identified early. Follow-up between sessions also ensures that progress is made in closing action items on schedule in the next team meeting. When interim follow-up does not occur, action items tend to stay open several days or weeks beyond the expected due dates. Delays in closing action items can have two detrimental effects on the overall success of a literacy initiative: (1) They can slow the roll-out of the initiative leading to increased costs, or (2) they can signal to stakeholders that the school or district leadership is not serious about making literacy reform happen—or even worse that they are unable to provide the direction, organization, and accountability needed to make the change happen. At BHS, Wayne recognized that getting closure on agreed-upon items was essential to maintaining momentum of changes they were trying to make. To underscore this, he frequently said, "We can't add new items to our list until we take one off—which one shall we really focus on so we can get it removed from the list?"

Conclusion

The principles described in this chapter are necessary but insufficient to ensure improvement in literacy outcomes in secondary schools. Why? The answer lies in the critical role leaders play in maintaining momentum. It is beyond this book's scope to dwell on leadership, but we must stress its importance in any attempt to improve adolescent literacy, whether via a single program or a coordinated combination of programs. In addition to his use of a School Improvement Team and the active involvement of his teaching staff, Wayne Sumner's leadership was a driving force behind the successful changes at BHS. Leaders like Wayne act as the "cog" that keeps a program rolling along. If that cog is out of place, spinning in a different direction, or composed of material that won't endure the intense friction and demands placed on it, then the chances of lasting literacy reform are dubious at best, regardless of the program selected. Moreover, although this chapter focused on one principal implementing one reform model, the principles of effective change and the importance of leadership we have detailed are not unique to that model. This chapter will best serve readers as a framework for planning and understanding the mechanisms and conditions of successful schoolwide literacy reform, regardless of program choices.

Wayne had a long career of leading high schools and school reform efforts to draw on during his tenure at BHS. It is critical to recognize that the array of skills he brought to bear is not easily attained. Moreover, the type of comprehensive and coordinated change Wayne took on at BHS is not likely to succeed without a specific capacity to manage change. Indeed, "Fundamentally, there is little recognition of the depth of change in the principal's role that will be required" to achieve the kind of widespread success elementary schools have experienced in school reform in middle and high schools (Fullan, 2003, p. 41). As the need for constant improvement grows (Bridges & Mitchell, 2000), in addition to possessing the more traditional personal attributes, administrative effectiveness, and organizational leadership associated with successful schools, principals and other leaders are expected to possess skills, competencies, and expertise that aid them in effectively planning, organizing, and sponsoring school reform efforts. These skills have been dubbed "change mastery skills" and are relatively new and important requirements of school leaders (Ulrich, 1997; Ulrich, Zenger, & Smallwood, 1999). In his ability to plan for change, to use a variety of tools to assess his school's readiness for and response to change, and to orchestrate coordinated and considered long-term action, Wayne certainly qualifies as one embodiment of change mastery skill. However, we urge readers unfamiliar with the concept to familiarize themselves both with the theory of change mastery (Ulrich, 1997; Ulrich et al., 1999) and to consider other embodiments described in other adolescent literacy publications (Berman & Biancarosa, 2005; National Association of Secondary School Principals, 2005; Short & Fitzsimmons, 2007). Principals, superintendents, and others who embark on one (or more) of the literacy initiatives presented in Part II of this book should have (or at least be developing) these change mastery skills because, as this chapter illustrates, the leadership required to achieve lasting literacy reform in middle and high schools is both significant and demanding.

Specific Instructional Programs

A PLETHORA OF PROGRAMS, PRODUCTS, AND PEDAGOGIES are available to the teacher or administrator looking for ways to improve the literacy curriculum in grades 4 through 12. Most educational publishers offer several products, targeted at different grades and types of students. Part II reviews 48 of the options currently available, describing their basic approach to instruction and to professional development and their evaluation and research bases. In addition, we compare the programs using several grids, which highlight the differences and similarities among the programs.

In general, we use the term *program* broadly to refer to the methods and curricula listed. All address adolescent literacy. However, some do so exclusively through preparing teachers in a pedagogical approach; others do so by providing a sequenced curriculum that can be delivered by any adult; and most use a combination of professional development and curriculum. By using the term *program*, we do not mean to imply that all of the listed options offer sequenced or systematic instruction but simply that all of the options offer an articulated approach to adolescent literacy instruction.

Criteria for Selecting Programs

Readers should note that, despite the large number of programs included, the list is by no means exhaustive. When considering programs to include in this book, we asked ourselves the following questions.

Is the program intended for the students targeted in this volume (i.e., struggling adolescent readers)?

The information in Part II originated a few years back as a summary of 16 programs intended to represent the range of curriculum options available in grades 4 to 12 that specifically cultivate high levels of reading comprehension. This original brief and representative list of programs has been expanded to include a broad array of curricula that address struggling adolescent readers.

With our focus on struggling students, we did not prioritize broader language arts or reading programs. Thus, although some of the curricula and programs detailed here are suitable for typically achieving and even advanced readers, this chapter offers a more thorough review of programs that target adolescents who struggle with one or more aspects of reading.

In keeping with this, we were also interested in whether or not programs targeted specific subsets of struggling readers. This was evidenced in primarily two ways. Some programs were originally developed for use with a specific population of struggling readers, such as students with learning disabilities or English-language learners. In other cases, evaluation and/or research has been conducted that specifically examines the effects of a program when used with a particular population of students.

In defining *adolescent readers*, we looked for programs and methods that were appropriate for middle and high school readers. Because of the dearth of programs developed specifically for students in the upper elementary grades who are in transition to middle school, we noted if the program or method addressed readers in grades 4 and 5 when applicable.

While we chose to focus on adolescent readers, many of the programs considered do address oral language, vocabulary, and writing skills.

Does this program offer literacy instruction?

As noted above, with our focus on literacy we tended to exclude language arts programs or basal reading programs that were intended for the typically developing reader. For the reader interested in such programs, it may be instructive to consider how they foster a range of reading skills in students. Our evaluative grids demonstrate how we thought about the range of reading skills we were looking for in programs. For instance, we did not simply ask whether programs addressed reading comprehension at all but tried to get a sense of the specific aspects of reading comprehension that were addressed.

Because of our stated belief in the importance of explicit instruction, we also did not strive to include the wide variety of programs, technology and/or print-based, that mainly offered teachers a series of workbooks or workbook-like activities. Nor did we include more than a smattering of the many programs that essentially "teach" reading and comprehension through postreading quizzes. Finally, we did not include basal series or high-interest, low-readability book series.

Are instruction and materials age-appropriate?

In choosing programs, we prioritized finding and including programs that were designed for adolescents. We looked for content and contexts that respected the higher cognitive abilities and interests of children in fourth grade and beyond. Programs that were "scaled up" to include higher grades were carefully considered. Of the included programs, we made an effort to note when programs were developed in this manner and the extent to which we found the materials and methods for older students to be different and appropriate.

Has the program been implemented widely in a variety of contexts and with a range of students?

In determining which programs to include, we prioritized programs that had been implemented widely over those that had not. We considered both geographic and demographic variety and strove to avoid programs that had only been implemented on a limited scale or by researchers alone rather than practicing teachers. Even so, on occasion we made exceptions for programs that were either well-known or seemed particularly promising.

The recent resurgence of interest in adolescent literacy has translated into some truly exciting and innovative developments by researchers, curriculum developers, and publishers. We include in our review only those programs that appeared to have sufficient details and supports available for interested teachers, schools, and districts to be able to easily obtain and implement them. Given the rapid state of development, we also include a list of curricula currently in development for those interested in the field's direction (see the Appendix).

Criteria for Evaluating Programs

Once a determination had been made to include a program, we evaluated each program by asking several more questions based on what research has found most effective in teaching reading. These questions included the following.

What type of professional development is offered to prepare teachers to implement the program?

As discussed in further detail throughout this book, research has shown that successful implementation of a literacy program requires that teachers learn not just how to present a curriculum but also that they understand the theory and rationale behind the instructional approaches. In addition, the most effective professional development model has consistently been shown to be sustained and ongoing, rather than the more common one-shot or short-term workshop model.

To what extent does the program incorporate assessment and employ data-driven tools that enable teachers to provide flexible and individualized instruction (i.e., based on students' assessed abilities, skills, and needs)?

Given what we know about the individuality of the struggling adolescent reader, we were somewhat biased in favor of programs that provide teachers with a means of evaluating students and of targeting instruction to their needs. When present, we detail the assessments used in programs and how they are linked to instruction. We also discuss how students' specific needs are met when programs or methods offer individualization.

Does this program contain features designed specifically to motivate and engage reluctant adolescent readers?

As discussed in greater detail in Chapters 1 and 2, motivation and engagement are critical to student learning during adolescence. Because of this, we evaluated each program for whether or not it specifically targeted these two factors. Different programs sought to motivate students with different techniques, but some of the most common were providing engaging reading materials, opportunities for success, and frequent feedback. Others programs, most commonly the technology-based programs, focused on age-relevant graphics and/or creating an incentives system.

How is technology used in this program?

Technological solutions are gaining popularity in schools, and this is certainly the case where literacy instruction and remediation are in demand. Particularly because technology-based programs often claimed to reduce teacher workload, offer easily administered and reported assessments, and/or opportunities for individualized instruction and practice, we did make an effort to include as many of the expanding array of technology-based programs as possible.

At the same time, educators must still be judicious in the curriculum choices they make because merely using technology will not necessarily produce benefits. In reviewing computer-based literacy programs, it is important to look for technological applications that are not merely "research based." Other important features to consider are a proven track record, the use of sound design principles, and programs that offer struggling students individualized instruction, ample opportunity to practice targeted skills, and supports for tackling grade-level texts they might not otherwise be able to read (e.g., Boone & Higgins, 2003; Hasselbring & Goin, 2004; Mayer, 2003).

Does the program promote the learning and/or transfer of reading skills across academic disciplines?

As discussed throughout this book and highlighted in Chapter 3, reading proficiency is crucial to success in each academic discipline. Because of this, we looked for evidence that programs sought to promote literacy across the curriculum. Because of the broad range of programs, we were open to the many ways in which this might occur. Some programs, for instance, were developed to be delivered schoolwide. In these cases, cross-curricular literacy learning was built into the very design of the program. Other programs were primarily meant to be implemented in only a single classroom, most often the language arts classroom. In these cases, we looked for evidence that explicit teaching for the transfer of reading skills was occurring within the program. Unfortunately, all too often this was not the case for these types of stand-alone programs.

How extensive is the evidence regarding the program's efficacy? Did the research base include the targeted students, or were evaluations conducted with other grades or types of students?

Readers will notice a great deal of variation in the extent of evaluation and research done on programs. Although many of the programs included have been in use for more than a decade, peer-reviewed articles made up a disappointingly small proportion of the research base for most programs. Even when a significant number of evaluations and studies existed, they often employed simple pretest and posttest data, did not necessarily include a control group, and rarely used experimental designs. Moreover, evaluations are usually funded or at the very least requested by publishers and unless published by independent third parties tend, therefore, to report only positive findings.

In summarizing the available research in each program profile, the more data that existed on a program's efficacy, the less we tended to belabor the details of the studies. Nevertheless, for readers considering a program, we highly recommend looking at the research data in detail. Whenever possible, we provide URLs for reports and articles to make this task less onerous. In addition, research studies (as opposed to descriptive articles) are identified by boldface type. When examining these studies, readers will want to consider how similar the students in the evaluation are to the readers' students, as well as how rigorous the design is. While improvements in percentile ranks or grade equivalents can seem impressive on their own, without a control group the reader cannot be certain such improvement would not have occurred without the program.

Using the Information Provided in Part II

In developing Part II, we have made every effort to include as many programs as we can. We have also taken extensive steps to ensure that the information is as relevant and up-to-date as possible.

In developing the list of programs to include, we first made a list of programs with which we (the authors) were familiar. We also combed several databases, did online searches, and consulted adolescent literacy researchers, experts, and policymakers to find additional programs. Along the way, several program developers who became aware of the project contacted us with information.

We then wrote a draft summary of each program. These summaries are intended to be descriptive and not evaluative in nature. We sent the summaries to a program developer or publisher for review and revision and made a minimum of two attempts to contact a representative for each program. In the cases where we received no response, we either used the summary that we had written or—in cases where we did not have sufficient information—omitted the program.

Despite the precautions we have taken, ensuring this information was current proved a daunting task, and it is important for the reader to understand the limitations we faced. More adolescent literacy programs are becoming available as attention to adolescent literacy issues increases. In addition, existing programs often are rapidly evolving. For example, some of the program websites and descriptions of their programs are virtually unrecognizable from when we began this project to now.

The next task we set for ourselves was to provide the reader tools for easy comparison of programs. To do this we created four matrixes comparing several types of program characteristics. In developing these matrixes, we primarily used published literature describing the programs, reviews of the programs, and information provided by the developers or publishers. Indeed, the decision to assign a checkmark was often made based solely on information given to us by the publisher of a program. For instance, if a program's website stated that the program was designed to "motivate and engage adolescent readers," the program received a check for motivation. Because in most cases we did not have the opportunity to review the program materials or observe the programs in action firsthand, we cannot comment on the quality of any particular characteristic of a program. *Thus, it is critical that the reader realize a checkmark in these matrixes does not convey evaluative information.*

In Matrix 1 (see page 122) we compare programs by the types of students for and by whom they were designed and used. Targeted student populations are categorized by grade and by characteristics such as whether readers are "typically developing," "struggling," "students with learning disabilities," or "English-language learners" (ELLs). Note that we do not represent whether programs address students below fourth grade. Because of our focus on locating programs that addressed struggling readers, 42 of the 48 programs were designed for this type of reader. In addition, 27 programs were developed with typically developing readers in mind and 28 for students with learning disabilities. It is interesting that only 17 of the programs were developed for ELLs. Although this catalog of programs is not exhaustive, the small number of programs that target struggling readers who are ELLs is telling. Moreover, educators must be wary of programs that claim to do everything for every type of reader, which 5 programs claim to do. Given the wide range of literacy abilities that students can have in later grades, it is extremely difficult for a program to meet equally the needs of all students. Similarly, particular attention should be paid to programs that cover all grades from 4 through 12. Instruction that is appropriate for a struggling 4th-grade student may not necessarily be effective for a struggling 10th-grade student. Specifically, the ideas and content that motivate them and that will prepare them for grade-level content and academic success are not the same. Thus, teachers and administrators should evaluate carefully for themselves whether the programs that claim to be appropriate for their adolescent students are appropriate.

In Matrix 2 (see page 124) we compare programs based on features. For instance, this matrix notes whether programs require or assume schoolwide implementation or an after-school implementation. Twelve programs were designed for schoolwide implementation and 5 for after-school implementation. In addition, the matrix notes whether they are core or supplementary reading or language arts programs. Only 12 programs were designated as full reading or language arts curricula, whereas 36 are curricular supplements. Core programs can replace an entire reading or language arts curriculum, whereas supplements are easily added to or used to modify existing curriculum. The matrix also denotes intervention programs, which offer specifically remedial instruction or components and may be either core or supplementary. There were 28 intervention programs. The skew toward supplementary and intervention programs reflects our focus on intervention for struggling readers when looking for programs.

Matrix 2 notes whether a program includes formative and summative assessments tools, although these may be optional. It also captures whether a program's instruction is structured to promote student motivation and engagement and explicitly addresses issues of transfer to reading across content areas. Twenty-seven programs include formative assessment tools, whereas 18 include summative tools. Formative assessment tools are intended to guide daily instruction, whereas summative assessment tools are intended for placement and evaluation purposes. Despite the central importance of motivation and engagement for adolescent readers and writers, only 30 of the 48 programs claim to have addressed this crucial factor. Similarly, although literacy in later grades becomes increasingly tied to learning in the content area, only 27 programs claim to intentionally foster transfer of taught literacy skills across content area materials and tasks. *Note that checkmarks for assessments, motivation, and transfer are based on program claims, and teachers and administrators should always examine sample program materials and lessons to determine whether the program truly meets their expectations in these critical areas.*

Matrix 3 (see page 126) provides some limited evaluative information about the programs. Programs that are primarily technology-based or require technology for a major part of the program are designated with a *T* in the technology category to distinguish them from programs that merely have technological supports or supplements available. Ten programs use technology to some degree, while an additional 14 programs are technology-based, requiring computers and other equipment in order to implement them fully. Programs wherein extended professional development is the primary or sole approach are noted with a *P* to distinguish them from programs that require or make available professional development but that have curriculum at their heart. Only 8 programs are extensive professional development approaches. Some of these programs include no other curricular components, while others do, and readers are encouraged to examine the program descriptions to find out more details. An additional 34 programs provide some amount of professional development; however, to find out the type and length of professional development, as well as whether it is optional or mandatory, the program descriptions must be consulted.

The last two columns in Matrix 3 report the amount of research support for programs. Note that all of the included programs claim to be based on research, and most could indeed be considered aligned to research. However, in evaluating the research support, we looked for research conducted specifically on the programs themselves. That is, we looked for evaluations of the programs and furthermore distinguished unpublished internal and third-party evaluations from those published in peer-reviewed research journals. In the Evaluation and Peer-Reviewed Research columns of this matrix, a star indicates we located 10 or more studies, a checkmark indicates fewer than 10 studies, and blanks indicate where no studies were found. Those two columns ought to be given much thought by teachers and administrators looking for a program. Although only three programs (Achieving Maximum Potential, Disciplinary Literacy, and LitART) had no research or evaluation information available at all, there was still a remarkable dearth of evidence of program efficacy across the vast majority of programs. Ten programs had fewer than 10 evaluation studies and no peer-reviewed studies. And 1 program had fewer than 10 peer-reviewed research studies but no evaluations available. Sixteen programs had 10 or fewer studies of both types. More telling still of the general lack of evidence of efficacy is how few programs had more than 10 studies of either kind. Only 7 programs had 10 or more evaluations, and only 8 had 10 or more research studies. Finally, a mere 3 (Accelerated Reader, Lexia Strategies for Older Students, and Success for All) had 10 or more of both types of studies, but even these were limited in that the students studied tended to be younger rather than older. In addition, note that checks and stars do not necessarily mean that effects of the programs reported are beneficial. While this is usually the case, it is not always so, especially in comparative studies.

Although some programs clearly have better evidence of effectiveness than others, teachers and administrators should take care to go the extra step of determining whether that evidence is for students similar to their own. Sometimes, even the fact that a program has solid evidence of efficacy can be misleading. For instance, for several programs with several studies demonstrating effectiveness, many of the studies were conducted with children in the primary grades. Similarly, although many of the programs claim to be effective for ELLs, few have peer-reviewed studies demonstrating that efficacy, and some have no evidence of effectiveness at all. Administrators and teachers should at the very least investigate the number and results of studies conducted with students similar to theirs.

Finally, in Matrix 4 (see page 128) we compare the programs on the skills, strategies, and knowledge they target. These include decoding and word recognition, fluency, and vocabulary. Twenty-six of the 48 programs address decoding, 25 fluency, and 33 vocabulary. Five of the decoding programs focus almost solely on decoding (sometimes in league with spelling, fluency, or basic comprehension). Of the fluency programs, only 1 focuses solely on fluency (READ RIGHT), and of the vocabulary programs only 1 focuses solely on vocabulary (Vocabulary Improvement Program).

The skills addressed by programs also include comprehension, which we broke down into four categories due to its importance in adolescent literacy. The first of these comprehension categories incorporates any instruction in basic comprehension skills instruction, such as finding the main idea, summarizing, locating details, and so forth. The vast majority of programs, 38 out of 48, addressing comprehension target these skills. The second comprehension category covers comprehension strategies, which include instruction in questioning, visualizing, predicting, and so forth. Twenty-two programs target these strategies.

The third comprehension category is metacognition and refers to explicit instruction aimed at helping readers monitor their own understanding of a text and recognize and repair breakdowns in comprehension. Although many would argue that comprehension strategies are by their very nature metacognitive, instruction in them does not necessarily explicitly invoke a metacognitive attitude in students. To earn a checkmark for this type of instruction, programs had to specifically note students' metacognition as an instructional goal fostered through instructional activities, and only 11 programs did so.

The fourth and final comprehension category is critical thinking, which is instruction in higher-level thinking about texts that might include critiques of texts and comparisons and synthesis across multiple texts. A mere 11 programs address critical thinking. It is possible that our focus on programs for struggling adolescent readers is responsible for the small number of programs targeting critical thinking, but the low number still points to the fact that struggling readers are less likely to gain these skills, which are so critical to academic and workplace success, through most programs.

The final three categories in Matrix 4 address the production of written language. Spelling and grammar are self-explanatory, and the writing category is meant to address instruction in writing extended running text. Sixteen of the 48 programs address spelling, 8 grammar, and 26 writing. Only 5 programs address all three areas of instruction: First Steps/STEPS, LANGUAGE!, READ 180, Success for All, and WriteToLearn. Notably, these 5 programs vary considerably in their approaches to instruction and the types of writing they target. The relatively low number of programs targeting spelling, grammar, and writing at all is in part the result of our focus on finding programs for struggling adolescent readers, but it does also point to a dissociation between reading and writing in many of programs we reviewed.

These matrixes are provided as a first step for locating potentially helpful programs based on a student's, classroom's, school's, or district's identified needs. The next step should be to review the program descriptions that follow these matrixes for more detail on the program. We also highly recommend contacting the program developers or publishers themselves before making a final decision. It is especially important to evaluate each program as to whether its claims as represented in the matrixes and descriptions are accurate. In fact, when you review the actual materials, you may find that the stated claims have not been met to your satisfaction. For instance, a comprehension program might only cover vocabulary by reviewing words before students read a text and not include explicit instruction in deriving word meanings and other independent vocabulary learning strategies. If you are seeking a program to enhance your students' comprehension and vocabulary this program's vocabulary instruction might not really meet your needs even though it technically does incorporate vocabulary. Finally, as is elaborated in Part I of this book, to be effective in attempts to improve adolescent literacy, the choice of a program should be informed not only by student characteristics and needs but also by the broader context, including school characteristics, the readiness of faculty for instructional change, and the human and financial resources available.

MATRIX 1. Adolescent Literacy Programs: Types of Students Served

Programs	Typically Developing or Advanced	Struggling	Students With Learning Disabilities	English-Language Learners	Grades Targeted
Academy of READING		✓			4 ——————→ 12
Accelerated Reader	✓	✓			4 ——————→ 12
Achieve3000	✓	✓	✓	✓	4 ——————→ 12
Achieving Maximum Potential Reading System		✓		✓	6 ——————→ 12
Advancement Via Individual Determination	✓	✓			5 ——————→ 12
AfterSchool KidzLit	✓			✓	4 ———→ 8
America's Choice—Ramp-Up Literacy		✓	✓	✓	6 9
Benchmark Word Detectives		✓	✓		4 ——————→ 12
Concept-Oriented Reading Instruction	✓	✓			4 →6
Corrective Reading		✓	✓	✓	4 ——————→ 12
Disciplinary Literacy	✓	✓	✓	✓	4 ——————→ 12
Failure Free Reading		✓	✓	✓	4 ——————→ 12
First Steps/STEPS	✓	✓	✓	✓	4 ———→7
Junior Great Books	✓				4 ——————→ 12
Knowledge Box	✓				4 →6
LANGUAGE!		✓	✓	✓	4 ——————→ 12
Learning Upgrade	✓	✓	✓		4 ——————→ 12
Lexia Strategies for Older Students		✓	✓	✓	4 ——————→ 12
Lindamood-Bell		✓	✓		4 ——————→ 12
LitART	✓				4 ———→ 8
My Reading Coach		✓	✓		4 ——————→ 12
Passport Reading Journeys		✓	✓		6 ——————→ 12
Peer-Assisted Learning Strategies	✓	✓	✓	✓	4 →6 9 ——→ 12
Phono-graphix		✓	✓		4 ——————→ 12

(continued)

Programs	Typically Developing or Advanced	Struggling	Students With Learning Disabilities	English-Language Learners	Grades Targeted
PLATO Learning	✓	✓	✓		4 ⟶ 12
Project CRISS	✓	✓			4 ⟶ 12
Puente	✓	✓		✓	9 ⟶ 12
Questioning the Author	✓	✓			4 ⟶ 12
READ 180		✓	✓	✓	4 ⟶ 12
READ RIGHT		✓	✓	✓	4 ⟶ 12
Reading Apprenticeship	✓	✓			6 ⟶ 12
Reading Is FAME (Girls and Boys Town)		✓	✓		7 ⟶ 12
Reading Power in the Content Areas	✓	✓			6 ⟶ 12
Reciprocal Teaching	✓	✓	✓		4 ⟶ 12
REWARDS		✓	✓	✓	4 ⟶ 12
Saxon Phonics Intervention		✓	✓		4 ⟶ 12
Scaffolded Reading Experience	✓	✓			4 ⟶ 12
Soar to Success		✓	✓		4 ⟶ 8
Spell Read P.A.T.			✓		4 ⟶ 12
Strategic Instruction Model	✓	✓	✓		9 ⟶ 12
Success for All	✓	✓			4 ⟶ 8 (9)
Talent Development High Schools	✓	✓			9 ⟶ 12
Thinking Reader	✓	✓	✓	✓	5 ⟶ 8
Transactional Strategies Instruction	✓	✓	✓		4 ⟶ 12
Vocabulary Improvement Program	✓			✓	4 ⟶ 6
Voyager TimeWarp Plus		✓			4 ⟶ 9
Wilson Reading System		✓	✓		6 ⟶ 12
WriteToLearn	✓	✓			5 ⟶ 12

MATRIX 2. Adolescent Literacy Programs: Included Features

Programs	Schoolwide Program	Out-of-School Time Program	Core Reading/Language Arts Program	Supplements Regular Curriculum	Intervention Program	Formative Assessment	Summative Assessment	Motivation and Engagement	Teaching for Transfer
Academy of READING				✓	✓	✓	✓	✓	
Accelerated Reader			✓		✓	✓		✓	
Achieve3000				✓		✓		✓	
Achieving Maximum Potential Reading System		✓	✓		✓	✓	✓	✓	✓
Advancement Via Individual Determination	✓			✓					✓
AfterSchool KidzLit		✓	✓				✓	✓	
America's Choice—Ramp-Up Literacy	✓		✓			✓	✓	✓	✓
Benchmark Word Detectives				✓	✓				
Concept-Oriented Reading Instruction				✓				✓	✓
Corrective Reading				✓	✓	✓			
Disciplinary Literacy	✓			✓					✓
Failure Free Reading				✓	✓	✓	✓	✓	
First Steps/STEPS	✓			✓		✓			✓
Junior Great Books			✓					✓	✓
Knowledge Box				✓			✓	✓	✓
LANGUAGE!				✓	✓	✓	✓		
Learning Upgrade				✓	✓		✓	✓	
Lexia Strategies for Older Students				✓	✓	✓		✓	
Lindamood-Bell				✓	✓	✓	✓		
LitART		✓		✓			✓	✓	✓
My Reading Coach				✓	✓	✓	✓		
Passport Reading Journeys	✓		✓		✓	✓	✓	✓	✓
Peer-Assisted Learning Strategies				✓				✓	
Phono-graphix				✓	✓	✓		✓	

(continued)

MATRIX 2. Adolescent Literacy Programs: Included Features (*continued*)

Programs	Schoolwide Program	Out-of-School Time Program	Core Reading/Language Arts Program	Supplements Regular Curriculum	Intervention Program	Formative Assessment	Summative Assessment	Motivation and Engagement	Teaching for Transfer
PLATO Learning				✓	✓	✓	✓	✓	✓
Project CRISS				✓				✓	✓
Puente	✓		✓		✓			✓	✓
Questioning the Author				✓				✓	✓
READ 180	✓		✓		✓	✓	✓		✓
READ RIGHT				✓	✓	✓			
Reading Apprenticeship	✓		✓					✓	✓
Reading Is FAME (Girls and Boys Town)				✓	✓	✓		✓	✓
Reading Power in the Content Areas	✓			✓		✓	✓		✓
Reciprocal Teaching				✓				✓	
REWARDS				✓	✓				✓
Saxon Phonics Intervention				✓	✓	✓		✓	
Scaffolded Reading Experience				✓				✓	
Soar to Success				✓	✓	✓			
Spell Read P.A.T.				✓	✓	✓			
Strategic Instruction Model	✓	✓		✓	✓			✓	✓
Success for All	✓		✓		✓				✓
Talent Development High Schools	✓		✓		✓	✓	✓	✓	✓
Thinking Reader				✓		✓	✓	✓	✓
Transactional Strategies Instruction				✓					✓
Vocabulary Improvement Program				✓				✓	✓
Voyager TimeWarp Plus		✓	✓		✓	✓	✓	✓	✓
Wilson Reading System				✓	✓	✓			
WriteToLearn				✓	✓	✓			✓

MATRIX 3. Adolescent Literacy Programs: Evaluated Features

Programs	Technology (T = technology-based)	Professional Development (P = primarily or solely)	Evaluation (★ ≥ 10)	Peer-Reviewed Research (★ ≥ 10)
Academy of READING	T	✓	✓	✓
Accelerated Reader	T	✓	★	★
Achieve3000	T	✓	✓	
Achieving Maximum Potential Reading System	T	✓		
Advancement Via Individual Determination		P	✓	✓
AfterSchool KidzLit		✓	✓	
America's Choice—Ramp-Up Literacy		✓	★	
Benchmark Word Detectives				★
Concept-Oriented Reading Instruction		P		★
Corrective Reading			✓	★
Disciplinary Literacy		P		
Failure Free Reading	T	✓	★	✓
First Steps/STEPS		P	✓	
Junior Great Books	✓	✓	✓	✓
Knowledge Box	T	✓	✓	
LANGUAGE!	✓	✓	★	✓
Learning Upgrade	T		✓	
Lexia Strategies for Older Students	T	✓	✓	✓
Lindamood-Bell	✓	✓	★	★
LitART		✓		
My Reading Coach	T	✓	✓	✓
Passport Reading Journeys	T	✓	✓	
Peer-Assisted Learning Strategies		✓		★
Phono-graphix	✓	✓	✓	✓

(continued)

Programs	Technology (T = technology-based)	Professional Development (P = primarily or solely)	Evaluation (★ ≥ 10)	Peer-Reviewed Research (★ ≥ 10)
PLATO Learning	T	✓	★	
Project CRISS		P	✓	
Puente		✓	✓	✓
Questioning the Author		✓		★
READ 180	T	✓	★	✓
READ RIGHT		P	✓	
Reading Apprenticeship		P	✓	✓
Reading Is FAME (Girls and Boys Town)	✓	✓		✓
Reading Power in the Content Areas		P	✓	
Reciprocal Teaching		✓		★
REWARDS		✓	✓	✓
Saxon Phonics Intervention		✓	✓	✓
Scaffolded Reading Experience	✓		✓	✓
Soar to Success		✓	★	
Spell Read P.A.T.	✓	✓	✓	✓
Strategic Instruction Model	✓	✓		★
Success for All		✓	★	★
Talent Development High Schools	✓	✓	✓	✓
Thinking Reader	T	✓	✓	
Transactional Strategies Instruction				★
Vocabulary Improvement Program			✓	✓
Voyager TimeWarp Plus		✓	★	
Wilson Reading System	✓	✓	✓	✓
WriteToLearn	T	✓	✓	✓

MATRIX 4. Adolescent Literacy Programs: Skills, Strategies, and Knowledge Taught

Programs	Decoding	Fluency	Vocabulary	Basic Comprehension Skills	Comprehension Strategies	Metacognition	Critical Thinking	Spelling	Grammar	Writing
Academy of READING	✓	✓	✓	✓						
Accelerated Reader		✓	✓	✓						✓
Achieve3000		✓	✓	✓		✓				✓
Achieving Maximum Potential Reading System	✓	✓	✓	✓	✓			✓	✓	
Advancement Via Individual Determination					✓		✓			✓
AfterSchool KidzLit			✓	✓	✓					✓
America's Choice—Ramp-Up Literacy	✓	✓	✓	✓	✓	✓	✓			✓
Benchmark Word Detectives	✓	✓	✓					✓		
Concept-Oriented Reading Instruction	✓	✓		✓	✓	✓	✓			✓
Corrective Reading	✓	✓	✓	✓						
Disciplinary Literacy			✓	✓	✓	✓	✓			✓
Failure Free Reading		✓	✓	✓				✓		
First Steps/STEPS				✓				✓	✓	✓
Junior Great Books		✓					✓			✓
Knowledge Box	✓		✓	✓			✓			✓
LANGUAGE!	✓	✓	✓	✓				✓	✓	✓
Learning Upgrade	✓		✓	✓						
Lexia Strategies for Older Students	✓	✓	✓	✓						
Lindamood-Bell	✓			✓						
LitART	✓	✓	✓	✓			✓	✓		✓
My Reading Coach	✓		✓					✓		✓
Passport Reading Journeys	✓	✓	✓	✓	✓			✓		
Peer-Assisted Learning Strategies		✓		✓	✓					
Phono-graphix	✓							✓		

(continued)

Programs	Decoding	Fluency	Vocabulary	Basic Comprehension Skills	Comprehension Strategies	Metacognition	Critical Thinking	Spelling	Grammar	Writing
PLATO Learning	✓		✓	✓	✓				✓	✓
Project CRISS			✓	✓	✓	✓				✓
Puente				✓			✓			✓
Questioning the Author				✓	✓	✓	✓			
READ 180	✓	✓	✓	✓				✓	✓	✓
READ RIGHT		✓								
Reading Apprenticeship		✓	✓	✓	✓	✓	✓			✓
Reading Is FAME (Girls and Boys Town)	✓	✓	✓	✓				✓		✓
Reading Power in the Content Areas			✓	✓	✓					
Reciprocal Teaching				✓	✓	✓				
REWARDS	✓	✓	✓	✓						✓
Saxon Phonics Intervention	✓							✓		
Scaffolded Reading Experience			✓	✓	✓					✓
Soar to Success	✓	✓		✓	✓					
Spell Read P.A.T.	✓	✓						✓		
Strategic Instruction Model	✓	✓	✓	✓	✓	✓				✓
Success for All	✓	✓	✓	✓	✓			✓	✓	✓
Talent Development High Schools		✓	✓	✓	✓					✓
Thinking Reader			✓	✓	✓	✓				
Transactional Strategies Instruction			✓	✓	✓	✓				
Vocabulary Improvement Program			✓							
Voyager TimeWarp Plus	✓	✓	✓	✓	✓		✓		✓	✓
Wilson Reading System	✓							✓		
WriteToLearn				✓				✓	✓	✓

Program Summaries

In the following pages, you will find summaries of 48 different adolescent literacy programs. The summaries are organized so that each includes the same basic information regarding each program: an instructional description, professional development details, research and evaluation findings, contact information, and bibliographic sources. Research has taught us a great deal about what instructional approaches are effective in teaching reading to adolescents. However, approaches are widely divergent across programs; thus, we attempted to provide as much detail as possible in a limited space. Professional development is detailed because it is consistently found that professional development is a key ingredient in the success of implementing successful programs in secondary schools. Next, we briefly describe what evaluation has been conducted to prove the effectiveness of a given program. Following these three descriptions, we provide you with contact information—whenever possible providing you with the name of a specific contact person—so that you can further evaluate these programs for use with your own students. Finally, we provide you with sources for all evaluation and research we could locate on a given program.

ACADEMY OF READING

Instructional Approach

The Academy of READING is a computer-based reading intervention program for struggling readers designed to supplement an existing reading and language arts curriculum. It focuses on improving fluency, phonemic awareness, and reading comprehension. The Academy of READING software program is offered by Autoskill and originated in the 1980s through the work of neurophysiologists Ronald Trites and Christina Fiedorowicz. According to the publisher, the program is suitable for readers of all ages and abilities.

Academy of READING offers self-paced, individualized instruction in component reading skills. It includes a management system that allows both teachers and students to keep track of students' performance. Academy of READING activities are designed to improve students' decoding ability, their ability to derive meaning from texts, and their engagement and motivation.

Professional Development

Professional development for Academy of READING is offered through a service called the Advantage Program, which has two versions. The Fundamental Package, intended primarily for teachers, offers unlimited instructional support in managing the software and keeping track of data and results. It also includes unlimited technical support through an 800 number, free software upgrades, and a monthly educator newsletter. The Administrator Package, intended for principals and district administrators, includes all of the components of the Fundamental Package plus additional tools and knowledge for establishing proof of efficacy and an hour-long consultation with literacy experts.

Program Evaluation

To date, Academy of READING has been evaluated through efficacy studies. However, it is part of the current National Study of the Effectiveness of Educational Technology Interventions, which is investigating the effectiveness of technology in improving reading achievement in first and fourth grade during the 2004–2005 and 2005–2006 school years (U.S. Department of Education, 2004). The Florida Center for Reading Research (2004) has also conducted an independent review of the program.

An efficacy study (Tucker, MacGregor, & Loh, 2003) in Tennessee using pre- and posttests, but no comparison group, demonstrated that third-grade students gained an average of 2.3 grade levels in a cloze measure of comprehension, 1.7 grade levels on a word recognition measure, and 0.9 grade levels on the STAR reading test published by Renaissance Learning. A similar efficacy study with eighth-grade students in Pennsylvania demonstrated comparable results (Michael & Strunk, 2004): Students gained 2.4 grade levels on the Stanford Diagnostic Reading Test and 2.1 grade levels on the cloze comprehension test. In this study, which also employed pre- and posttests but no comparison group, time on task was also measured and shown to be positively correlated with outcomes. Finally, in a larger scale study of 2,154 students in grades K–11 from nine schools in Leavenworth, Kansas, overall gains in reading proficiency of 1.3 grade levels were demonstrated on the STAR reading test (Loh, 2004).

Contact Information

Address: AutoSkill International, Inc.
　　　　　 555 Legget Drive
　　　　　 Suite 600, Tower B
　　　　　 Ottawa, ON
　　　　　 Canada K2K 2X3
Phone:　　 800-288-6754
E-mail:　　 info@autoskill.com
Website:　 www.autoskill.com/products/reading

Sources

Fiedorowicz, C. (1986). Training of component reading skills. *Annals of Dyslexia, 36*, 318–334.

Fiedorowicz, C., & Trites, R. (1986). *AutoSkill pilot reading project* (Education Report). Wellington, TX: Wellington High School.

Fiedorowicz, C., & Trites, R. (1987). *An evaluation of the effectiveness of computer-assisted component reading subskills training.* Toronto, ON: Queen's Printer for Ontario.

Fiedorowicz, C., & Trites, R. (1990). *Follow-up study of the effectiveness of the AutoSkill CRS program.* Toronto, ON: Queen's Printer for Ontario.

Florida Center for Reading Research. (2004, November). *Academy of Reading.* Tallahassee, FL: Author. Retrieved January 14, 2007, from http://www.fcrr.org/FCRRReports/PDF/AcademyReadingFinal.pdf

Kubinec, S., Pepper, K., & Loh, E. (2005). *Review of student gains in reading proficiency based on training with the AutoSkill Academy of READING: Independence Middle School, Bethel Park School District, Pennsylvania, 2004–2005 school year.* Ottawa, ON: AutoSkill.

Loh, E. (2004). *Evaluation of the effectiveness of the AutoSkill Academy of READING skills training program in K–11 students in the Leavenworth school district.* Ottawa, ON: AutoSkill.

Loh, E. (2005). *Building reading proficiency in high school students: Examining the effectiveness of the Academy of READING for striving readers.* Ottawa, ON: AutoSkill.

Michael, E., & Strunk, C. (2004, January). *Examination of gains in reading proficiency by students training on the AutoSkill Academy of READING software intervention program in the Chambersburg Area School District, 2001–2002 school year.* Ottawa, ON: AutoSkill. Retrieved January 14, 2007, from http://www.autoskill.com/pdf/Chambersburg_EfficacyStudy.pdf

Tucker, B., MacGregor, D., & Loh, E.A. (2003). *Improvements on reading scores: Effects of Academy of READING intervention program in Sweetwater Elementary School, Sweetwater, TN.* Ottawa, ON: AutoSkill. Retrieved January 14, 2007, from http://www.autoskill.com/pdf/Sweetwater_Report.pdf

U.S. Department of Education. (2004, February 13). Department to study technology's role in raising student achievement [Press release]. Retrieved January 14, 2007, from http://www.ed.gov/news/pressreleases/2004/02/02132004.html

ACCELERATED READER

Instructional Approach

Accelerated Reader is one of several Renaissance Learning computer-based learning information systems. It provides detailed information about student learning and encourages students to read books within their "zone of proximal development." Students read books and answer a series of comprehension questions. Students and teachers are then provided with a report of student progress, which shows how many questions the student answered correctly.

Additional learning information systems are available, which include Accelerated Vocabulary, Fluent Reader, and Accelerated Writer. The Accelerated Vocabulary offers students a list of vocabulary words before reading each book and gives a vocabulary quiz upon completing the reading. Fluent Reader is a system where students select a passage at the appropriate reading level and read along with a recorded reader until they feel they have read it fluently and then complete a comprehension quiz for which a report is provided. Accelerated Writer provides students with a series of expertly scored writing samples to score and provides feedback as to how the students' scoring matches the experts' scoring. It also provides teachers with a series of lessons, rubrics, and writing prompts to assist in lesson planning.

Professional Development

Renaissance Learning offers optional training seminars for each of the learning information systems. These seminars address alignment of the program with U.S. federal requirements, integrating the curriculum in the classroom and use of the assessment piece effectively. There are several options for participating in professional development, including school-based training by a visiting

Renaissance representative and Web-based courses. In addition, continuing education credit is offered through an accredited university.

Program Evaluation

An unusual amount of outside research has been conducted on Accelerated Reader and its component pieces. In addition, several evaluations of the program as implemented in schools have been published in peer-reviewed journals and in dissertations. These studies have most often shown gains in reading comprehension as measured by Accelerated Reader quiz score gains, as well as increased time spent reading. The Florida Center for Reading Research (2006) has also conducted an independent review of the program.

Contact Information

Address: Renaissance Learning, Inc.
           PO Box 8036
           Wisconsin Rapids, WI 54495-8036
Phone: 866-846-7323
E-mail: answers@renlearn.com
Website: www.renlearn.com/reading.htm

Sources

Algozzine, B. (2004). Effects of Read Now on adolescents at risk for school failure. *Journal of At-Risk Issues, 10*(2), 1–8.

Biggers, D. (2001). The argument against Accelerated Reader. *Journal of Adolescent & Adult Literacy, 45,* 72–75.

Carter, B. (1996). Hold the applause! Do Accelerated Reader (TM) and Electronic Bookshelf (TM) send the right message? *School Library Journal, 42*(10), 22–25.

Cuddeback, M., & Ceprano, M. (2002). The use of Accelerated Reader with emergent readers. *Reading Improvement, 39*(2), 89–96.

Facemire, N.E. (2000). *The effect of the Accelerated Reader on the reading comprehension of third graders.* Unpublished master's thesis, Salem-Teikyo University, WV. (ERIC Document Reproduction Service No. ED442097; www.eric.ed.gov/content delivery/servlet/ERICServlet?accno=ED442097)

Florida Center for Reading Research. (2006, September). *Accelerated Reader.* Tallahassee, FL: Author. Retrieved January 14, 2007, from http://www.fcrr.org/FCRR Reports/PDF/Accelerated_Reader.pdf

Goodman, G. (1998, November). *The Reading Renaissance/Accelerated Reader program* (Pinal County School-to-Work Evaluation Report). Tucson, AZ: Creative Research Associates. (ERIC Document Reproduction Service No. ED427299; www.eric. ed.gov/contentdelivery/servlet/ERICServlet?accno=E D427299)

Hamilton, B. (1997). Using Accelerated Reader with ESL students. *MultiMedia Schools, 4*(2), 50–52.

Howard, C.A. (1999). *An evaluation of the Accelerated Reader program in grades 3–5 on reading vocabulary, comprehension, and attitude in an urban southeastern school district in Virginia.* Unpublished doctoral dissertation, Old Dominion University, Norfolk, VA. (ERIC Document Reproduction Service No. ED465987; www.eric.ed.gov/contentdelivery/servlet/ ERICServlet?accno=ED465987)

Johnson, R.A., & Howard, C.A. (2003). The effects of the Accelerated Reader program on the reading comprehension of pupils in grades three, four, and five. *The Reading Matrix, 3*(3), 87–96.

Kambarian, V.N., Jr. (2001). *The role of reading instruction and the effect of a reading management system on at-risk students.* Unpublished doctoral dissertation, Saint Louis University, MO. (ERIC Document Reproduction Service No. ED461835; www.eric. ed.gov/contentdelivery/servlet/ERICServlet?accno=E D461835)

Krashen, S.D. (2003). The (lack of) experimental evidence supporting the use of Accelerated Reader. *Journal of Children's Literature, 29*(2), 16–30.

Mallette, M., Henk, W., & Melnick, S. (2004). The influence of Accelerated Reader on the affective literacy orientations of intermediate grade students. *Journal of Literacy Research, 36,* 73–84.

McDurmon, A. (2001). *The effects of guided and repeated reading on English language learners.* Unpublished master's thesis, Berry College, Mount Berry, GA.

McGlinn, J., & Parrish, A. (2002). Accelerating ESL students' reading progress with Accelerated Reader. *Reading Horizons, 42*(3), 175–189.

Melton, C., Smothers, B., Anderson, E., Fulton, R., Replogle, W., & Thomas, L. (2004). A study of the effects of the Accelerated Reader program on fifth grade students' reading achievement growth. *Reading Improvement, 41*, 18.

Nunnery, J.A., & Ross, S.M. (in press). A randomized experimental evaluation of the impact of Accelerated Reader/Reading Renaissance implementation on reading achievement in grades 3 to 6. *Journal of Education for Students Placed at Risk*.

Palumbo, T.J. (2004, April). *Effects of the Fluent Reader program on reading performance*. Unpublished master's thesis, University of Minnesota, Minneapolis. Retrieved January 14, 2007, from http://www.tc.umn.edu/~samue001/papers.htm

Paul, T.D. (2003). *Guided independent reading: An examination of the reading practice database and the scientific research supporting guided independent reading as implemented in Reading Renaissance*. Wisconsin Rapids, WI: Renaissance Learning.

Paul, T.D., Swanson, S., Zhang, W., & Hehenberger, L. (2000). *Learning information system effects on reading, language arts, math, science, and social studies*. Madison, WI: The Institute for Academic Excellence.

Paul, T.D., VanderZee, D., Rue, R., & Swanson, S. (1996, October). *Impact of Accelerated Reader on overall academic achievement and school attendance*. Paper presented at the National Reading Research Center Conference on Literacy and Technology for the 21st Century, Atlanta, GA.

Pavonetti, L., Brimmer, K., & Cipielewski, J. (2002). Accelerated Reader: What are the lasting effects on the reading habits of middle school students exposed to Accelerated Reader in elementary grades? *Journal of Adolescent & Adult Literacy, 46*, 300–311.

Peak, J.P., & Dewalt, M.W. (1994). Reading achievement: Effects of computerized reading management and enrichment. *ERS Spectrum, 12*(1), 31–34.

Persinger, J. (2001). What are the characteristics of a successful implementation of Accelerated Reader? *Knowledge Quest, 29*(5), 30–35.

Peterson, C.L., Caverly, D.C., Nicholson, S.A., O'Neal, S., & Cusenbary, S. (2000). *Building reading proficiency at the secondary level: A guide to resources*. Austin, TX: Southwest Educational Development Laboratory.

Poock, M. (1998). The Accelerated Reader: An analysis of the software's strengths and weaknesses and how it can be used to its best potential. *School Library Media Activities Monthly, 14*(9), 32–35.

Renaissance Learning. (2001). *California students achieve 28 percent higher Stanford 9 Reading scores after only one semester of Accelerated Reader implementation* (Renaissance Independent Research Reports No. 20). Madison, WI: Author.

Rogers, L. (2003). Computerized reading management software: An effective component of a successful reading program. *Journal of Children's Literature, 29*(2), 16–30.

Ross, S.M., & Nunnery, J.A. (2005). *The effect of School Renaissance on student achievement in two Mississippi school districts*. Memphis, TN: University of Memphis, Center for Research in Educational Policy. Retrieved January 14, 2007, from http://crep.memphis.edu/web/research/pub/Mississippi_School_Renaissance_FINAL_4.pdf

Sadusky, L.A., & Brem, S.K. (2002). *The integration of Renaissance programs into an urban Title I elementary school, and its effect on school-wide improvement* (Technical Report). Tempe, AZ: Arizona State University. Retrieved January 14, 2007, from http://www.public.asu.edu/~sbrem

Samuels, S.J., Lewis, M., Wu, Y., Reininger, J., & Murphy, A. (2003). *Accelerated Reader vs. non-accelerated reader: How students using the Accelerated Reader outperformed the control condition in a tightly controlled experimental study* (Technical Report). Minneapolis, MN: University of Minnesota.

Scott, L.S. (1999). *The Accelerated Reader program, reading achievement, and attitudes of students with learning disabilities*. Unpublished master's thesis, Georgia State University, Atlanta. (ERIC Document Reproduction Service No. ED434431; http://www.eric.ed.gov/contentdelivery/servlet/ERICServlet?accno=ED434431)

Stevenson, J., & Camarata, J. (2000). Imposters in whole language clothing: Undressing the Accelerated Reader program. *Talking Points, 11*(2), 8–11.

Topping, K.J., & Fisher, A.M. (2003). Computerised formative assessment of reading comprehension: Field trials in the U.K. *Journal of Research in Reading, 26*, 267–279.

Topping, K.J., & Paul, T.D. (1999). Computer-assisted assessment of practice at reading: A large scale survey using Accelerated Reader data. *Reading and Writing Quarterly, 15*, 3.

Topping, K.J., & Sanders, W.L. (2000). Teacher effectiveness and computer assessment of reading: Relating value-added and learning information systems data. *School Effectiveness and School Improvement, 11*, 305–337.

Vollands, S.R., Topping, K.J., & Evans, R.M. (1999). Computerized self-assessment of reading comprehension with Accelerated Reader: Action research. *Reading and Writing Quarterly, 15*, 197–211.

Walberg, H.J. (2001). *Final evaluation of the reading initiative* (Report to the J.A. & Kathryn Albertson Foundation, 2001). Retrieved January 29, 2007, from http://jkaf.org/publications/pdfs/readevw.pdf

Instructional Approach

Achieve3000 publishes KidBiz3000 and TeenBiz3000, Web-based, individualized reading and writing instruction for grades 2–8. Achieve3000 distributes the same assignment to the entire class but tailors it according to each student's reading level using student Lexile levels. KidBiz3000 is aimed at second- through eighth-grade students, while TeenBiz3000 is for high school students. The program is based on the philosophy that the only way to enable students to reach and then exceed the appropriate level is to individualize instruction and texts.

Students' reading levels are assessed by Achieve3000's Level Set, a built-in reading comprehension assessment inventory. KidBiz3000 (or TeenBiz3000) then engages students in a five-step process to improve vocabulary, comprehension and reading fluency, as well as writing skills. During this sequence, students receive reading materials and follow-up activities matched to their learning abilities. The five steps are setting a schema, reading for information, demonstrating mastery, constructing meaning, and forming an opinion.

In the first step, students set a schema by reading and replying to a daily e-mail, which sets the stage for what they are about to read. The informal environment is intended to encourage students to make text-to-self connections. In the second step, students read an appropriately leveled nonfiction article for information as directed by the e-mail. Taken from current events, the article is intended to engage students through real-world topics. Students have the opportunity to listen to the article read aloud, so they can hear models of oral reading. In the third step, students demonstrate mastery by answering questions that monitor comprehension, vocabulary, and higher-order thinking skills. In the fourth step, students construct meaning by writing responses to open-ended questions. In the fifth and final step, students form an opinion by participating in a poll about the article.

The KidBiz3000 and TeenBiz3000 interface varies by grade level and was designed with input from adolescents to make it engaging and appealing. Each Friday, teachers receive e-mails outlining the next week's articles and activities so that they may plan ahead which days they want their students to use the program. Weekly e-mails also provide updates on student usage and performance. Teachers can also print customized reports. Achieve3000 recommends the programs be used at least twice weekly for at least 20 minutes per session and up to 40 minutes for older readers. The programs are most frequently used in language arts classes but can also be used in social studies.

Professional Development

Achieve3000 provides training that can be customized to districts' unique schedules and needs. In the initial three-hour training session, which can be conducted on-site or online, educators are given the skills to understand and implement KidBiz3000 and TeenBiz3000. Follow-up training sessions focus on reporting capabilities and more advanced workshops on using the programs to instruct students on different reading comprehension or writing strategies.

Program Evaluation

Two independent studies have demonstrated a correlation between use of the programs and improvement on standardized tests. A year-long longitudinal study (Tracey & Young, 2004) evaluated the effects of a year-long intervention using KidBiz3000 on 219 fifth-grade students' performance in reading, language use, technology knowledge, and motivation. There were two experimental conditions—differentiated and nondifferentiated use of KidBiz3000—and one control group. When comparing students in differentiated versus nondifferentiated classrooms, students in the differentiated classrooms outperformed students in the nondifferentiated classrooms on the Scholastic Reading Inventory (SRI) and TerraNova.

The other study investigated the impact of KidBiz3000 and TeenBiz3000 on low-income, low-achieving students, using performance data in 12 Chicago Public Schools (Young, 2004). All of the participating schools had been identified as needing improvement under No Child Left Behind. They were all Title I schools, with 90% or more of students eligible for free/reduced-cost lunch. This study found that schools using the Achieve3000 programs demonstrated dramatically higher gains on end-of-year standardized reading tests, including the Iowa Test of Basic Skills. Specifically, schools using KidBiz3000 showed a statistically significant increase in their average national percentile from the 30th percentile at the beginning of the school year to the 34th percentile at the end of the year. In comparison, the schools that did not use KidBiz demonstrated a small, nonsignificant increase from the 32nd to the 33rd percentile.

Contact Information

Address: Susan Gertler
            Achieve3000
            1091 River Avenue
            Lakewood, NJ 08701
Phone: 201-692-7917
E-mail: Susan.gertler@achieve3000.com
Website: www.achieve3000.com

Sources

Perez, M. (2005). KidBiz3000. *Learning and Leading With Technology, 33*(1), 40–41.

Tracey, D.H., & Young, J.W. (2004). *Evaluation of KidBiz3000: Bayonne study final report.* Howell, NJ: Achieve3000.

Young, J.W. (2004). *Evaluation study: Chicago Public Schools 2003–2004.* Howell, NJ: Achieve3000.

ACHIEVING MAXIMUM POTENTIAL READING SYSTEM

Instructional Approach

Produced by Pearson/AGS Globe, Achieving Maximum Potential (AMP) Reading System was authored by Timothy Shanahan of the University of Illinois at Chicago. AMP is designed for striving middle and high school readers who are reading at a third- to fifth-grade level. The AMP curriculum is a three-year, three-level sequence intended to accelerate students' comprehension, vocabulary, and fluency. Each level is a course in reading intervention according to student reading grade level; the three levels together are designed to move struggling readers to a sixth-grade reading level.

AMP aims to improve comprehension by introducing one reading comprehension strategy at a time; increase fluency through guided oral reading, teacher modeling, and direct instruction; and build vocabulary by focusing on academic words students will encounter across the content areas. Thirty-two words are taught in each of the seven units per level, and students are exposed to these words at least 10 times in varying contexts within a unit. Materials are 85% nonfiction and colorful and are designed to be age-appropriate in order to keep older struggling readers motivated and engaged in the reading process. In addition, students produce written responses during each lesson, and structured writing lessons at the end of each unit focus on writing skills, including sentence and paragraph structure.

Materials include teacher's editions (two per level/year), student guides (two per level/year), library books (seven per level/year), and a training CD-ROM. Books are also available on audio CD-ROM and in the online library. Student guides include passages, over 85% of which are nonfiction. The online library provides access to the library books in an interactive, multimedia format; includes reading comprehension strategy tips; and is customizable to three different levels of scaffolding. Developed in consultation with the Center for Applied Special Technologies, online supports include the ability for students to learn vocabulary definitions and hear the book read aloud, which also models fluency. The teacher technology component helps teachers manage lessons plans and monitor student data.

Additionally, AMP includes Assessment Masters that provide mid-unit and end-unit tests for each of the seven units per level, and these are intended to help diagnose student problems and monitor progress. Also included in AMP are customized guidance for content area teachers in the application of the taught reading comprehension strategies. Every lesson in AMP includes specific strategies for supporting English learners through differentiated instruction and additional vocabulary learning supports. Abbreviated versions of the levels, called Short Courses, are available for summer school or one-semester use.

Professional Development

Professional development in the AMP Reading System is delivered through the training CD-Rom and a DVD and is also embedded in the curriculum's teacher guides. The DVD provides models of successful teaching and features commentary by educators and Timothy Shanahan. These materials are designed for use by teachers across the content areas. Professional development opportunities embedded into the teacher guides provide teachers with references to research and FYI Notes that elaborate on concepts like direct instruction and on topics such as implementation, assessment, grouping, pacing, and meeting special needs.

Program Evaluation

No evidence of the curriculum's effectiveness was available at the time this publication went to press.

Contact Information

Address: Pearson/AGS Globe
              Customer Service Center
              145 South Mount Zion Road
              PO Box 2500
              Lebanon, IN 46052-3009
Phone: 800-328-2560
E-mail: k12cs@custhelp.com
Website: www.agsglobe.com/amp

Sources

Pearson AGS Globe. (2005). *AMP Digest*. Shoreview, MN: Author. Retrieved October 15, 2006, from http://www.agsglobe.com/amp/files/digest.pdf

Pearson AGS Globe. (2005). *Research points to a successful intervention approach to improving comprehension skills of struggling readers*. Shoreview, MN: Author.

Retrieved October 15, 2006, from http://www.agsglobe.com/amp/files/research.pdf

Pearson AGS Globe. (2006). *AMP Reading System overview*. Shoreview, MN: Author. Retrieved October 15, 2006, from http://www.agsglobe.com/amp/files/overview.pdf

ADVANCEMENT VIA INDIVIDUAL DETERMINATION

Instructional Approach

Advancement Via Individual Determination (AVID) is a program requiring whole-school participation. Over 2,300 schools in 36 states have adopted the AVID program. The program is also used internationally, with participating schools located in Canada and Department of Defense Dependent Schools around the world. The program is designed to prepare students in grades 4 through 12 for college eligibility and success by placing academically average students in advanced classes. The program is targeted to students in the academic middle without a college-going tradition in their families.

The AVID Elective prepares students to compete in their school's most rigorous classes through the use of curriculum materials focusing instruction on reading, writing, study skills, test-taking skills, organization, critical thinking, goal-setting, choosing a college, and preparing for college entrance exams. Reading strategies are also taught, including clarifying and questioning; however, emphasis is placed on synthesis and critique. Through the Path Series, content area teachers also learn techniques for bringing out the best in average students. In this way, AVID students are supported in content area classrooms as well as in the AVID elective.

Within the classroom, the Socratic method and study groups are emphasized, with the teacher's role redefined from lecturer to advocate and guide. A model of writing to learn, inquiry, collaboration, and critical reading forms the basis of the curriculum, with reading and writing emphasized in all subjects.

Professional Development

Professional development is a key ingredient in implementing the AVID program, and participating schools are offered an array of professional development options. Two-day preimplementation awareness and program planning sessions are scheduled throughout the year. In these sessions, educators learn what is needed to implement the AVID program from experienced AVID teachers, current students, and graduates. Week-long summer institutes introduce new site teams to AVID and also offer higher-level AVID strands for experienced AVID teams. Institutes also provide sessions for the AVID interdisciplinary site teams, focusing on research, advocacy, and the development of a site plan for the school year around college access. The AVID District Leadership Training (ADL) is a two-year program that offers extensive training on the AVID Essentials as well as the site and district change process. A regional or district liaison also attends training at the AVID Center in order to provide continual on-site assistance.

In addition, the AVID Center provides workshops for content area teachers using AVID's Write Path materials. This training emphasizes the use of writing, inquiry, collaboration, and reading as tools for learning in the content areas. Additional activities include note-taking and the effective use of rubrics and graphic organizers.

Program Evaluation

AVID has been the subject of multiple research studies. The AVID website offers an overview of research examining the success of schools implementing the program. This includes company-sponsored research, outside evaluation reports, and studies published in peer-reviewed journals. These studies show positive results in terms of college-going and academic achievement for students participating in the AVID program. The materials are based on U.S. national teaching standards.

Contact Information

Address: Robert Gira, Executive Vice-President
AVID Center
5120 Shoreham Place, Suite 120
San Diego, CA 92122
Phone: 858-623-2843
E-mail: rgira@avidcenter.org
Website: www.avidonline.org

Sources

Cunningham, A., Redmond, C., & Merisotis, J. (2003). *Investing early: Intervention programs in selected U.S. states* (Millennium Research Series No. 2). Montreal, QC: Canada Millennium Scholarship Fund.

Guthrie, L.F., & Guthrie, G.P. (2000). *Longitudinal research on AVID 1999–2000: Final report*. Burlingame, CA: Center for Research, Evaluation and Training in Education.

Guthrie, L.F., & Guthrie, G.P. (2002). *The magnificent eight: AVID best practices study, final report*. Burlingame, CA: Center for Research, Evaluation and Training in Education.

Hayward, G.C., Brandes, B.G., Kirst, M.W., & Mazzeo, C. (1997). *Higher education outreach programs: A synthesis of evaluations* (Policy Analysis for California Education Report). Oakland, CA: University of California, Office of the President.

Mehan, H., Villanueva, I., Hubbard, L., Lintz, A., & Okamoto, D. (1996). *Constructing school success: The consequences of untracking low achieving students*. New York: Cambridge University Press.

Talley, S., & Martinez, D.H. (1998). *Tools for schools: School reform models supported by the National Institute on the Education of At-Risk Students*. Washington, DC: U.S. Department of Education, Office of Educational Research and Improvement.

Watt, K.M., Powell, C.A., & Mendiola, I.D. (2004). Implications of one comprehensive school reform model for secondary school students underrepresented in higher education. *Journal of Education for Students Placed at Risk, 9*, 241–259.

Watt, K.M., Yanez, D., & Cossio, G. (2002/2003). AVID: A comprehensive school reform model for Texas. *National Forum of Educational Administration and Supervision Journal, 19*(3), 43–59.

AFTERSCHOOL KIDZLIT

Instructional Approach

AfterSchool KidzLit is a language arts enrichment curriculum designed for use in after-school programs. Produced by the Development Studies Center (DSC), the curriculum is differentiated into three grade-level sets, with one curriculum for Kindergarten through third-grade students, another for third- through sixth-grade students, and the third for sixth- through eighth-grade students. It is designed for use with typically achieving students, but the curriculum's focus on vocabulary and engagement can also be supportive of English-language learners and children achieving below grade level.

The KidzLit 3–5 package includes five 10-book sets with guides for each; themes center on relationships and points of view. The 6–8 package includes two 10-book sets with guides, and the themes are divided between nonfiction tales of courage and perseverance and fiction tales about diversity, responsibility, and individuality. Each book comes with a leader's guide, and each set comes with a book of tips and insights. It is also possible to purchase each thematic set of 10 separately. A youth questionnaire and an interview that can be used to assess students' feelings about reading and amount of reading, among other things, are available through DSC. Math and science curricula designed specifically for out-of-school time are also available. DSC also offers curricula designed to be implemented by credentialed teachers in either in-school or after-school settings; these include a phonics program called SIPPS and a reading comprehension program called Making Meaning.

At all grade levels, the program uses a five-part process to develop youngsters' literacy skills, written expression, core values, connections, and thinking skills. The core values center on social skills, while thinking skills and connections engage students in using reading comprehension skills and strategies and a range of responses to reading activities. The five-part process is built on a before-, during-, and after-reading structure, with the focus falling on after-reading activities. The primary literacy skills focused on include vocabulary, identifying main ideas and themes, making predictions, visualizing, using graphic organizers, brainstorming, and writing journal responses. It is recommended that the program be implemented for 30 to 90 minutes per day (depending on student age and program day length) and two to three times a week.

Professional Development

Professional development is designed to introduce program leaders, new and veteran, to the curriculum. This includes experiencing curriculum implementation and learning strategies to enhance cooperation and literacy skills in students. Activities include hands-on enactment, coaching, and modeling of the five-part teaching process used in the curriculum. Follow-up support is also available and may include planning, observation, modeling, co-teaching, and coaching as needed. An on-site support kit for program users wanting to train their own staff is also available. It includes a handbook, six videos, three copies of sample materials and journals, and a CD-ROM containing additional support materials.

Program Evaluation

KidzLit has been evaluated in 23 after-school sites affiliated with CORAL (Communities Organizing Resources to Advance Learning) in Fresno, Long Beach, Pasadena, Sacramento, and San Jose, California. Conducted by Public/Private Ventures, early results from the evaluation indicate that 70% of the students began the program reading below grade level. At the end of an average five-month period in the study, students' overall reading levels increased about a third of a grade level. Students who were reading at two or more levels below their grade showed an increase of approximately three-quarters of a grade level, and students who were English-language learners showed average gains similar to those of students deemed proficient in English.

In another study, researchers from the National Center for Research on Evaluation, Standards, and Student Testing (CRESST) conducted an evaluation of KidzLit at 13 sites affiliated with a Los Angeles after-school enrichment program, LA's BEST in 2001–02. Seven of the sites implemented the program, the other 6 served as a control group. When compared with the control group, the KidzLit students had significantly better attitudes toward academic reading at the end of the evaluation period.

Finally, a third evaluation of the KidzLit program's effects on second- and fourth-grade students attending eight after-school sites in Los Angeles used a pretest/posttest design to assess changes over eight months. Both second and fourth graders reported increased amounts of reading and feelings of self-efficacy in reading. Although no significant effects were shown for vocabulary, quality of implementation appeared to relate to how much improvement in vocabulary students demonstrated, and Spanish-speaking students appeared to benefit significantly.

Contact Information

Address: Developmental Studies Center
2000 Embarcadero, Suite 305
Oakland, CA 94606-5300
Phone: 800-666-7270, ext. 289
E-mail: megan_weber@devstu.org
Website: www.devstu.org/index.html

Source

Developmental Studies Center. (2003). *Summary of AfterSchool KidzLit evaluation*. Oakland, CA: Author.

AMERICA'S CHOICE–RAMP-UP LITERACY

Instructional Approach

Ramp-Up Literacy was developed by America's Choice, Inc., a for-profit subsidiary of the National Center on Education and the Economy. The course curriculum and teacher and student materials evolved over a six-year period through collaboration between program evaluators and classroom teachers. Ramp-Up Literacy is designed for entering middle and high school students (typically grades 6 and 9) who are two or more years below grade level in reading. Ramp-Up students meet for a double period block of 90 minutes daily for an academic year. This double block class is intended to replace the regular

English language arts (ELA) class taken by sixth- and ninth-grade students. The Ramp-Up program is typically part of larger whole-school design efforts; however, only the Ramp-Up literacy curriculum is reviewed here.

The Ramp-Up curriculum is segmented into three 18-week units, which move from texts and concepts traditionally encountered in ELA to texts and concepts central to social studies and science. The program is based on a workshop model, and a standard lesson structure is used that includes whole-group, small-group, and individualized instruction. A typical session begins with independent reading time, followed by vocabulary study, a read-aloud–think-aloud, a classroom discussion, a lesson on a particular comprehension strategy, and individualized teacher–student conferences.

Readings include both nonfiction and high-interest adolescent literature. Ramp-Up is designed to motivate students and to enable them to develop the reading, writing, speaking and listening skills they need to succeed. Comprehension strategies and metacognition are woven throughout the materials. Students are given instruction in "thinking about thinking" through the read-aloud–think-aloud activity. Comprehension instruction also emphasizes the use of strategy charts and discussion of texts, text features, and knowledge structures of the disciplines. Students also produce writing that emerges from what they are reading. Writing assignments are genre specific as are the rubrics that call for genre features, critical thinking, and appropriate use of conventions.

Ramp-Up assessments include a measure of reading comprehension, based on the structure used in the PISA (Programme for International Student Assessment) study; a measure of fluency; a vocabulary assessment, based on the words taught in the given unit of study; and a writing assessment, employing prompts designed for evaluation of persuasive writing ability. These regular assessments allow America's Choice to monitor the progress of students in these four areas, using a standardized measure across all Ramp-Up programs; in addition, they allow teachers to refocus and differentiate instruction throughout the school year.

Professional Development

Professional development is central to implementing the Ramp-Up approach. English or reading teachers who will teach the Ramp-Up to Literacy course attend off-site professional development where they learn the course strategies and content and how to implement the course. Generally, teachers attend a five-day summer institute with 2 two-day follow-up sessions during the year. Administrators or supervisors of Ramp-Up teachers also attend a one-day training in order to understand the structures of the course and its goals and strategies. Additional support is provided to teachers through online lessons, and feedback on student learning is provided through a suite of student assessments developed by the Australian Council on Educational Research.

Program Evaluation

The Consortium of Policy research in Education (CPRE) at the University of Pennsylvania was contracted to conduct the external evaluation of the America's Choice in 1998. Each year CPRE designs and conducts a series of targeted studies on the implementation and impacts of the America's Choice design. Among the studies that have been published are evaluations of implementation in Florida, Georgia, New Jersey, and New York. Case studies of school, district, and state implementations are also available at the America's Choice website. Independent analyses comparing schoolwide reform models have shown positive results, but the impact has varied (Borman, Hewes, Overman, &, Brown, 2003; Legters, Balfanz, & McPartland, 2002; Mason, 2005).

Contact Information

Address: Judy Aaronson, Special Assistant to the President
America's Choice, Inc.
555 13th Street, NW
Suite 500-West
Washington, DC 20004

Phone: 202-783-3668

E-mail: schooldesign@ncee.org

Website: http://americaschoice.org

Sources

Bach, A.J., & Supovitz, J.A. (2003, November). *Teacher and coach implementation of writers workshop in America's Choice schools, 2001 and 2002.* Philadelphia, PA: Consortium for Policy Research in Education, University of Pennsylvania, Graduate School of Education. Retrieved January 14, 2007, from http://www.cpre.org/Publications/AC-07.pdf

Borman, G.D., Hewes, G.M., Overman, L.T., & Brown, S. (2003). Comprehensive school reform and achievement: A meta-analysis. *Review of Educational Research, 73,* 125–230.

Corcoran, T., Hoppe, M., Luhm, T., & Supovitz, J.A. (2000, February). *America's Choice comprehensive school reform design: First-year implementation evaluation summary.* Philadelphia, PA: Consortium for Policy Research in Education, University of Pennsylvania, Graduate School of Education. Retrieved January 14, 2007, from http://www.cpre.org/Publications/AC.pdf

Legters, N., Balfanz, R., & McPartland, J. (2002). *Solutions for failing high schools: Converging visions and promising models.* Washington, DC: Office of Vocational and Adult Education.

Mason, B. (2005). *Achievement effects of five comprehensive school reform designs implemented in Los Angeles Unified School District.* Santa Monica, CA: Pardee RAND Graduate School.

May, H., Supovitz, J.A., & Lesnick, J. (2004, July). *The impact of America's Choice on writing performance in Georgia: First-year results.* Philadelphia, PA: Consortium for Policy Research in Education, University of Pennsylvania, Graduate School of Education. Retrieved January 14, 2007, from http://www.cpre.org/Publications/AC-09.pdf

May, H., Supovitz, J.A., & Perda, D. (2004, July). *A longitudinal study of the impact of America's Choice on student performance in Rochester, New York, 1998–2003.* Philadelphia, PA: Consortium for Policy Research in Education, University of Pennsylvania, Graduate School of Education. Retrieved January 14, 2007, from http://www.cpre.org/Publications/AC-10.pdf

Poglinco, S.M., Bach, A.J., Hovde, K., Rosenblum, S., Saunders, M., & Supovitz, J. (2003, May). *The heart of the matter: The coaching model in America's Choice schools.* Philadelphia, PA: Consortium for Policy Research in Education, University of Pennsylvania, Graduate School of Education. Retrieved January 14, 2007, from http://www.cpre.org/Publications/AC-06.pdf

Supovitz, J.A., & Klein, V. (2003, November). *Mapping a course for improved student learning: How innovative schools systematically use student performance data to guide improvement.* Philadelphia, PA: Consortium for Policy Research in Education, University of Pennsylvania, Graduate School of Education. Retrieved January 14, 2007, from http://www.cpre.org/Publications/AC-08.pdf

Supovitz, J.A., & May, H. (2003, January). *The relationship between teacher implementation of America's Choice and student learning in Plainfield, New Jersey.* Philadelphia, PA: Consortium for Policy Research in Education, University of Pennsylvania, Graduate School of Education. Retrieved January 14, 2007, from http://www.cpre.org/Publications/AC-05.pdf

Supovitz, J.A., & May, H. (2004). A study of the links between implementation and effectiveness of the America's Choice comprehensive school reform design. *Journal of Education for Students Placed at Risk, 9,* 389–419.

Supovitz, J.A., & Poglinco, S.M. (2001, December). *Instructional leadership in a standards-based reform.* Philadelphia, PA: Consortium for Policy Research in Education, University of Pennsylvania, Graduate School of Education. Retrieved January 14, 2007, from http://www.cpre.org/Publications/AC-02.pdf

Supovitz, J.A., Poglinco, S.M., & Bach, A. (2002, April). *Implementation of the America's Choice literacy workshops.* Philadelphia, PA: Consortium for Policy Research in Education, University of Pennsylvania, Graduate School of Education. Retrieved January 14, 2007, from http://www.cpre.org/Publications/AC-03.pdf

Supovitz, J.A., Poglinco, S.M., & Snyder, B.A. (2001). *Moving mountains: Successes and challenges of the America's Choice comprehensive school reform design.* Philadelphia, PA: Consortium for Policy Research in Education, University of Pennsylvania, Graduate School of Education. Retrieved January 14, 2007, from http://www.cpre.org/Publications/AC-01.pdf

Supovitz, J.A., Taylor, B.S., & May, H. (2002, October). *The impact of America's Choice on student performance in Duval County, Florida.* Philadelphia, PA: Consortium for Policy Research in Education, University of Pennsylvania, Graduate School of Education. Retrieved January 14, 2007, from http://www.cpre.org/Publications/AC-04.pdf

BENCHMARK WORD DETECTIVES

Instructional Approach

The Benchmark program evolved from the curriculum in place at the Benchmark School in Pennsylvania. The school, which began in 1970 as a part-time program, enrolls struggling readers aged 6 to 14 who tend to score between the 1st and 35th percentile on standardized measures of reading. The school's approach to teaching decoding is the basis of the Word Detectives curriculum.

The Benchmark Word Detectives program teaches decoding by analogy, which is an approach that focuses on teaching children spelling patterns using "key words." Once children have memorized the spelling pattern of a key word, that word can be used to successfully decode and spell words that sound like it. High-frequency words (such as *some*, *the*, or *was*) that do not follow these patterns reliably are also taught and memorized. The program has three levels. Level one is for preprimary learners through second grade. Level two is for second through fifth grades. And level three, which is split into two parts, is for fifth grade and beyond. In 2000, the level-two curriculum was adapted for learners in fifth grade or above in order to address older learners with lower levels of decoding.

The lessons in the curriculum are 30 minutes in length and focus on decoding and vocabulary with the aim of building reading fluency. Depending on the level of curriculum in use, between 150 and 165 lessons are included, providing instruction in the approach of decoding by analogy itself and substantial practice reading nonfiction. Brief lessons are taught to the class as a whole, and then children work individually or in pairs or small groups.

Professional Development

Professional development for the use of this program is achieved by teachers reviewing the materials independently.

Program Evaluation

While a great deal has been published regarding the program's effectiveness within the Benchmark School, no large-scale evaluations of its effectiveness in other contexts were apparent. The Southwest Educational Development Laboratory rated the Benchmark Word Detectives Program as promising (Peterson, Caverly, Nicholson, O'Neal, & Cusenbary, 2000). However, program evaluations and research on the program were not found.

Contact Information

Address: Benchmark School
           2107 North Providence Road
           Media, PA 19063-1898
Phone: 610-565-3741
E-mail: benchmarkinfo@benchmarkschool.org
Website: www.benchmarkschool.org/index.htm

Sources

Gaskins, I.W. (1998). A beginning literacy program for at-risk and delayed readers. In J. Metsala & L. Ehri (Eds.), *Word recognition in beginning literacy* (pp. 209–232). Mahwah, NJ: Erlbaum.

Gaskins, I.W. (1998). There's more to teaching at-risk and delayed readers than good reading instruction [Distinguished Educator series]. *The Reading Teacher, 51*, 534–547.

Gaskins, I.W. (2003). A multidimensional approach to beginning literacy. In D.M. Barone & L.M. Morrow (Eds.), *Literacy and young children: Research-based practices* (pp. 45–60). New York: Guilford.

Gaskins, I.W. (2004). Word detectives. *Educational Leadership, 61*, 70–73.

Gaskins, I.W., Cuncelli, E., & Satlow, E. (1992). Implementing an across-the-curriculum strategies program: Reaction to change. In J. Pressley, K. Harris, & J. Guthrie (Eds.), *Promoting academic competence and literacy in school* (pp. 411–426). Boston: Academic.

Gaskins, I.W., Downer, M., Anderson, R., Cunningham, P., Gaskins, R., Schommer, M., et al. (1988). A metacognitive approach to phonics: Using what you know to decode what you don't know. *Remedial and Special Education, 9*, 36–41.

Gaskins, I.W., Ehri, L.C., Cress, C., O'Hara, C., & Donnelly, K. (1997a). Procedures for word learning: Making discoveries about words. *The Reading Teacher, 50*, 312–327.

Gaskins, I.W., Ehri, L.C., Cress, C., O'Hara, C., & Donnelly, K. (1997b). Analyzing words and making discoveries about the alphabetic system: Activities for beginning readers. *Language Arts, 74*, 172–184.

Gaskins, I.W., & Elliot, T.T. (1991). *Implementing cognitive strategy instruction across the school: The Benchmark manual for teachers*. Cambridge, MA: Brookline.

Gaskins, R.W., Gaskins, I.W., Anderson, R.C., & Schommer, M. (1995). The reciprocal relationship between research and development: An example involving a decoding strand for poor readers. *Journal of Reading Behavior, 27*, 337–377.

Gaskins, R.W., Gaskins, J.C., & Gaskins, I.W. (1991). A decoding program for poor readers—and the rest of the class, too! *Language Arts, 68*, 213–225.

Gaskins, R.W., Gaskins, J.C., & Gaskins, I.W. (1992). Using what you know to figure out what you don't know: An analogy approach to decoding. *Reading and Writing Quarterly, 8*, 197–221.

Peterson, C.L., Caverly, D.C., Nicholson, S.A., O'Neal, S., & Cusenbary, S. (2000). *Building reading proficiency at the secondary level: A guide to resources*. Austin, TX: Southwest Educational Development Laboratory.

Instructional Approach

Concept-Oriented Reading Instruction (CORI) is a research-based curriculum emphasizing reading engagement, reading comprehension, and conceptual learning in science. Students receive explicit instruction in comprehension strategies in the context of a science inquiry. Thus, both reading strategies and content relate directly to students' experiences. The curriculum is based on the premise that the use of authentic knowledge and concept-oriented goals for reading instruction promotes motivation and a deep engagement with reading, and thereby a deeper understanding of texts and ownership of strategies and content.

CORI was designed to improve on previous reading comprehension strategy instruction models by providing teachers with engaging practices intended to be enacted long term. Specifically, CORI units last 12–16 weeks, teach students multiple strategies, integrate easily with science and language arts curricular goals, and target the whole class. CORI teachers support students' engagement in reading through five motivational practices: (1) focusing on content goals in a conceptual theme, (2) affording choices and control to students, (3) providing hands-on activities to pique students' interest in the theme's topics, (4) using interesting texts that are related to the concepts being learned, and (5) organizing effective collaboration to enable learning from text.

Each unit progresses through four phases: observe and personalize (where students help set inquiry goals for the unit); search and retrieve (where students research their topics); comprehend and integrate (where students learn strategies for understanding, retaining, and organizing the information); and communicate to others (where students demonstrate their learning by engaging in thoughtful text-based writing). The core reading strategies covered include activating background knowledge; student questioning; searching for and summarizing information; organizing information graphically; monitoring comprehension; and synthesizing information into a communicative product (such as a chapter book, information book, persuasive essay, or story). Typical CORI instruction is supplemented for students who struggle with decoding; these students are grouped together to receive additional instruction in decoding skills and practice fluent expressive reading.

Professional Development

Although CORI is a curricular approach, it relies heavily on substantial and ongoing professional development for successful implementation. The current scale-up of CORI involves teachers in 10 half-day workshops during the summer before implementation. Teachers learn the theory behind CORI, see and experience models of effective CORI instruction, and plan their own CORI units. Ongoing support is provided through a project website that includes links to journal articles, book lists, model lessons, student sample work, and forums for discussions among the teachers themselves, as well as with their students and the researchers. In addition, teachers attend monthly workshops where they see additional modeling, share their ongoing experiences, and collaborate with one another to improve their own practice.

Program Evaluation

Evaluation of CORI's effectiveness is available through published research articles. Using quasi-experimental designs, CORI researchers have investigated the effects of the approach on third-, fourth-, and fifth-grade teachers and their students. They have found that students in CORI classrooms outperformed students in traditional classrooms in motivation to read and strategy use (Guthrie, Wigfield, & VonSecker, 2000) and in conceptual learning from text, motivated strategy use, and reading comprehension (Guthrie, Anderson, Alao, & Rinehart, 1999). They have also found that after a full year of CORI instruction, students had significantly improved their strategy use and that better strategy use mediated better conceptual knowledge; furthermore, these effects were more pronounced for third-grade than fifth-grade students (Guthrie et al., 1998).

Although the curriculum was originally implemented on a classroom-by-classroom basis, a recent Interagency Education Research Initiative grant has enabled the program designers to "scale up." The scale-up studies compared the CORI program (i.e., explicit support for both cognitive and motivational processes of reading) with a strategy instruction (SI) program (i.e., explicit support for cognitive processes of reading) and a traditional instruction (TI) control group (i.e., support for comprehension through the use of basal reading materials). In these 12-week treatment studies, CORI showed significant benefits in elementary students' reading comprehension (both for multiple-text reading and short-passage reading), content knowledge acquisition, reading engagement, and growth in strategic reading (Guthrie, Wigfield, Barbosa, et al., 2004; Wigfield, Guthrie, Tonks, & Perencevich, 2004). These studies also used standardized reading comprehension tests to show generalizablity of the results.

Contact Information

Address: Concept-Oriented Reading Instruction Project Office
University of Maryland
Department of Human Development
3304 Benjamin Building
College Park, MD 20742
Phone: 301-314-8448
E-mail: jguthrie@umd.edu
Website: www.cori.umd.edu

Sources

Guthrie, J.T. (2003). Concept-oriented reading instruction: Practices of teaching reading for understanding. In A.S. Sweet & C.E. Snow (Eds.), *Rethinking reading comprehension* (pp. 115–140). New York: Guilford.

Guthrie, J.T. (2004a). Classroom contexts for engaged reading: An overview. In J.T. Guthrie, A. Wigfield, & K. Perencevich (Eds.), *Motivating reading comprehension: Concept-Oriented Reading Instruction* (pp. 97–123). Mahwah, NJ: Erlbaum.

Guthrie, J.T. (2004b). Teaching for literacy engagement. *Journal of Literacy Research, 36,* 1–30.

Guthrie, J.T., Anderson, E., Alao, S., & Rinehart, J. (1999). Influences of Concept-Oriented Reading Instruction on strategy use and conceptual learning from text. *The Elementary School Journal, 99,* 343–366.

Guthrie, J.T., & Davis, M.H. (2003). Motivating struggling readers in middle school through an engagement model of classroom practice. *Reading & Writing Quarterly, 19,* 59–85.

Guthrie, J.T., & Humenick, N.M. (2004) Motivating students to read: Evidence for classroom practices that increase reading motivation and achievement. In. P. McCardle & V. Chhabra (Eds.), *The voice of evidence in reading research* (pp. 329–354). Baltimore, MD: Brookes.

Guthrie, J.T., Schafer, W.D., VonSecker, C., & Alban, T. (2000). Contributions of integrated reading instruction and text resources to achievement and engagement in a statewide school improvement program. *Journal of Educational Research, 93,* 211–225.

Guthrie, J.T., Van Meter, P., Hancock, G.R., Alao, S., Anderson, E., & McCann, A. (1998). Does Concept-Oriented Reading Instruction increase strategy-use and conceptual learning from text? *Journal of Educational Psychology, 90,* 261–278.

Guthrie, J.T., Wigfield, A., Barbosa, P., Perencevich, K., Taboada, A., Davis, M., et al. (2004). Increasing reading comprehension and engagement through Concept-Oriented Reading Instruction. *Journal of Educational Psychology, 96,* 1–21.

Guthrie, J.T., Wigfield, A., & Perencevich, K.C. (Eds.). (2004). *Motivating reading comprehension: Concept-Oriented Reading Instruction.* Mahwah, NJ: Erlbaum.

Guthrie, J.T., Wigfield, A., & VonSecker, C. (2000). Effects of integrated instruction on motivation and strategy use in reading. *Journal of Educational Psychology, 92,* 331–341.

Ozgungor, S., & Guthrie, J.T. (2004). Interactions among elaborative interrogation, knowledge, and interest in the process of constructing knowledge from text. *Journal of Educational Psychology, 96,* 437–443.

Swan, E.A. (2003). *Concept-Oriented Reading Instruction: Engaging classrooms, lifelong learners.* New York: Guilford.

Wang, J.H., & Guthrie, J.T. (2004). Modeling the effects of intrinsic motivation, extrinsic motivation, amount of reading, and past reading achievement on text comprehension between U.S. and Chinese students. *Reading Research Quarterly, 39,* 162–186.

Wigfield, A., Guthrie, J.T., Tonks, S., & Perencevich, K. (2004). Children's motivation for reading: Domain specificity and instructional influences. *Journal of Educational Research, 97,* 299–309.

CORRECTIVE READING

Instructional Approach

The Corrective Reading program was designed to aid readers who "misidentify, reverse, or omit words, who have little recall and limited attention span and who read without understanding" (as noted on the Corrective Reading website, www.sraonline.com/productsamples.html?show=2&gid=2713&tid=14, January 26, 2007). The program was developed in 1973 according to the precepts of Direct Instruction and has two strands: decoding and comprehension. The decoding strand focuses on improving decoding skills so that readers may direct their attention to comprehension, while the comprehension strand develops vocabulary, background knowledge, and thinking skills.

Materials include workbooks, books, teacher guides and presentation books, placement and mastery tests, and a series guide. Both the decoding and comprehension strands of Corrective Reading have three levels, which proceed from basics to more advanced strategies and skills and, finally, to extended practice and application. At the start of the program, students are given decoding and comprehension placement tests, and results are used to start them at the appropriate level in the Corrective Reading program sequences. Teacher guides provide a series of scripted lessons.

Professional Development

It was not clear from Corrective Reading sources whether professional development is included in the purchase of the program, or what such professional development might entail.

Program Evaluation

Corrective Reading is one of the older intervention programs available, and both published and unpublished evaluation and research of its effects exist. Much of this work is summarized on the program's website. Many of the studies employed comparison groups, and those studies showed positive effects for Corrective Reading on decoding, vocabulary, and comprehension. Effects were consistent across subgroups of students, including learning-disabled, struggling, at-risk, and limited-English-proficient students. Corrective Reading is also one of four intervention programs under evaluation by the Power4Kids Research Initiative in a randomized experiment (as noted on the Haan Foundation website, www.haan4kids.org/power4kids/exec_summary_0306.html, January 26, 2007). The study will compare the programs in terms of impact, fidelity of treatment, and neurological effects. In addition, the Florida Center for Reading Research has conducted an independent review of the program.

One of the most recently published studies examined the effects of Corrective Reading for rural, high school students with learning disabilities (Marchand-Martella, Martella, Orlob, & Ebey, 2000). Students received the intervention for an academic year and were pre- and posttested using the Gates–MacGinitie vocabulary and reading comprehension tests. Students placed in the lowest level of the Corrective Reading program improved by 1.5 years in vocabulary and 1 year in reading comprehension, while those placed at higher levels of the program improved by 1 year in vocabulary and 1.5 years in reading comprehension. The program was used in concert with peer tutoring and repeated reading, obscuring its unique contribution to the observed effects.

Contact Information

Address: SRA/McGraw-Hill
          220 East Danieldale Road
          DeSoto, TX 75115-2490
Phone: 888-SRA-4543
E-mail: SRA_CustomerService@mcgraw-hill.com

Website: www.sraonline.com/index.php/home/curriculumsolutions/di/
          correctivereading/102

Sources

Campbell, M.L. (1984). Corrective Reading program evaluated with secondary students in San Diego. *ADI News*, 7, 15–17.

Clunies-Ross, G. (1999). Some effects of direct instruction in comprehension skills on intellectual performance. *Behavior Change*, 7, 84–89.

Florida Center for Reading Research. (2004, March). *SRA Corrective Reading*. Tallahassee, FL: Author. Retrieved January 14, 2007, from http://www.fcrr.org/FCRRReports/PDF/corrective_reading_final.pdf

Gregory, R.P., Hackney, C., & Gregory, N.M. (1982). Corrective Reading programme: An evaluation. *British Journal of Educational Psychology*, 52, 33–50.

Harris, R., Marchand-Martella, N., & Martella, R. (2000). Effects of a peer-delivered corrective reading program. *Journal of Behavioral Education*, 10(1), 21–36.

Hempenstall, K.J. (1997). *The effects on the phonological processing skills of disabled readers of participating in direct instruction reading programs*. Unpublished doctoral dissertation, Royal Melbourne Institute of Technology, Australia.

Marchand-Martella, N., Martella, R.C., Bettis, D.F., & Blakely, M.R. (2004). Project Pals: A description of a high school-based tutorial program using Corrective Reading and peer-delivered instructions. *Reading & Writing Quarterly*, 20, 179–201.

Marchand-Martella, N., Martella, R.C., Orlob, M., & Ebey, T. (2000). Conducting action research in a rural high school setting using peers as Corrective Reading instructors for students with disabilities. *Rural Special Education Quarterly*, 19(2), 20–29.

Polloway, E.A., Epstein, M.H., Polloway, C.H., Patton, J.R., & Ball, D.W. (1986). Corrective Reading program: An analysis of effectiveness with learning disabled and mentally retarded students. *Remedial and Special Education*, 7(4), 41–47.

Steventon, C.E., & Fredrick, L.D. (2003). The effects of repeated readings on student performance in the Corrective Reading program. *Journal of Direct Instruction*, 3, 17–27.

Strong, A., Wehby, J., Falk, K., & Lane, K. (2004). The impact of a structured reading curriculum and repeated reading on the performance of junior high students with emotional and behavioral disorders. *School Psychology Review*, 33(4), 561–581.

Thorne, M.T. (1978). Payment for reading: The use of the Corrective Reading scheme with junior maladjusted boys. *Remedial Education*, 13, 87–89.

Torgesen, J., Myers, D., Schirm, A., Stuart, E., Vartivarian, S., Mansfield, W., et al. (2006). *National assessment of Title I: Interim report. Volume II: Closing the reading gap: First year findings from a randomized trial of four reading interventions for striving readers*. Washington, DC: National Center for Education Evaluation and Regional Assistance, Institute of Education Sciences, U.S. Department of Education. Retrieved January 14, 2007, from http://www.ed.gov/rschstat/eval/disadv/title1interimreport/vol2.pdf

Vitale, M., Medland, M., Romance, N., & Weaver, H.P. (1993). Accelerating reading and thinking skills of low-achieving elementary students: Implications for curricular change. *Effective School Practices*, 12, 26–31.

DISCIPLINARY LITERACY

Instructional Approach

Developed by the Institute for Learning at the University of Pittsburgh, Disciplinary Literacy is a professional development program designed for secondary school administrators, coaches, and lead teachers. A requirement of the program is that whole districts participate and that these districts have the infrastructure available to support the implementation of the program districtwide. The program is designed to prepare participating schools to include all students, regardless of their academic skills, in complex thinking tasks based on rigorous academic content material. The training introduces instructional approaches for secondary teachers in the content areas of English language arts (ELA), history, mathematics, and science.

While each strand addresses discourse skills, the ELA strand addresses secondary students' reading literacy skills most directly by making teachers aware of the need to determine areas of potential difficulty in text, both for all students and for English-language learners. In addition, teachers are trained to consider students' cultural background and help all students develop an understanding of academic reading and writing as defined by each discipline. Finally, vocabulary is taught through reading, writing, and thinking activities.

The history strand addresses literacy by making explicit the reading practices historians employ when working with primary- and secondary-source documents. Students are explicitly taught how to comprehend text by learning how to situate the text in its historical context, how to think about the author's intent within that context, and how to corroborate the text with others from the same time period dealing with the same historical issues. Vocabulary is taught in context as well, taking into account the type of document in which the word appears (political speech, personal letter, article of legislation) and the author's intent in using that word to support the development of specific historical ideas and arguments within the document. In mathematics, learners learn mathematics by actually doing mathematics. The mathematical activities in which students engage require them to explore concepts, make and test conjectures, verify outcomes, predict results, and generalize beyond a given case. Students reflect on what they are doing in mathematics and communicate about it to others. Students talk, write and listen, share their methods for solving problems, respond to questions posed by their peers, make sense of other students' solutions, and ask questions to ensure their own understanding. The science strand, in addition to providing specific support for writing scientific explanations, offers support to enhance students' ability to describe, explain, and predict natural phenomena in speech and in writing.

Professional Development

This professional development program is rigorous, with participation in the Disciplinary Literacy program requiring prior participation in a year-long preparatory course introducing the Institute for Learning's Principles of Learning, which link pedagogical practice and decades of learning research to help educators analyze the quality of instruction and opportunities for learning that they offer to students. Upon completion of this course, participating districts are eligible to apply to participate in the Disciplinary Literacy training. Acceptance into the programs will depend on each program's staff assessment of the district's readiness and on space availability.

Within the training course, participants engage in cycles of study and activity in which they plan, teach, and analyze sequences of subject-matter content lessons that enable high levels of literate thinking and reasoning. At the school and district levels, the Disciplinary Literacy course provides a set of coaching structures and strategies, along with a focus on how to organize professional learning in ways that support disciplinary apprenticeships.

Program Evaluation

Research and evaluation on Disciplinary Literacy was not available when this volume went to press.

Contact Information

Address: Nancy Israel
               Institute for Learning
               University of Pittsburgh
               3939 O'Hara Street, 310 LRDC
               Pittsburgh, PA 15260
Phone: 412-624-7093
E-mail: nisrael@pitt.edu
Website: www.instituteforlearning.org

Source

Matsumara, L.C., Slater, S.C., et al. (2006). *Measuring the quality of reading comprehension and mathematics instruction in urban middle schools.* Los Angeles: National Center for Research on Evaluation Standards and Student Testing.

FAILURE FREE READING

Instructional Approach

Failure Free Reading is a computerized reading program designed for struggling readers, English as a second language (ESL), special education, at-risk, and minority students who score repeatedly in the 0–15th percentile on reading tests. Students are not excluded on the basis of label or prior reading ability, and the program is designed to provide a high-impact, high-intensity reading intervention. The program was designed especially for "phonetically deaf" children who do not benefit from a phonics approach to reading instruction.

Failure Free Reading is built on the premise that with adequate repetition of lessons and practice, appropriately challenging syntax, and meaningful story content, even the most challenged readers will thrive. The program is designed to supplement existing reading and language arts programs by having students learn to read a series of age-appropriate graded stories. Every lesson begins with an explicit, structured, language development exercise designed to enhance listening comprehension, vocabulary development, and speaking. Completion of a lesson ends with the students reading a story passage with full fluency and comprehension. Repeated readings are the key instructional fluency procedure. Students learn a new part of the story in every lesson. Eventually they are taught how to read the entire story.

Failure Free Reading's materials include a combination of print, talking software, and teacher-directed lessons. Classroom kits include scripted teachers' manuals, reinforcement activities, student workbooks, independent reading booklets, instructional readers, flashcards, parent communication letters, and certificates of accomplishments. Software lessons and texts are aligned with the print materials. The software includes spelling, fluency, comprehension, language development activities and assessments and also has Spanish audio resources for Spanish-speaking students. There are several levels of materials that are grade appropriate for kindergarten through adult learners who are not yet efficient readers of text. Higher-level instructional materials are also available. Failure Free Reading includes features such as an online diagnostic prescriptive assessment and the use of high-interest–high-comprehensible supplementary reading materials for adolescent nonreaders. The program also includes a management system for collecting and summarizing data.

Professional Development

The Failure Free Reading professional development courses are designed such that the participants play an active role with guidance from a facilitator. Participants receive brief introductory overviews of the material they will cover. After the overview, they are given materials that guide them through the learning activities. Upon completion of the activities they must produce a product or presentation that demonstrates thorough knowledge of the material and how they will apply what they learned.

Failure Free Reading materials include a teacher's manual with completely scripted lessons, designed for use by parents or teaching aides. Samples of the teacher's manuals are also downloadable from the support website. Additional support is available via e-mail, phone, and Web conference.

Program Evaluation

The Failure Free Reading website offers a summary of evaluations of the program's effectiveness (Failure Free Reading, n.d.). According to this summary, Failure Free Reading has shown positive effects in independent quasi-experimental studies. For example, one high school study found that ESL, special education, and at-risk students using the Failure Free Reading program improved by 2.77 grade equivalents on the Stanford Achievement Test over the course of one academic year. Similar students at the same school who did not use the program improved by only 1.06 grade equivalents during the same time period.

Over a half a dozen studies of Failure Free Reading's effectiveness in the primary grades have been published in journals. One available published study investigated the program's effectiveness for randomly selected, third- through fifth-grade students with severe learning disabilities (Rankhorn, England, Collins, Lockavitch, & Algozzine, 1998). The study found that, after seven months of Failure Free Reading instruction, students had improved significantly in letter–word identification, word attack, and comprehension. Failure Free Reading is also one of four intervention programs selected for inclusion by the Power4Kids Research Initiative in a randomized experiment (as noted on the Power4Kids website). The study will compare the programs in terms of impact, fidelity of treatment, neurological effects, and cost-effectiveness. The Florida Center for Reading Research (2004) has also conducted an independent review of the program.

Contact Information

Address: Dr. Joseph Lockavitch
             Failure Free Reading
             140 Cabarrus Avenue W
             Concord, NC 28025
Phone: 704-786-7838
E-mail: Joe.lockavitch@failurefree.com
Website: www.failurefree.com

Sources

Algozzine, B., & Lockavitch, J.F. (1998). Effects of failure free reading on students at-risk for reading failure. *Special Services in the School, 13*, 95–105.

Algozzine, B., Lockavitch, J.F., & Audette, R. (1997). Effects of Failure Free Reading on students at-risk for serious school failure. *Australian Journal of Learning Disabilities, 2*(3), 14–17.

Failure Free Reading. (n.d.). *Failure Free Reading's continuum of Effectiveness: Research summary.* Concord, NH: Author. Retrieved January 14, 2007, from http://www.failurefree.com/downloads/FFR_White_Paper.pdf

Florida Center for Reading Research. (2004, June). *Failure Free Reading.* Tallahassee, FL: Author. Retrieved January 14, 2007, from http://www.fcrr.org/FCRRReports/PDF/failure_free_reading.pdf

Lockavitch, J.F., & Algozzine, B. (1998). Effects of intensive intervention on students at-risk for reading failure. *Florida Reading Journal, 35*(2), 27–31.

Lockavitch, J.F., Morgan, L., & Algozzine, B. (1999). Accelerating the growth curve: Improving opportunities for children at-risk for reading failure. *Proven Practice, 1*, 60–67.

Rankhorn, B., England, G., Collins, S.M., Lockavitch, J.F., & Algozzine, B. (1998). Effects of the Failure Free Reading program on students with severe reading disabilities. *Journal of Learning Disabilities, 31*(3), 307–312.

Slate, J., Algozzine, B., & Lockavitch, J.F. (1998). Effects of intensive remedial reading instruction. *Journal of At-Risk Issues, 5*, 30–35.

Torgesen, J., Myers, D., Schirm, A., Stuart, E., Vartivarian, S., Mansfield, W., et al. (2006). *National assessment of Title I: Interim report. Volume II: Closing the reading gap: First year findings from a randomized trial of four reading interventions for striving readers.* Washington, DC: National Center for Education Evaluation and Regional Assistance, Institute of Education Sciences, U.S. Department of Education. Retrieved January 14, 2007, from http://www.ed.gov/rschstat/eval/disadv/title1interimreport/vol2.pdf

Instructional Approach

First Steps is a professional development program that prepares teachers to implement effective literacy strategies across the curriculum in grades K through 5. The professional development program for grades 6 through 12 was formerly called Stepping Out and is currently under revision and called STEPS. First Steps was developed by the Education Department of Western Australia through a collaboration of classroom teachers and university researchers attempting to build research-based practice, was sold through Heinemann Publishers for several years, and is now distributed by Steps Professional Development and Consulting based in Salem, Massachusetts. First Steps is used widely in elementary schools throughout Australia.

A central component of both the First Steps and STEPS programs is a diagnostic framework or Developmental Continua, which helps teachers determine where students are functioning in the areas of reading, writing, spelling, and oral language as a basis for guiding instruction. Because of the diagnostically driven instruction, the program is designed to support all students and has been used in educating both second-language learners and special needs students. The professional development courses stress classroom practices of modeling, guided practice, independent practice, and cooperative learning. Another focus of the professional development is to assist teachers to help students understand reading strategies as a set of tools to be used in a variety of settings. The STEPS professional development also focuses on understanding how text structures and comprehension strategies apply to specific content areas, as well as how to address the needs of struggling readers.

Professional Development

A schoolwide approach encourages all teachers within the school to participate in two-day courses in the component that has been identified by the school for implementation. In addition, some teachers within the school can become First Steps Tutors, which requires an extra eight days of training. These Tutors function as on-site trainers, in all four components, and coaches to the teachers in the school as they implement the program. Workshops for principals are also available.

Program Evaluation

Program evaluation appears to have mostly been conducted on students in elementary schools and in Australia. A report by Bank Street College of Education, New York, shows that teachers implement the strategies after receiving training. Several publications have also listed First Steps as an effective research-based program.

Contact Information

Address: STEPS Professional Development & Consulting
97 Boston Street
Salem, MA 01970

Phone: 866-505-3001

E-mail: info@stepspd.org

Website: www.stepspd.org

Sources

Australian Council for Educational Research. (n.d.). *The impact of First Steps on the reading and writing ability of year 5 students* (An interim report to the Curriculum Development Branch Western Australian Ministry of Education). Retrieved May 31, 2006, from http://www.stepspd.org/research/res6.html

Australian Council for Educational Research. (n.d.). *The impact of First Steps on schools and teachers* (An interim report to the Curriculum Development Branch Western Australian Ministry of Education). Retrieved May 31, 2006, from http://www.stepspd.org/research/res7.html

Deschamp, P. (n.d.). *Case studies of the implementation of the First Steps Project in twelve schools.* Retrieved June 16, 2006, from http://www.stepspd.org/research/res4.html

Deschamp, P. (n.d.). *The development and implementation of the First Steps Project in Western Australia.* Retrieved June 16, 2006, from http://www.stepspd.org/research/res1.html

Deschamp, P. (n.d.). *The implementation of the literacy component of the First Steps Project in ELAN schools.* Retrieved June 16, 2006, from http://www.stepspd.org/research/res3.html

Deschamp, P. (n.d.). *The study of effects of First Steps teaching on student achievement.* Retrieved June 16, 2006, from http://www.stepspd.org/research/res8.html

Deschamp, P. (1994). *A survey of the implementation of the literacy component of the First Steps Project in Western Australia.* Retrieved June 16, 2006, from http://www.stepspd.org/research/res2.html

Dewsbury, A. (n.d.). *Supporting linguistic and cultural diversity through First Steps: The Highgate project.* Retrieved June 16, 2006, from http://www.stepspd.org/research/res11.html

Freidus, H., McNamara, M., & Groseis, C. (1998). *First Steps study: The year two progress report.* New York: Bank Street College of Education. Retrieved June 16, 2006, from http://www.stepspd.org/research/bankstreet.pdf

Peterson, C.L., Caverly, D.C., Nicholson, S.A., O'Neal, S., & Cusenbary, S. (2000). *Building reading proficiency at the secondary level: A guide to resources.* Austin, TX: Southwest Educational Development Laboratory.

St. John, E.P., Loescher, S.A., & Bardzell, J.S. (2003). *Improving reading and literacy in grades 1–5: A resource guide to research-based programs.* Thousand Oaks, CA: Corwin.

JUNIOR GREAT BOOKS

Instructional Approach

The Junior Great Books program is a literature-based English language arts (ELA) program designed to teach students how to read with comprehension. Designed by the Great Books Foundation, the program provides low-cost, age-appropriate reading series for students in grades 2 through 12. It can function as the core ELA curriculum or as a supplement to an existing curriculum in ELA or other content area classes.

The program is built on a model of shared inquiry, and participating teachers are prepared to guide students in analysis and critical discussions of a wide range of literature. Teachers are provided with suggested interpretive strategies for each reading selection and, throughout the curriculum, students are encouraged to support their ideas with examples from text as they answer open-ended questions. The emphasis is on guiding students to become critical and self-reliant readers capable of communicating complex ideas and supporting their reasoning with evidence.

Each series for grades 2 through 6 includes a student anthology with 12 selections of classic and modern fiction; audiotapes of the reading selections; student activity books; and a teacher's edition, which includes copies of students' reading selections and activity pages, lesson plans, and activity guides. For grades 7 through 12, each series includes a student anthology with 12 selections of short stories, novellas, and selections from novels; however, the series for grades 10 through 12 also incorporate selections from classic nonfiction works of philosophy, history, politics, and other content areas. Each of the series for grades 7 through 12 also includes a leader's guide, which includes the selections and questions for prereading and postreading, as well as vocabulary and note-taking activities and suggests writing activities and passages for in-depth textual analysis. A number of supplementary series are available that allow for in-depth exploration of additional themes and topics, such as life sciences, environmental science, poetry, human rights, and cultural assimilation.

Professional Development

School personnel must participate in preimplementation planning to ensure that the program is a good fit for the school and district. It is recommended that, at a minimum, all teachers implement the curriculum within a given school. However, books may also be purchased separately without Great Books professional development, and the program's flexibility allows various levels of implementation. For schools implementing a schoolwide approach, the Great Books Foundation provides staff to conduct two-day, on-site training to schools and districts implementing the program. Participants in the training receive a manual and an instructional guide. At the end of the first year, lead teachers are identified and then receive additional instruction. An on-site coordinator receives additional professional development in how to coordinate and support the program and ongoing coaching is offered, with follow-up consultation required for the first two years of implementation. The Great Books Foundation also offers a Web-based tutorial on the shared inquiry discussion method and online discussion forums.

Program Evaluation

Several dissertation studies have been conducted on the effects of the Great Books curricula. One showed that low-performing third-grade students made significant gains in supporting their opinions with evidence from text when compared with a control group. In another study, low-performing fifth-grade students made gains in literal and inferential comprehension as measured by a researcher-designed pretest and an end-of-study administration of the Iowa Test of Basic Skills. The remaining dissertation studies showed gains in critical thinking and positive attitudes toward reading within the sample but were similar to the fifth-grade study cited above in that no comparison group was included in the study.

Contact Information

Address: Tom Kershner
The Great Books Foundation
35 East Wacker Drive, Suite 2300
Chicago, IL 60601-2298
Phone: 800-222-5870 ext. 255
E-mail: jgb@greatbooks.org
Website: www.greatbooks.org

Sources

Bird, J.J. (1984). *Effects of fifth graders' attitudes and critical thinking/reading skills resulting from a Junior Great Books program*. Unpublished doctoral dissertation, Rutgers University, New Brunswick, NJ.

Biskin, D.S., Hoskisson, K., & Modlin, M. (1976). Prediction, reflection, and comprehension. *The Elementary School Journal*, 77, 131–139.

Criscuola, M. (1994). Read, discuss, reread: Insights from the Junior Great Books program. *Educational Leadership*, 51(5), 58–61.

Criscuola, M., & Hare, V.C. (1992). *The Junior Great Books curriculum of interpretive reading, writing, and discussion: A proposal submitted to the Program Effectiveness Panel for the National Diffusion Network of the U.S. Department of Education*. Chicago: The Great Books Foundation.

Graup, L.B. (1985). *Response to literature: Student-generated questions and collaborative learning as related to comprehension*. Unpublished doctoral dissertation, Hofstra University, Long Island, New York.

Gursky, D. (1998, March). What works for reading. *American Teacher*, 82, 12–13.

Heinl, A.M. (1988, December). *The effects of the Junior Great Books program on literal and inferential comprehension*. Paper presented at the annual meeting of the National Reading Conference, Tucson, AZ.

Kelly, J., Benson, M., & Benson, D. (1996). *Junior Great Books: Summary of program implementation and evaluation*. Castleberry, TX: Castleberry Independent School District.

Killion, J. (1997). *What works in the middle: Results-based staff development*. Oxford, OH: National Staff Development Council.

Killion, J. (1998). Scaling the elusive summit. *Journal of Staff Development*, 19(4), 12–16.

Killion, J. (2002a). *What works in the elementary school: Results-based staff development*. Oxford, OH: National Staff Development Council.

Killion, J. (2002b). *What works in the high school: Results-based staff development*. Oxford, OH: National Staff Development Council.

Killion, J. (2003). Use these 6 keys to open doors to literacy. *Journal of Staff Development*, 24(2), 10–16.

Lang, G. (1995). *Education programs that work: The catalogue of the National Diffusion Network (NDN). "Linking the nation with excellence."* Longmont, CA: Sopris West. Retrieved April 25, 2006, from http://www.ed.gov/pubs/EPTW/index.html

National Clearinghouse for Comprehensive School Reform. (n.d.). Website. Retrieved April 24, 2004, from http://www.nwrel.org/scpd/catalog

Peterson, C.L., Caverly, D.C., Nicholson, S.A., O'Neal, S., & Cusenbary, S. (2000). *Building reading proficiency at the secondary level: A guide to resources*. Austin, TX: Southwest Educational Development Laboratory.

Sandora, C., Beck, I., & McKeown, M. (1999). A comparison of two discussion strategies on students' comprehension and interpretation of complex literature. *Journal of Reading Psychology*, 20, 177–212.

Wheelock, A. (1999). Junior Great Books: Reading for meaning in urban schools. *Educational Leadership*, 57, 47–50.

Instructional Approach

Knowledge Box is a K–6 software system designed to support reading and language arts, as well as other subject areas. Published by Pearson Digital Learning, Knowledge Box makes use of broadband Internet technology to offer the program anywhere in a school and to keep the program up-to-date. Students interact with video, text, and Internet sources in order to think, process, research, organize, and present content aligned with standards. In addition, the product offers teachers an array of materials and media for use in daily teaching and a system for tracking student progress.

Knowledge Box reading lessons focus on phonics and comprehension skills. Explicit instruction is given in early literacy skills, such as phonological awareness, including practice in the alphabetic principle, letter–sound correspondence, word families, blending, and segmenting. Students also receive instruction in word meanings and other conventions of written English. Comprehension is further aided through multimedia reading activities. Students are also taught to use graphic organizers and are prompted to write summaries and responses to what they read. In addition, numerous genres are covered, including literature, myths, fables, poetry, and songs. Skills taught are practiced across the other subject areas included in Knowledge Box: math, science, and social studies.

Professional Development

Professional development for Knowledge Box is accomplished through on-site training for coordinators and faculty by Pearson Digital Learning personnel. Training includes the basics of using the product and an introduction to its instructional topics and potential. Teachers also receive a written guide, and a video guide is built into the product. Finally, ongoing support is offered through a toll-free number, and a trainer can follow up on-site if desired.

Program Evaluation

No published studies were available on Knowledge Box's efficacy. However, some effects were summarized on the product website (www.pearsondigital.com/knowledgebox). Positive effects were reported in regular teacher and student use of the product and the facilitation of home–school links. Knowledge Box is also part of the National Study of the Effectiveness of Educational Technology Interventions, which is investigating the effectiveness of technology in improving reading achievement in fourth grade during the 2004–2005 school year (U.S. Department of Education, 2004).

Contact Information

Address: Pearson Digital Learning
6710 East Camelback Road
Scottsdale, AZ 85251

Phone: 888-977-7900

E-mail: pdlinfo@pearson.com

Website: www.pearsondigital.com/knowledgebox

Sources

Pearson Digital Learning. (2006). *Knowledge Box successes*. Upper Saddle River, NJ: Pearson Education. Retrieved May 2, 2006, from http://www.pearson digital.com/successes/products.cfm

U.S. Department of Education. (2004, February 13). Department to study technology's role in raising student achievement [Press release]. Retrieved January 14, 2007, from http://www.ed.gov/news/pressreleas es/2004/02/02132004.html

LANGUAGE!

Instructional Approach

LANGUAGE! is a comprehensive, research-based literacy curriculum designed for at-risk and English as a second language (ESL) students, grades 3–12. The curriculum is characterized as sequential, cumulative, and integrated. In its third edition, each LANGUAGE! unit of instruction incorporates six steps: phonemic awareness and phonics, word recognition and spelling, vocabulary and morphology, grammar and usage, listening and reading comprehension, and speaking and writing. Fluency is considered a component of all six steps. Readability level of reading selections ranges from primer to high school.

Students are placed in the curriculum based on their performances on norm-referenced assessments, which are part of the curriculum package along with unit mastery tests and summative tests. The curriculum provides teachers with information for grouping students with similar proficiency levels. In addition to whole-group instruction, the curriculum provides opportunities for independent practice. Materials include teacher editions, student texts, interactive texts, teacher kit, assessment kit, ESL kit, and technology.

Professional Development

While not mandatory, professional development is strongly encouraged. Nationally certified LANGUAGE! trainers are available to travel to schools to provide training that lasts from three to five days. Training includes instruction in the linguistic bases of literacy as well as the research underlying the design of the program. Participants are specifically taught to teach the curriculum content, to administer and interpret the standardized and curriculum-based assessments, to plan lessons, and to prepare other teachers. Instruction in the program's technology components is provided through ongoing inservice training sessions. Training sessions can accommodate up to 60 participants, and college or continuing education credit can also be arranged.

Program Evaluation

A study evaluating the LANGUAGE! curriculum was authored by Jane Fell Greene (1996), who is the author of the curriculum. The study provides data on a sample of 45 middle and high school juvenile offenders (43 males, 2 females; ages 13–17) engaged in the curriculum for up to a year (individual student participation averaged 22.73 weeks). Results demonstrated that students using the LANGUAGE! curriculum showed significantly greater gains than did a control group in reading, comprehension, composition, and spelling as measured by several outcome measures: the Gray Oral Reading Test (GORT–III); the PIAT Test of Written Expression; and the Spelling and Word Identifications Tests of the Wide-Range Achievement Test (WRAT–R). The publisher reports that numerous independent studies by schools and districts across the United States implementing the program have also demonstrated significant gains made by students in the program. Results from these evaluations are available from the publisher on request. The Florida Center for Reading Research (2002) has also conducted an independent review of the program.

Contact Information

Address: Sopris West
4093 Specialty Place
Longmont, CO 80504
Phone: 800-547-6747
E-mail: customerservice@sopriswest.com
Website: www.teachlanguage.com

Sources

Florida Center for Reading Research. (2002, November). *LANGUAGE!* Tallahassee, FL: Author. Retrieved January 15, 2007, from http://www.fcrr.org/FCRRReports/PDF/Language.pdf

Greene, J.F. (1996). Effects of an individualized structured language curriculum for middle and high school students. *Annals of Dyslexia, 46,* 97–121.

Sopris West Educational Services. (n.d.). *Implementation results with LANGUAGE! at elementary grades three through six.* Longmont, CO: Author. Retrieved May 25, 2006, from http://www.teachlanguage.com/PDFs/Implementation_Data_Grades_3-6.pdf

Sopris West Educational Services. (n.d.). *Implementation results with LANGUAGE! at the middle and high school grades.* Longmont, CO: Author. Retrieved May 25, 2006, from http://www.teachlanguage.com/PDFs/Implementation_Data_Middle&High_%20School.pdf

Sopris West Educational Services. (n.d.). *Implementation results with LANGUAGE! of students who are limited English proficient.* Longmont, CO: Author. Retrieved May 25, 2006, from http://www.teachlanguage.com/PDFs/Implementation_Data_Limited_English_Proficiency.pdf

Instructional Approach

Learning Upgrade offers a sequenced series of two online reading courses—Reading Upgrade and Comprehension Upgrade—designed to be used by individual students in a classroom or individual setting. The program was developed by Learning Upgrade LLC and is sold and distributed by this San Diego–based company. Each program consists of a series of 50 Web-based lessons that are designed to be self-paced and can be completed over a period of three to eight weeks in 30- to 60-minute sessions.

Teachers are directed to place a student in the Reading Upgrade program if the student is "a struggling reader reading at grade level 4 or below, who pauses frequently when reading out loud, who has trouble sounding out unfamiliar words, or who reads very slowly." They are directed to place typically developing students at the fifth-grade level or beyond in the Comprehension Upgrade program. The central component of both programs is original pop music, video, and games designed to teach reading skills.

Professional Development

Professional development is not required for implementing this program. After teacher decision as to student placement in a course, students are expected to be able to complete lessons without assistance.

Program Evaluation

The developer claims that students completing one of the courses typically make gains of one to two years in reading. The website lists several evaluations conducted for the Reading Upgrade and Comprehension Upgrade programs in schools and single classrooms.

Contact Information

Address: Vinod Lobo
11655 Lindly Court
San Diego, CA 92131
Phone: 800-998-8864
E-mail: info@learningupgrade.com
Website: www.learningupgrade.com

Sources

Cole, J.M. (2004). *Research project summary: Effect of Web-based intervention on elementary students' reading performance and motivation*. San Diego, CA: Learning Upgrade. Retrieved May 25, 2006, from http://www.learningupgrade.com/html/ruucsdlchs03.htm

Cole, J.M. (2005). *Final report: An efficacy study of Comprehension Upgrade at Valencia Park Elementary*

School & Casa De Oro Elementary School. San Diego, CA: Learning Upgrade. Retrieved May 25, 2006, from http://www.learningupgrade.com/html/CompUp2004UCStudyReport.pdf

Lohman-Hawk, P. (n.d.). *Effect of Reading Upgrade program with adolescent struggling readers with specific language impairment*. San Diego, CA: Learning Upgrade. Retrieved May 25, 2006, from http://www.learningupgrade.com/html/rulohmanhawk.htm

LEXIA STRATEGIES FOR OLDER STUDENTS

Instructional Approach

Lexia Learning Systems' Strategies for Older Students (SOS) is a computer-based supplemental reading program designed to help older students master basic reading skills by providing independent practice in basic and advanced word decoding, word identification, and comprehension skills. The activities range from simple sound–symbol correspondences and short vowel skills to advanced skills such as decoding multisyllabic words, Latin prefixes and suffixes, special accent patterns, and Greek combining forms. The activities are designed to build word-level fluency and enhance vocabulary knowledge.

The software program consists of a series of 24 activities, ranging in difficulty from basic to advanced, that can be used independently in either a classroom or lab setting. The exercises branch automatically, either providing additional practice in a given skill or moving to a higher level of difficulty when students exhibit mastery. The program supports upper elementary, middle, and high school students in need of remedial reading instruction and is available with Spanish-language directions that facilitate the use of the program by Spanish-speaking students. The activities are designed to be engaging for an older audience, and the program provides detailed reports of student progress.

Professional Development

Lexia provides optional basic training services for teachers preparing to implement a Lexia program in their classroom. This training is delivered on-site or over the Internet and can be scheduled via a local sales representative. The training includes an overview of the scope and sequence of the program's offering, as well as training on how to access and interpret student performance data generated for each participating student or group of students. Software support is also available for purchase to participating schools.

Program Evaluation

Lexia Learning Systems has conducted research with academic partners examining the success of its programs since 1996, and their website offers information on these studies and the programs' effectiveness. The publishers report that this research has found that students have benefited from using Lexia Learning

Systems software. To date, most of these studies have examined the effectiveness of the SOS program when used with early elementary students (Macaruso, Hook, & McCabe, 2006). The Florida Center for Reading Research (2005) has also conducted an independent review of the program.

Contact Information

Address: Lexia Learning
            2 Lewis Street
            PO Box 466
            Lincoln, MA 01773
Phone: 800-435-3942
E-mail: info@lexialearning.com
Website: www.lexialearning.com/products/reading/sos.cfm

Sources

Faux, R. (2004, June). *Evaluation of Lexia software in Boston Public Schools* (Report by Davis Square Associates presented to Boston Public Schools, MA). Retrieved January 15, 2007, from http://www.lexialearning.com/upload/research/fauxt.pdf

Florida Center for Reading Research. (2005, September). *Lexia Reading S.O.S.* Tallahassee, FL: Author. Retrieved January 15, 2007, from http://www.fcrr.org/FCRRReports/PDF/LexiaReadingSOSFINAL.pdf

Macaruso, P., Hook, P.E., & McCabe, R. (2006). The efficacy of computer-based supplementary phonics pro-grams for advancing reading skills in at-risk elementary students. *Journal of Research in Reading, 29,* 162–172.

Macaruso, P., Hook, P., McCabe, R., & Walker, D. (2006). *Research report: Lexia software improves reading achievement by supporting instruction* (Report by Revere, MA, Public Schools and Lexia Learning Systems). Lincoln, MA: Lexia Learning Systems.

Stevens, D.A. (2000, March). *Leveraging technology to improve test scores: A case study of low-income Hispanic students.* Paper presented at the International Conference on Learning With Technology, Philadelphia, PA.

LINDAMOOD-BELL

Instructional Approach

Lindamood-Bell has developed three sensory-cognitive instructional programs designed to provide an integrated approach to address the language processing needs of students. These are Lindamood Phoneme Sequencing (LiPS), Seeing Stars for Symbol Imagery (SI), and Visualizing and Verbalizing (V/V). Each program is a diagnostically driven instructional system of intervention, and together the three programs are designed to address the full spectrum of developmental and remedial language processing needs of students.

Both the LiPS and SI programs address decoding issues. The LiPS program focuses more on phonemic awareness, while the SI program focuses more on orthographic awareness. In the LiPS program, the student develops an understanding of how their mouths look, and hence feel, while articulating specific speech sounds and this awareness aids them in distinguishing these sounds. The ability to create mental representations for sounds and letters within words is developed through the SI program. The V/V program addresses comprehension issues. The V/V program is designed to develop the ability to create mental representations for the gist of what is read or heard in order to improve comprehension.

In each of the three programs, instruction is guided by assessment of individual students' strengths and weaknesses and can be delivered one-on-one, in small groups, or as whole-class instruction. The program creators suggest that daily intensive instruction—in any of the three programs—is required for at least eight weeks in order to achieve accelerated growth. A Web-based test-scoring program offers the capacity to assess, diagnose, and track students, as well as to report progress. The Lindamood-Bell research staff can provide quarterly progress reports suitable for parents and school boards. A research manual is also included in the materials.

Professional Development

Lindamood-Bell offers a variety of professional development opportunities, but each must be purchased separately. These include on-site and off-site workshops of 1 to 12 days for teachers and administrators. There is also an annual international conference. Support is also offered to aid in school and districtwide implementation.

Program Evaluation

Most published research on Lindamood-Bell programs refer to the previous incarnation of LiPS: Auditory Discrimination in Depth. Most recently, the LiPS program has been found to be effective for 8- to 10-year-old students with severe reading disabilities (Torgesen et al., 2001). Students showed significant gains in all reading skills measured, including comprehension. Gains were largely maintained or improved relative to norming samples up to two years later. Notably, second-language speakers were excluded from the study. Earlier studies conducted with kindergarteners have found that the LiPS–related program produced consistently and significantly better results than comparison programs and controls, but that word-reading benefits did not necessarily generalize to spelling or reading comprehension skills two years later (Torgesen, Wagner, & Rashotte, 1997; Torgesen et al., 1999). The LiPS program has been reviewed independently by the Florida Center for Reading Research (2006).

In a 1997 evaluation, fourth-grade students who received V/V instruction outperformed comparison students who did their normal language arts curriculum, with students receiving V/V making significantly larger gains than comparison students in reading comprehension (Lindamood, Bell, & Lindamood, 1997). The Florida Center for Reading Research (2006) has also conducted an independent review of the V/V program. The Lindamood-Bell website offers extensive information on school and clinical evaluations of its programs.

Contact Information

Address: Paul Worthington
Director of Research & Development
Lindamood-Bell Learning Processes
416 Higuera Street
San Luis Obispo, CA 93401

Phone: 800-233-1819

E-mail: pworthington@lblp.com

Website: www.lindamoodbell.com

Sources

Adair, J., Nadeau, S., Conway, T., Gonzalez-Rothi, L., Heilman, P., Green, I., et al. (2000). Alterations in the functional anatomy of reading induced by rehabilitation of an alexic patient. *Neuropsychiatry, Neuropsychology and Behavioral Neurology, 13*(4), 303–311.

Alexander, A., Anderson, H., Heilman, P., Voeller, K., & Torgesen, J. (1991). Phonological awareness training and the remediation of analytic decoding deficits in a group of severe dyslexics. *Annals of Dyslexia, 41,* 193–206.

Bell, N. (1991). Gestalt imagery: A critical factor in language comprehension. *Annals of Dyslexia, 41,* 246–260.

Burke, C., Howard, L., & Evangelou, T. (2005). *A project of hope: Lindamood-Bell Center in a school project final evaluation report.* Retrieved January 29, 2007, from http://lindamoodbell.com/research/research articles.html

Conway, T., Heilman, P., Gonzalez-Rothi, L., Alexander, A., Adair, J., Crosson, B., et al. (1998). Treatment of a case of phonological alexia with agraphia using the Auditory Discrimination in Depth (ADD) program. *Journal of the International Neuropsychological Society, 4,* 608–620.

Eden, G.F., Jones, K.M., Cappell, K., Gareau, L., Wood, F.B., Zeffiro, T.A., et al. (2004). Neural changes following remediation in adult developmental dyslexia. *Neuron, 44*(3), 411–422.

Florida Center for Reading Research. (2006, April). *Lindamood Phoneme Sequencing Program for Reading, Spelling, and Speech (LiPS).* Tallahassee, FL: Author. Retrieved January 15, 2007, from http://www.fcrr.org/FCRRReports/PDF/LIPs.pdf

Florida Center for Reading Research. (2006, April). *Visualizing and Verbalizing.* Tallahassee, FL: Author. Retrieved January 15, 2007, from http://www.fcrr.org/FCRRReports/PDF/VisualizingVerbalizing.pdf

Johnson-Glenberg, M.C. (2000). Training reading comprehension in adequate decoders/poor comprehenders: Verbal vs. visual strategies. *Journal of Educational Psychology, 92*(4), 772–782.

Kennedy, K., & Backman, J. (1993). Effectiveness of the Lindamood Auditory Discrimination in Depth Program with students with learning disabilities. *Learning Disabilities Research and Practice, 8*(4), 253–259.

Lindamood, P., Bell, N., & Lindamood P. (1997). Sensory-cognitive factors in the controversy over reading instruction. *The Journal of Developmental and Learning Disorders, 1*(1), 143–182.

Pokorni, J., Worthington, C., & Jamison, P. (2004). Phonological awareness intervention: Comparison of Fast ForWord, Earobics, and LiPS. *Journal of Educational Research, 97,* 147–157.

Sadoski, M., & Willson, V. (2006). Effects of a theoretically based large-scale reading intervention in a multicultural urban school district. *American Educational Research Journal, 43,* 137–154.

Simos, P., Fletcher, J., Bergman, E., Breier, J., Foorman, B., Castillo, E., et al. (2002). Dyslexia-specific brain activation profile becomes normal following successful remedial training. *Neurology, 58,* 1203–1212.

Torgesen, J., Alexander, A., Wagner, R., Rashotte, C., Voeller, K., Conway, T., et al. (2001). Intensive remedial instruction for children with severe reading disabilities: Immediate and long-term outcomes from two instructional approaches. *Journal of Learning Disabilities, 34,* 33–58.

Torgesen, J., Wagner, R., & Rashotte, C. (1994). Longitudinal studies of phonological processing and reading. *Journal of Learning Disabilities, 27,* 276–286.

Torgesen, J., Wagner, R., & Rashotte, C. (1997). Approaches to the prevention and remediation of phonologically based reading disabilities. In B. Blachman (Ed.), *Foundations of reading acquisition and dyslexia: Implications for early intervention* (pp. 287–304). Hillsdale, NJ: Erlbaum.

Torgesen, J., Wagner, R., Rashotte, C., Rose, E., Lindamood, P., Conway, T., et al. (1999). Preventing reading failure in young children with phonological processing disabilities: Group and individual responses to instruction. *Journal of Educational Psychology, 91,* 579–593.

Truch, S. (1994). Stimulating basic reading processes using Auditory Discrimination in Depth. *Annals of Dyslexia, 44,* 60–80.

Instructional Approach

LitART is an after-school literacy curriculum for use in grades 1 through 8. Each grade level includes a year's worth of lesson series organized around eight themes. Because it is designed for an after-school context, the lessons are designed to develop oral language and reading and writing skills, in addition to math skills, through engaging activities.

Each lesson begins with an activity designed to invite students to articulate their thoughts. The rest of the lesson is broken into activities with differing foci. These include read-alouds of quality, age-appropriate children's literature with before-, during-, and after-reading questions, and prompts designed to support and improve students' comprehension. Students complete entries in a response journal after reading. Students also engage in math and word games. Follow-up activities include art projects, dramatic enactments, and social games based on the literature read. The word games have varying purposes, which include promoting students' vocabulary, phonemic awareness, and phonics skills.

Evaluation tools are included with the curriculum. A three-part evaluation framework guides programs in evaluating the efficacy of the curriculum and in promoting continual improvement of implementation. An evaluation notebook and tools are provided.

Professional Development

A two-day training is recommended to introduce the curriculum to after-school teachers. LitART also offers a series of monthly three-hour workshops focusing in more depth on different aspects of literacy instruction, such as reading, writing, and oral language, and can also support classroom management and the introduction of each new theme throughout the school year. Finally, on-site visits in which trainers coach teachers, demonstrate techniques, and observe instruction are also possible.

Program Evaluation

No evidence of the curriculum's effectiveness was available at the time this publication went to press.

Contact Information

Address: Global Learning
            1001 SE Water Avenue, Suite 310
            Portland, OR 97214
Phone: 888-548-2787
E-mail: info@litart.com
Website: www.litart.com

Sources

No published research, evaluations, or descriptions were available.

MY READING COACH

Instructional Approach

My Reading Coach is a software program developed to identify phonics and phonemic awareness problems, to give students the basic tools they need to correctly identify the words they read, and to teach students to comprehend the ideas behind those words. The design of the program is based on the premise that a large percentage of reading comprehension problems are due to poor decoding skills.

The program offers direct and explicit instruction in decoding and spelling. Students are first taught phonemic awareness. They are introduced to letters and combinations of letters. They then learn phonics rules and simple sight words that do not follow phonics rules. Finally, they learn ways to handle progressively longer multisyllabic words.

Based on an initial assessment, each student is placed within the program. Each student then progresses at his or her own pace based on evidence of mastery and receives individualized feedback. Students occasionally take review tests that cover all previously mastered material, and the program reassigns lessons if students perform poorly on a previously mastered skill. Teachers also receive reports based on students' usage, patterns of mistakes, and progress.

Program lessons include multimedia instruction and activities. Activities give students practice but do not use games. The program is designed with an eye to age-appropriate contexts for learning and practicing skills. Lessons are frequently supplemented by worksheets completed outside the program. These worksheets cover reading comprehension, spelling, writing, and memory aids for rules. The reading comprehension activities use words previously covered in the program and are intended to help students begin to learn to comprehend as they read. It is recommended that students in second grade or above use the program for at least 30 to 40 minutes daily. The full version of the program includes software, a teaching guide, a blackline master book, Web-based training, and one year of free technical support.

Professional Development

Web-based training uses video to help teachers understand the settings and options in the program. One year of free phone and e-mail technical support is also provided. Every other month, teachers receive a newsletter containing tips on using the program, success stories, and answers to common questions. Finally, a support website also offers technical support.

Program Evaluation

Summaries of pilot studies conducted in a variety of contexts, including in middle and high schools, can be found on the program's website. In one pilot study of the effects of using My Reading Coach with middle school students, 12 out of 17 students completed the program and improved between 2 and 5 stanines on the Degrees of Reading Power (DRP) reading comprehension test. The five students who did not complete the program showed an average increase of 1 stanine. A similar study with 20 high school students in a remedial English class found that on average students improved 12 percentile rank points on the DRP reading comprehension test after completing the program during one school year. Nine of these students used the program again the following year when an additional 42 remedial-English students were introduced to the program. The 42 new users also showed a 12 percentile rank improvement, and the repeat users improved an additional 9 percentile rank points. The repeat users all had limited English proficiency. However, none of the studies conducted with adolescents used comparison groups. The Florida Center for Reading Research (2004) has conducted an independent review of the program.

Contact Information

Address: MindPlay
440 S. Williams Boulevard, Suite 206
Tucson, AZ 85711
Phone: 520-888-1800
E-mail: mail@mindplay.com
Website: www.myreadingcoach.com

Sources

Crews, J.M. (2003). Helping poor readers: A case study of a computer assisted instruction reading tutorial. *Ninth Americas Conference on Information Systems: Information Technology in Education* (pp. 618–629). Retrieved January 28, 2007, from http://www.myreadingcoach.com/results/HelpingPoorReaders.pdf

Crews, J.M. (2003). *An investigation of the effectiveness of using My Reading Coach to improve 2nd graders' reading comprehension*. Retrieved July 6, 2005, from http://www.myreadingcoach.com/results/ocotillo prelim.html

Florida Center for Reading Research. (2004, October). *My Reading Coach*. Tallahassee, FL: Author. Retrieved January 15, 2007, from http://www.fcrr.org/FCRR Reports/PDF/MyReadingCoachFinal.pdf

My Reading Coach pilots and studies. (n.d.). Retrieved July 6, 2005, from http://www.myreadingcoach.com/results

Instructional Approach

Produced by Voyager Expanded Learning, Passport Reading Journeys (PRJ) is designed for middle and secondary struggling readers who are at least two years behind in reading. PRJ students receive targeted core reading instruction in five components of reading instruction: phonemic awareness, phonics, fluency, vocabulary, and comprehension. Designed to fit a 50-minute classroom schedule and be implemented by a single teacher teaching up to 30 students per class, lessons are taught in 15 two-week units called Expeditions. Expeditions are launched by DVD presentations delivered by teen hosts, and topics are designed to be of interest to adolescents. Instruction progresses from teacher-led whole group, to flexible small group, to partnered work, to independent reading and response opportunities in Strategic Online Learning Opportunities (SOLO). SOLO is Web-based and can be accessed by students outside school. Students needing additional support also receive focused small-group instruction in target areas.

Prior to placement in PRJ, students are universally screened using a Reading Benchmark based on the Lexile Framework for vocabulary and comprehension and using Voyager's Vital Indicators of Progress (VIP) Reading Connected Text fluency measure. Universal screening provides baseline information, and instruction is adjusted based on continual progress-monitoring measures, which are also recorded in an online data base. Formal assessments include criterion-referenced assessments at the end of each Expedition and reading benchmarks given at the beginning, middle, and end of the year. PRJ students are also informally assessed in daily lessons.

PRJ includes four core components: word study, vocabulary, fluency, and comprehension. All PRJ students receive instruction in advanced word study, which provides increasingly more sophisticated applications of the alphabetic principle, including spelling and syllable patterns. Students needing intensive, targeted intervention also receive phonics and, in some cases, phonemic awareness instruction. Skills and words are taught in isolation, as well as in connected texts. The vocabulary component comprises explicit instruction of word meanings and development of strategies to determine unknown words through morpheme analysis. An initial word introduction is supported by numerous repetitions of the word in oral discussions, reading passages, online reading opportunities, and student application activities. In the fluency component, fluency is modeled by teachers and SOLO using a wide variety of selections, and students practice reading texts that vary in topic, genre, and organization using a rate/accuracy/correction procedure that gives immediate online feedback. Passage length and complexity increases in small increments to increase reading stamina. The comprehension component emphasizes the flexible use of several comprehension strategies that students can apply before, during, and after reading. Strategy instruction includes explicit instruction and teacher modeled think-alouds in the Expeditions, and students practice using expository passages in the classroom and in SOLO. Students also receive text feature instruction. Much of student work occurs in collaborative learning groups and pairs. Reading materials are leveled and include anthology, library, SOLO selections, and online books.

Professional Development

Prior to implementation, Voyager representatives meet with administrators, department chairpersons, literacy coaches, and other key individuals in the district to define specifics of the implementation based on district needs. Teachers and other critical personnel receive training designed to successfully start the intervention through demonstrations of key reading strategies and assessment administration practice. The session prepares participants to successfully launch the implementation and meet ongoing support needs. The PRJ Training Kit includes a videotape, tutorial booklets, a DVD tutorial for the SOLO component, and a practice manual that includes sample lessons. Additional support is provided through online resources, which teachers are trained to use, and via telephone, e-mail, and the Voyager website. Voyager representatives also meet periodically with principals to provide information regarding implementation fidelity and to ensure they are able to monitor online student progress data.

Program Evaluation

Voyager monitors student growth in its reading programs through VIP results, as well as other curriculum-based measures. Data from Benchmarks 1 and 2 in spring 2006 indicated that PRJ students, who had completed 12 weeks of instruction, showed an increase of 59.2 Lexiles among a group of 813 seventh graders, an increase of 108.8 Lexiles among a group of 561 eighth graders, and an increase of 152.9 Lexiles among a group of 195 struggling ninth graders. Special education students, under the same instructional circumstances, showed an overall increase of 32.9 Lexiles among a group of 12 seventh graders and an increase of 150 Lexiles among a group of 8 eighth graders. An independent evaluation available on the Voyager website showed that students in Florida after 26 weeks of PRJ made about twice the gain in Lexiles that Metametrics would predict for students with comparable Lexile scores at the beginning of the school year.

Contact Information

Address: Peggy Marrin
            National Director of Reading
            Voyager Expanded Learning, L.P.
            1800 Valley View Lane, Suite 400
            Dallas, TX 75234

Phone: 214-932-3233
E-mail: pmarrin@voyagerlearning.com
Website: www.voyagerlearning.com

Sources

Voyager Expanded Learning Research and Development. (2005). *Research foundations and design: Passport Reading Journeys*. Dallas, TX: Author. Retrieved October 15, 2006, from http://www.voyagerlearning.com/ResearchStudyDocuments/Voyager_Passport_Journeys_White_Paper.pdf

Voyager Expanded Learning. (2006). *Florida's middle and high school students accelerate their reading skills with Passport Reading Journeys*. Dallas, TX: Author. Retrieved October 15, 2006, from http://www.voyagerlearning.com/ResearchStudyDocuments/Florida_Statewide_Journeys_2006.pdf

PEER-ASSISTED LEARNING STRATEGIES

Instructional Approach

Peer-Assisted Learning Strategies (PALS) is a whole-class peer tutoring program and was developed by Doug Fuchs and Lynn Fuchs, professors of special education and Kennedy Center investigators at Vanderbilt University. In this program, the teacher pairs students to work together on reading skills. In each session, each student takes a turn as a "coach" and then as a "reader." The coach listens to the reader and offers feedback. Students are instructed in how to offer feedback when coaching. This model is intended to allow teachers to individualize instruction to the needs of specific student pairs and to give teachers the freedom to observe students and give individual remedial instruction while students are working in pairs. The program is not a comprehensive reading program but rather is designed to supplement an English-language arts program. No special reading materials must be purchased to implement the program as teachers may use the peer coaching model with any reading materials.

PALS for students in grades 2–6 focuses on reading fluency and comprehension and consists of three activities: Partner Reading, Paragraph Shrinking, and Prediction Relay. Originally developed for use with general education students in grades 2–6, the program has been expanded to serve high school students by modifying the motivational strategies and the type of assistance offered by the peer coach. PALS for high school students is primarily used in special education settings and by remedial reading teachers. Most recently, PALS has been used in a middle school setting.

Professional Development

There is a PALS teaching manual and video that can be purchased from Vanderbilt University, where the developers are faculty members. Implementation of the PALS program does not require professional development. However, the developers recommend at least a one-day training workshop, which is offered at locations throughout the United States and can also be arranged on-site. Follow-up training is also available.

Program Evaluation

The developers have published several articles describing the research that led to the development of the PALS program. Several studies of its effectiveness have also been published. In these studies, the developers have used either experimental or quasi-experimental designs, involving large numbers of schools, teachers, and students. PALS has been found to be successful with low-achieving, average-achieving, and high-achieving students, as well as mainstreamed students with learning disabilities and English-language learners with learning disabilities. While the majority of these studies have examined the effects of PALS in working with very young children, three studies have found the program to be successful in improving reading for high school students. An additional recent study investigated the effect of PALS combined with a peer-mediated phonological intervention on middle school students with reading disabilities and found the combined interventions had significantly larger positive impacts on word reading and comprehension than did a comparable intervention. In addition, PALS is currently participating in a federally funded scale-up study designed to validate and support larger scale implementation.

Contact Information

Address: Vanderbilt University
          Attn: Flora Murray
          Box 328 Peabody
          230 Appleton Place
          Nashville, TN 37203-5701
Phone: 615-343-4782
E-mail: flora.murray@vanderbilt.edu
Website: http://kc.vanderbilt.edu/kennedy/pals

Sources

Allor, J.H., Fuchs, D., & Mathes, P. (2001). Do students with and without lexical retrieval weaknesses respond differently to instruction? *Journal of Learning Disabilities, 34,* 264–275.

Calhoon, M.B. (2005). Effects of a peer-mediated phonological skill and reading comprehension program on reading skill acquisition for middle school students with reading disabilities. *Journal of Learning Disabilities, 38,* 424–433.

Fuchs, D., & Fuchs, L.S. (1998). Researchers and teachers working together to adapt instruction for diverse learners. *Learning Disabilities Research and Practice, 13,* 126–137.

Fuchs, D., Fuchs, L.S., & Burish, P. (2000). Peer-Assisted Learning Strategies: An evidence-based practice to promote reading achievement. *Learning Disabilities Research and Practice, 15,* 85–91.

Fuchs, D., Fuchs, L.S., Mathes, P.G., & Martinez, E. (2002). Preliminary evidence on the social standing of students with learning disabilities in PALS and No-PALS classrooms. *Learning Disabilities Research and Practice, 17,* 205–215.

Fuchs, D., Fuchs, L.S., Mathes, P.G., & Simmons, D.C. (1997). Peer-Assisted Learning Strategies: Making classrooms more responsive to diversity. *American Educational Research Journal, 34,* 174–206.

Fuchs, D., Fuchs, L.S., Thompson, A., Yen, L., Al Otaiba, S., Nyman, K., et al. (2001). Peer-Assisted Learning Strategies in reading: Extensions for kindergarten, first grade, and high school. *Remedial and Special Education, 22*, 15–21.

Fuchs, L.S., Fuchs, D., & Kazdan, S. (1999). Effects of Peer-Assisted Learning Strategies on high-school students with serious reading problems. *Remedial and Special Education, 20*, 309–318.

Fuchs, L.S., Fuchs, D., Kazdan, S., & Allen, S. (1999). Effects of Peer-Assisted Learning Strategies in reading with and without training in elaborated help giving. *The Elementary School Journal, 99*, 201–219.

Locke, W.R., & Fuchs, L.S. (l995). Effects of peer-mediated reading instruction on the on-task behavior and social interactions of children with behavior disorders. *Journal of Emotional and Behavioral Disorders, 3*, 92–99.

McMaster, K.N., Fuchs, D., & Fuchs, L.S. (2005). Responding to nonresponders: An experimental field trial of identification and intervention methods. *Exceptional Children, 71*, 445–463.

McMaster, K.N., Fuchs, D., & Fuchs, L.S. (2006). Research on Peer-Assisted Learning Strategies: Promise and limitations on peer mediation. *Reading and Writing Quarterly, 22*(1), 5–25.

Rohrbeck, C.A., Ginsburg-Block, M.D., Fantuzzo, J.W., & Miller, T.R. (2003). Peer-assisted learning interventions with elementary school students: A meta-analytic review. *Journal of Educational Psychology, 95*, 240–257.

Saenz, L.M., Fuchs, L.S., & Fuchs, D. (2005). Peer-Assisted Learning Strategies for English language learners with learning disabilities. *Exceptional Children, 71*, 231–247.

Simmons, D.C., Fuchs, D., Fuchs, L.S., Pate, J., & Mathes, P. (1994) Importance of instructional complexity and role reciprocity to classwide peer tutoring. *Learning Disabilities Research and Practice, 9*, 203–212.

Simmons, D., Fuchs, L.S., & Fuchs, D. (l995). Effects of explicit teaching and peer tutoring on the reading achievement of learning disabled and low-performing students in regular classrooms. *The Elementary School Journal, 95*, 387–408.

PHONO-GRAPHIX

Instructional Approach

Phono-graphix is a program designed to develop word reading and spelling skills in readers of all ages. Using constructivist pedagogy, students are given lessons in phonemic awareness and taught how to segment and blend the phonemes in words. A book on the method, called *Reading Reflex* (McGuiness & McGuiness, 1999), is available from U.S. booksellers and represents the core of the Phono-graphix program. Support materials designed for the program are available to teachers (and parents) through the Read America website. Classroom materials include a lesson-planning workbook, student support workbooks, word cards, manipulatives, stickers, wall charts, and games. One-on-one tutoring is available through an online "virtual" clinic, certified Phono-graphix therapists, and at the Read America Clinic in Orlando, Florida. The program also has versions available internationally.

Included in Reading Reflex are Phono-graphix diagnostic tests, instructions in and illustrations of the Phono-graphix method, and sample lessons. The book also includes an assortment of exercises and reproducible materials, such as manipulatives, games, and work sheets. The Phono-graphix program is based on the premise that three skills underlie the ability to read words. Students are taught to realize that letters are really pictures that represent sounds and that sometimes multiple letters represent a single sound. They are also taught that most sounds can be represented by more than one letter or letters. Finally, they are taught that most letters and letter combinations can represent more than one sound.

Students exercise this knowledge by segmenting words into component sounds, blending component sounds into words, and manipulating sounds within words to change the words.

Professional Development

Professional development is available separately. Training may take place as a single-day, on-site internship or as a five-day certification course. Some materials are only available to those certified in Phono-graphix, and certification requires the purchase of some materials. Training is also available through third parties, such as Advantage Learning Services. A general discussion board is also available on the Read America website.

Program Evaluation

Published research on Phono-graphix's effectiveness is limited. One study conducted by the program creators reported that students (ages 6 to 16) in a one-on-one clinical setting trained with Phono-graphix made consistent gains in phonemic awareness and word-reading skills (McGuiness, McGuiness, & McGuiness, 1996). A small-scale study using the program to tutor prison inmates also procured a standard deviation's improvement after 30+ hours of tutoring (McCarty, 2002). Neither of these studies employed comparison groups. A number of pilot and efficacy studies are also available on the Phono-graphix website. The Florida Center for Reading Research (2002) has also conducted an independent review of the program, but only for grades K–5.

Contact Information

Address: Read America
          PO Box 1246
          Mount Dora, FL 32756
Phone: no phone support available
E-mail: RAchat@aol.com
Website: www.readamerica.net

Sources

Curran, L., Guin, L., & Marshall, L. (2002). *Improving reading ability through the use of cross-age tutoring, Phono-Graphix, and reciprocal teaching.* Chicago: Saint Xavier University.

Florida Center for Reading Research. (2002, November). *Phono-Graphix.* Tallahassee, FL: Author. Retrieved May 31, 2006, from http://www.fcrr.org/FCRRReports/PDF/Phono_Graphix_Report.pdf

McCarty, R. (2002). Reading therapy project. *Research and Teaching in Developmental Education, 18*(2), 51–56.

McGuiness, C., McGuiness, D., & McGuiness, G. (1996). Phono-graphix: A new method for remediation of reading difficulties. *Annals of Dyslexia, 46,* 73–96.

McGuiness, C., & McGuiness, G. (1999). *Reading Reflex: The foolproof Phono-graphix method for teaching your child to read.* New York: Fireside.

Read America. (n.d.). *Read America research.* Mount Dora, FL: Author. Retrieved June 10, 2004, from http://www.readamerica.net/research.asp

Instructional Approach

PLATO Learning offers computer-based software products for teaching reading and writing to intermediate and secondary-level students. PLATO Learning's products are designed to be used separately or together as needed to support existing reading and language arts curricula.

One product, PLATO Writing Process and Practice, focuses solely on writing and is intended for students writing at levels commensurate with grades 7–12. It offers students instruction in the writing process, including strategies, grammar, and mechanics. Strategies include coaching students' awareness of audience and purpose and how these influence the writing process. Instruction is broken down into tutorials, applications (or practice opportunities, both online and off), and mastery tests.

Among the reading products offered by PLATO Learning is the PLATO Reading Strategies series. This series is targeted at teaching students 10 reading comprehension strategies, including summarizing and interpreting graphical information. It is available in a spiral-bound curriculum at fundamental (grades 5–6), intermediate (grades 7–8), and advanced (grades 9–14) levels. Additional programs are available that target other skill sets; PLATO Essential Reading Skills, designed to remediate skills generally taught in grades 3–4, refreshes students' basic reading skills, and PLATO Vocabulary and Reading Comprehension teaches third- through ninth-grade–level vocabulary and reading comprehension skills to secondary students. All lessons are self-paced and offer interactive opportunities for practicing skills both online and off.

In both PLATO Writing Process and Practice and PLATO Reading Strategies series, cognitive strategies are taught as open-ended, problem-solving experiences in either individual study or small-group collaborative learning settings. Using multimedia technology, young-adult mentors introduce and model strategies to students by explaining their usefulness in daily life. Each strategy is summarized step-by-step, and then students are given multiple opportunities for practicing and generalizing the strategies through scaffolded interactions. Lessons are designed to be age-appropriate for secondary students and incorporate instruction with real-world scenarios, allowing learners to apply newly acquired reading skills to real-life situations through self-paced instruction.

Professional Development

PLATO Learning customizes training around an individual client's needs, so training programs can vary considerably. Consultants help plan and implement professional development, using a four-step cycle: assess, align, instruct, and evaluate. Ongoing professional development opportunities are also available online.

Program Evaluation

Peer-reviewed research on PLATO Learning's reading and writing programs was not available, but an evaluation series on various PLATO Learning products is available through either PLATO Learning or ERIC document reproduction services. One such study demonstrated that 70% of students who had failed a benchmark test for entry into 10th grade passed the test after a five-week summer intervention program utilizing PLATO reading products (Quinn & Quinn, 2001). A year-long study in a remedial lab for secondary students showed that 85% of students who had previously failed their state test passed after using PLATO courseware (Hannafin, 1999). In a study at a career-center high school using the ACT Work Keys test, 47% of students progressed at least one Work Keys level, compared to a statewide decline in performance (Snyder & Gohringer, 1998).

Contact Information

Address: Chris Bueschler
            PLATO Learning, Inc.
            10801 Nesbitt Avenue
            Bloomington, MN 55437
Phone: 952-832-1541
E-mail: cbuecksler@plato.com
Website: www.plato.com

Sources

Brush, T. (2002). *Terry High School, Lamar Consolidated ISD, Rosenberg, TX: PLATO evaluation series.* Bloomington, MN: PLATO Learning.

Hannafin, B. (1999). *Lawrence Central High School, Indianapolis, IN: PLATO evaluation series.* Bloomington, MN: PLATO Learning.

Hannafin, B. (2001). *Lakeland Senior High School, Lakeland, FL: PLATO evaluation series.* Bloomington, MN: PLATO Learning.

Hannafin, B. (2002). *Central Cabarrus High School, North Carolina: PLATO evaluation series.* Bloomington, MN: PLATO Learning.

Quinn, D.W., & Quinn, N.W. (2001). *Jobs for Youth–Boston, Madison Park Technical-Vocational High School, Boston, Massachusetts: PLATO evaluation series.* Bloomington, MN: PLATO Learning.

Quinn, N.W., & Quinn, D.W. (2002). *Skill Development PLATO use at Reuther Alternative High School, Kenosha, Wisconsin: PLATO evaluation Series.* Bloomington, MN: PLATO Learning.

Quinn, N.W., & Quinn, D.W. (2003). *Skill Development PLATO use at Miami Valley CTC Youth Connections, Dayton, OH: PLATO evaluation series.* Bloomington, MN: PLATO Learning.

Snyder, P., & Gohringer, K. (1998). *Columbus, Ohio Public Schools Career Centers: PLATO evaluation series.* Bloomington, MN: PLATO Learning.

PROJECT CRISS

Instructional Approach

Project CRISS, CReating Independence through Student-owned Strategies, is an interdisciplinary professional development program designed to help teachers incorporate reading, writing, and studying strategies into their regular content instruction. Project CRISS was originally developed in the late 1970s by Carol

Santa and a team of middle and high school teachers from Kalispell School District in Montana. Lynn Havens, previously a secondary math and science teacher, is the project director.

Project CRISS is a professional development program for teachers and administrators to help adolescents become more proficient readers, writers, and learners. Content teachers incorporate CRISS principles and philosophy as part of their regular classroom instruction using a model of direct, explicit comprehension instruction. Project CRISS is based on the philosophy that comprehension and learning can be improved when students build on their prior knowledge and are actively involved in the learning process through discussion, extensive writing, and organizing information. The goals are for students to incorporate this philosophy as they apply strategies for learning content and gain a metacognitive understanding of when and how to use them. After students become comfortable with the strategies, their teachers encourage them to select their own learning goals and to use the strategies that work best for them.

Project CRISS was approved as a National Diffusion Network program in 1985 and again in 1993. The program continues to be revised to incorporate new techniques and research about learning processes. Based on principles of cognitive psychology and brain research, it is designed for all learners with a particular emphasis on students in grades 4–12.

To support teacher instruction of the CRISS principles and strategies, the CRISS authors developed a semester class for students in grades 6–9. Through a series of CRISS strategic learning plans, based on the trade book *Tough Terminators* by Sneed B. Collard III, students are introduced to most of the CRISS principles and strategies. They spend time learning and practicing the strategies, reflecting on their successes and failures, and applying the principles and strategies to learning tasks in their other classes.

Professional Development

A 12-to-18-hour inservice begins to prepare teachers and administrators to implement Project CRISS principles and instructional strategies within their own curriculum. A direct, explicit instruction model is used to help participants learn ways to teach their students how to interact with text, understand text structure, have productive discussions, engage actively in learning processes, organize for learning, write to learn, write reports and essays, and learn new vocabulary. Teachers also learn how to guide their students to become more reflective (metacognitive) about their learning processes. Students begin to see how they can apply strategies in a flexible manner and how to monitor their own learning.

Participants in Project CRISS workshops receive a 300+-page book (*Project CRISS: Helping Teachers Teach and Learners Learn*; Santa, Havens, & Valdes, 2005) that assists them in implementing the project in their own teaching contexts. A free quarterly newsletter is also available for additional support. The project is disseminated to educators (teachers, administrators, and support personnel) across the United States through a network of national and district CRISS-certified trainers. Project CRISS is being used by teachers and administrators in 26 states and two Canadian provinces.

Program Evaluation

The effects of Project CRISS have been examined using experimental research designs conducted by personnel from Project CRISS and schools and districts implementing Project CRISS. The two major research questions evaluated are these: Do students in CRISS classrooms improve their reading, learning, and retention of content significantly more than students in non-CRISS classrooms? Do CRISS students have a better understanding of their own learning processes than non-CRISS students? Results consistently show that students in CRISS classrooms—regardless of location, grade level, or subject area—demonstrate significantly more improvement than do control students in reading and retaining information as measured by age-appropriate content reading selections. The data extend over a span of 20 years and involve more than 21 different comparison groups.

Contact Information

Address: Lynn Havens
            40 Second Street East, Suite 249
            Kalispell, MT 59901
Phone: 406-758-6440
E-mail: info@projectcriss.com
Website: www.projectcriss.com

Sources

Killion, J. (1997). *What works in the middle: Results-based staff development*. Oxford, OH: National Staff Development Council.

Killion, J. (2002). *What works in the elementary school: Results-based staff development*. Oxford, OH: National Staff Development Council.

Killion, J. (2002). *What works in the high school: Results-based staff development*. Oxford, OH: National Staff Development Council.

Peterson, C.L., Caverly, D.C., Nicholson, S.A., O'Neal, S., & Cusenbary, S. (2000). *Building reading proficiency at the secondary level: A guide to resources*. Austin, TX: Southwest Educational Development Laboratory.

Project CRISS. (2004). *Comments From CRISS, 17*, 2.

Santa, C.M. (1993). *Project CRISS: Evidence of effectiveness*. Retrieved May 25, 2006, from http://www.projectcriss.com/prc/pages/research/research_home.html

Santa, C.M. (1995). *Project CRISS: Evidence of effectiveness*. Retrieved May 25, 2006, from http://www.projectcriss.com/prc/pages/research/research_home.html

Santa, C.M. (2000). The National Reading Panel report supports CRISS. *Comments From CRISS, 14*(1), 1–3.

Santa, C.M. (2004). Project CRISS: A history of reliable, replicable research. *Comments From CRISS, 18*(1), 1–3.

Santa, C.M. (2004). *Project CRISS: Evidence of effectiveness*. Retrieved May 25, 2006, from http://www.projectcriss.com/prc/pages/research/research_home.html

Santa, C.M., & Havens, L. (2005). CRISS on the cutting edge: Support from the Reading Next report. *Comments From CRISS, 18*(2), 1, 5–7.

Santa, C.M., Havens, L., & Valdes, B. (2005). *Project CRISS: Helping teachers teach and learners learn*. Kalispell, MT: Project CRISS.

Instructional Approach

Puente is an academic preparation program that aims to increase the number of Latino and educationally underserved students who graduate high school and attend four-year colleges and universities. In 1981, Patricia McGrath and Felix Galaviz initiated Puente as a program to support Latino and Mexican American students in community colleges. In 1993, Puente began an expansion that over four years led to a full four-year support program for 18 high schools. At the end of the pilot, all 18 schools institutionalized the program, and now Puente is in 36 high schools across California. The program is included here for its focus on literacy, especially writing.

The Puente high school program targets nonimmigrant Latino and Mexican American students when they enter ninth grade. Puente students are selected from a wide range of ability levels based on their desire to improve and excel academically. Puente students are chosen for participation if they demonstrate this attitude and a vision of higher education as a stepping-stone to bettering their lives and communities. However, students who read more than three years below grade level are excluded from Puente. Students selected for Puente participation are then divided into four categories based on whether they previously have demonstrated high or low academic performance and high or low effort (Gandara & Moreno, 2002).

Although Puente involves substantial components focused on counseling and mentoring students, the main academic focus is improving students' writing. Writing is targeted because of the fundamental role it plays in academic achievement in any subject. The writing curriculum is aligned with state standards and uses a portfolio approach. Using small cooperative groups, students are led through a developmental writing program and cultivate their critical thinking skills by engaging in university-level reading and writing.

The Puente English curriculum emphasizes the importance of knowing and understanding not only the academic strengths and weaknesses of students but also their cultural background and conditions (Pradl, 2002). From this foundation, the Puente model asks teachers to abandon old transmission models of teaching and instead to scaffold their students' interpretation of reading and writing skills and knowledge. This is achieved through the use of multicultural and challenging texts, the consistent employment of strategies and exploration of ideas over extended periods of time and multiple texts, and the cultivation of a classroom atmosphere of mutual respect and answer seeking (Pradl, 2002).

Students' writing is developed through a writing process approach and is documented in a portfolio of at least five writing samples. Students select pieces and write a cover letter describing the pieces they chose and how they represent their growth as writers. Among the five required pieces is a baseline essay written in response to a common prompt across all Puente sites at the beginning of the school year. In addition, a variety of genres are taught and emphasized.

Professional Development

Training sessions are available for teachers, counselors, and mentors year-round. Development begins with a two-week summer training and is followed up regionally with two-day workshops that provide the time to explore a few core ideas, to practice new skills, and to reflect on both. One core idea is that in order to teach writing effectively, teachers themselves must practice writing regularly. Other core topics include portfolio assessment, integrating multicultural literature, and leading true discussions. Furthermore, as time goes on, training is differentiated depending on demonstrated and emerging needs. Because of Puente's approach to English instruction, more than 400 teachers who are not directly involved in Puente programs have participated in and benefited from the Puente training program (Pradl, 2002).

Program Evaluation

The Puente program has undergone extensive internal evaluation. Program state offices maintain a database of all implementations to facilitate inquiries. In addition, independent evaluations have been conducted. In the original expansion of Puente to a high school context, Puente students enrolled in four-year colleges at about twice the rate of matched controls: 43% versus 24% respectively (Gandara, 1998). In another study of the same data, Puente students outperformed Latino and other non-Puente students on a myriad of attitude and college-preparedness measures (Gandara, 2002). In addition, across all ability levels a higher percentage of Puente students than non-Puente students completed the courses required for enrollment by the University of California. However, Puente students did not earn significantly higher grade-point averages than non-Puente students (Gandara, 2002).

In a follow-up study, 31 of the Puente students and 31 matched non-Puente students were interviewed two years later (Moreno, 2002). The study revealed that 72% of the Puente students did enroll in a four-year or community college compared to 52% of the matched non-Puente students, and that essentially the same proportions of these students were still in school two years later.

Contact Information

Address: Puente Project
300 Lakeside Drive
7th Floor
Oakland, CA 94612
Phone: 510-987-9548
E-mail: puente@ucop.edu
Website: www.puente.net

Sources

Cazden, C. (2002). A descriptive study of six high school Puente classrooms. *Educational Policy*, *16*, 496–521.

Cooper, C.R. (2002). Five bridges along students' pathways to college: A developmental blueprint of families, teachers, counselors, mentors, and peers in the Puente Project. *Educational Policy*, *16*, 607–622.

Gandara, P. (1998). *Final report of the evaluation of High School Puente, 1993–1998.* New York: Carnegie Corporation.

Gandara, P. (2002). A study of High School Puente: What we have learned about preparing Latino youth for postsecondary education. *Educational Policy*, *16*, 474–495.

Gandara, P. (2004). Building bridges to college. *Educational Leadership*, *62*(3), 56–60.

Gandara, P., & Bial, D. (2001). *Paving the way to secondary education: K–12 intervention programs for underrepresented youth.* Washington, DC: U.S. Department of Education, National Center for Education Statistics.

Gandara, P., & Moreno, J.F. (2002). The Puente Project: Issues and perspectives on preparing Latino youth for higher education. *Educational Policy*, *16*, 463–473.

Grubb, W.N., Lara, C.M., & Valdez, S. (2002). Counselor, coordinator, monitor, mom: The roles of counselors in the Puente program. *Educational Policy*, *16*, 547–571.

Hayward, G.C., Brandes, B.G., Kirst, M.W., & Mazzeo, C. (1997). *Higher education outreach programs: A synthesis of evaluations* (Policy Analysis for California Education Report). Oakland: University of California, Office of the President.

Moreno, J.F. (2002). The long-term outcomes of Puente. *Educational Policy*, *16*, 572–587.

Pradl, G.M. (2002). Linking instructional intervention and professional development using the ideas behind Puente High School English to inform educational policy. *Educational Policy*, *16*, 522–546.

Puente. (n.d.). *Research update: Excerpts of recent research studies about the Puente Project, 2001–2002.* Oakland, CA: Author. Retrieved May 25, 2006, from http://www.puente.net/r.update2.pdf

QUESTIONING THE AUTHOR

Instructional Approach

Questioning the Author (QtA) is an approach to teaching reading comprehension that is designed to promote deep comprehension and critical thinking. QtA has been implemented in grades 3 through 12 and in about 200 schools across the United States. The approach was developed originally as a way of coping with inadequate content area texts used in intermediate-grade classrooms, and of stimulating engaged reading and building meaning from texts. These goals arose because Isabel Beck and Margaret McKeown had observed in their research that students rarely went beyond a surface-level comprehension of texts, often due to a lack of engagement and motivation.

QtA asks teachers to reconceptualize the questions they ask during reading discussions as open-ended queries. The distinction is important because traditional questions tend to have answers that are easily retrievable from text. In contrast, queries are intended to stimulate grappling with text ideas and comprehension, rather than to assess it. Students are asked to consider not only what the text says but also what the author intended the reader to understand. The approach encourages students to realize that texts are written by fallible authors, and that their confusion while reading may sometimes be the fault of the author. The approach fosters critical thinking in that students consider the author's intent and how writing can be used to achieve purposes that are not openly stated. In short, QtA is designed to engage students in their reading in a deep and thoughtful way.

Implementation of QtA is left largely up to the teacher and works well as a supplement to most reading plans. The approach may be used with both content area and language arts texts and is easily adapted to whole-class read-alouds.

Professional Development

Although QtA is not a purchasable curriculum, sources for training are available. A detailed book describing the QtA method by its originators is available (Beck, McKeown, Hamilton, & Kucan, 1997). A companion volume presents an examination of issues that may arise during implementatin in a case study format (McKeown, Beck, Hamilton, & Kucan, 1999). For additional information on potential training opportunities, the QtA authors can be contacted directly. Training can be given over the course of one or two days and can also include training participants as district trainers. The Wright Group at McGraw-Hill also offers training in using QtA.

Program Evaluation

Anecdotal and observational accounts reveal more coherent and critical contributions from students during discussions of texts, as well as increased engagement (e.g., Beck & McKeown, 2002; Beck, McKeown, Hamilton, & Kucan, 1998; McKeown, 1993). In addition, three peer-reviewed studies of QtA's effectiveness have been published. In the first (Beck, McKeown, Sandora, Kucan, & Worthy, 1996), QtA decreased the amount of teacher talk and increased the amount of student talk during classroom discussions in one inner-city, fourth-grade classroom. Additionally, teachers' questions focused more on drawing out student thought, and students' contributions increased in complexity. In the second study (Sandora, Beck, & McKeown, 1999), researchers compared QtA with the Junior Great Books approach in one school's sixth- and seventh-grade classrooms. The researchers found that the sixth-grade students, who received QtA instruction, outperformed the seventh-grade students, who received Junior Great Books instruction, in their ability to recall more of the texts and answer open-ended questions. For the third study, (McKeown & Beck, 2004) researchers developed a resource to be used by teachers independently and investigated the implementation by teachers using the resource in place of detailed feedback. This study also found that student talk increased, and both teachers' and students' contributions focused more on meaning and less on text retrieval. The Florida Center for Reading Research (2004) has also conducted an independent review of the QtA program.

Contact Information

Address: Dr. Margaret McKeown
           646 Learning Research and Development Center

University of Pittsburgh
Pittsburgh, PA 15260

Phone: 412-624-7068

E-mail: mckeown@pitt.edu

Website: www.wrightgroup.com/index.php/home/profdevelopment/in
sight/researchbasedwrkshps/comprehensionpd/121#explicitguidin
gofcomprehension:questioningtheauthorapproach(grades3-12)

see also http://edr1.educ.msu.edu/CompStrat/login.asp
(*username: demo; password: demo*)

Sources

Almasi, J.F., McKeown, M.G., & Beck, I.L. (1996). The nature of engaged reading in classroom discussions of literature. *Journal of Literacy Research*, 28(1), 107–146.

Beck, I.L., & McKeown, M.G. (2001). Inviting students into the pursuit of meaning. *Educational Psychology Review*, 13(3), 225–241.

Beck, I.L., & McKeown, M.G. (2002). Questioning the Author: Making sense of social studies. *Educational Leadership*, 30(3), 44–47.

Beck, I.L., McKeown, M.G., Hamilton, R.H., & Kucan, L. (1997). *Questioning the Author: An approach for enhancing student engagement with text*. Newark, DE: International Reading Association.

Beck, I.L., McKeown, M.G., Hamilton, R.H., & Kucan, L. (1998). Getting at the meaning: How to help students unpack difficult text. *American Educator*, 22, 1–2, 66–71, 85.

Beck, I.L., McKeown, M.G., Sandora, C., Kucan, L., & Worthy, J. (1996). Questioning the Author: A yearlong classroom implementation to engage students with text. *The Elementary School Journal*, 96(4), 385–414.

Comprehension Professional Development. (n.d.). *Explicit guiding of comprehension: Questioning the Author approach (3–12)*. Chicago: Wright Group. Retrieved July 25, 2005, from http://www.wright group.com/index.php/home/profdevelopment/in sight/researchbasedwrkshps/comprehensionpd/121

Florida Center for Reading Research. (2004, October). *Questioning the Author*. Tallahassee, FL: Author. Retrieved January 15, 2007, from http://www.fcrr. org/FCRRReports/PDF/QuestioningAuthorFinal.pdf

Killion, J. (2002a). *What works in the elementary school: Results-based staff development*. Oxford, OH: National Staff Development Council.

Killion, J. (2002b). *What works in the high school: Results-based staff development*. Oxford, OH: National Staff Development Council.

McKeown, M.G. (1993). Grappling with text ideas: Questioning the Author. *The Reading Teacher*, 46, 560–566.

McKeown, M.G. (1998). Discussion of text for understanding. In T.E. Raphael & K.H. Au (Eds.), *Literature-based instruction: Reshaping the curriculum* (pp. 365–370). Norwood, MA: Christopher-Gordon.

McKeown, M.G., & Beck, I.L. (1998). Talking to an author: Readers taking charge of the reading process. In R. Calfee & N. Nelson (Eds.), *The reading–writing connection: Ninety-seventh yearbook for the National Society for the Study of Education* (pp. 112–130). Chicago: National Society for the Study of Education.

McKeown, M.G., & Beck, I.L. (1999). Getting the discussion started. *Educational Leadership*, 5(3), 25–28.

McKeown, M.G., & Beck, I.L. (2001). Designing questions toward thinking and understanding rather than answers. *Perspectives*, 27(2), 21–24.

McKeown, M.G., & Beck, I.L. (2004). Transforming knowledge into professional development reSources Six teachers implement a model of teaching for understanding text. *The Elementary School Journal*, 104(5), 391–408.

McKeown, M.G., Beck, I.L., Hamilton, R., & Kucan, L. (1999). *"Questioning the Author" accessibles: Easy access resources for classroom challenges*. Bothell, WA: Wright Group.

McKeown, M.G., Beck, I.L., & Sandora, C.A. (1996) Questioning the Author: An approach to developing meaningful classroom discourse. In M.G. Graves, B.M. Taylor, & P. van den Broek (Eds.), *The first R: Every child's right to read* (pp. 97–119). New York: Teachers College Press.

Sandora, C., Beck, I., & McKeown, M. (1999). A comparison of two discussion strategies on students' comprehension and interpretation of complex literature. *Journal of Reading Psychology*, 20, 177–212.

Instructional Approach

READ 180 is a comprehensive reading intervention program offered by Scholastic and available in three stages—Stage A for grades 3 to 6, Stage B for middle school, and Stage C for high school. Starting in 1985, Ted Hasselbring and his colleagues at Vanderbilt University developed an approach to motivating and improving middle school literacy achievement that had technology at its core. The full program was piloted in 1994 and began wide dissemination in 1999. In 2002, the curriculum was extended to high school.

Instruction is delivered in 90-minute, workshop-like periods. Students receive 30 minutes of whole-group instruction with the teacher in two sessions that bookend the reading block. In between, students rotate in small groups through 20 minutes of small-group instruction with the teacher, 20 minutes of independent reading time with optional modeled reading and audio support, and 20 minutes of exercises delivered via READ 180's individualized software program. The *rBook*, a consumable student work text, presents linked readings on nonfiction content area topics, literature, and poetry, and is the basis of large- and small-group instruction. Instructional activities build academic vocabulary, comprehension, writing, grammar, and other skills through repeated reading, text marking, writing, and other scaffolded activities. An *rBook* anchor DVD builds background for the readings.

The READ 180 software, recently improved through collaboration with the Center for Applied Special Technologies, provides teachers with ongoing information about students' strengths and difficulties with particular skills and current reading level (reported in Lexiles). Students' reading levels are determined when they take the Scholastic Reading Inventory three times during the school year. The software individualizes instruction in reading comprehension, word reading, and spelling based on student performance. The reading comprehension part of the program includes a video to build and activate prior knowledge, content area passages written at multiple levels so that students of all reading levels are exposed to the same content, and multiple-choice comprehension questions that offer immediate feedback. The reading passages have tools for practicing fluent reading and also include highlighted words, which students can double-click with a mouse to get a definition (in English, Spanish, Cantonese, Hmong, Haitian Creole, and Vietnamese). The word-reading portion of the software teaches students how to decode content vocabulary words and offers practice and assessment opportunities as well. Finally, the spelling portion quizzes students on spelling in a variety of ways. Once students have passed the benchmarks in all three portions of the software for a particular passage, they take various comprehension assessments and record themselves reading the passage aloud.

Scholastic also offers several other program and curriculum options for struggling readers. These include ReadAbout, a content area reading coaching system, and Thinking Reader, among others. Offered in collaboration with Tom Snyder Productions, Thinking Reader is described in this volume and is intended to support readers of varying abilities in their reading of grade-level quality children's literature.

Professional Development

Professional development for READ 180 is provided by qualified Scholastic reading specialists through one day of introductory implementation training for administrators and one day of training for teachers and coaches. At the training, participants receive a *Teacher Implementation Guide* that provides them with overview tools, checklists, and the key steps to getting started with the program and resources. A second day of follow-up training occurs about 8 to 10 weeks after the program is first implemented when teachers learn to use key data from the program to make instructional decisions. Teachers also have the option of taking an online course that incorporates key research-based principles of teaching reading to older struggling readers as well as direction on how to use program components. The curriculum itself comes with support materials: an introductory video, resource guides, lesson plans, and an organizational planning guide. Throughout the school year, Scholastic offers the READ 180 Seminar Series, including eight half-day seminars that can be customized to meet a school district's needs. Phone support and on-site technical support are available for one year.

In addition, the *rBook Teacher's Edition* includes explicit teaching instructions for using the *rBook*, as well as strategic CheckPoints that explain when and how to provide data-driven, differentiated instruction. Integrated professional development articles provide support for planning and classroom management. Teaching instructions include guidance in using instructional routines and structured engagement techniques, such as the use of oral cloze, think-pair-share, sentence starters, and other strategies that have been shown to be effective with older struggling readers (Feldman, 2002).

Program Evaluation

READ 180 was originally piloted in 1994 with middle school students and was found to significantly improve the self-esteem, standardized reading achievement, and spelling of students identified as having both reading and behavioral problems (Hasselbring, Goin, Taylor, Bottge, & Daley, 1997). Since wide-scale dissemination, schools and districts have provided data on the efficacy of the program and third parties have analyzed and summarized the data for Scholastic. Schools and districts implementing READ 180 generally show significant improvements in student achievement. For instance, in the Los Angeles Unified School District, READ 180 students improved on the SAT9 reading and language arts tests relative to national norms, whereas comparison students' scores in the same district declined relative to national norms (Policy

Studies Associates, 2002). Similar results were obtained for English-language learners (ELLs) in this same district (Scholastic Research and Evaluation Department, 2004a). Some evidence that the program is also effective with special education students has been collected, but these data lack comparison groups (Palmer, 2003). READ 180 is also part of the National Study of the Effectiveness of Educational Technology Interventions, which is investigating the effectiveness of technology in improving reading achievement in 4th grade during the 2004–2005 school year (U.S. Department of Education, 2004). The READ 180 website includes links to evaluation studies in 17 schools and districts, many of which were implemented with ELLs and special education students. The Florida Center for Reading Research (2004) has also conducted an independent review of the program, but only for grades 6–8.

Contact Information

Address: Peter Cipkowski
             Scholastic, Inc.
             524 Broadway, 8th Floor
             New York, NY 10012
Phone: 212-965-7428
E-mail: Pcipkowski@scholastic.com
Website: www.scholastic.com/Read180

Sources

Feldman, K. (2002). *Engaged literacy learning: Strategies to maximize student participation.* New York: Scholastic Red.

Florida Center for Reading Research. (2004, October). *READ 180.* Tallahassee, FL: Author. Retrieved May 31, 2006, from http://www.fcrr.org/FCRRReports/PDF/READ180Final.pdf

Hasselbring, T.S., Goin, L., Taylor, R., Bottge, B., & Daley, P. (1997). The computer doesn't embarrass me. *Educational Leadership, 55*(3), 30–33.

Interactive, Inc. (2002). *An efficacy study of READ 180 Council of Great City Schools: A print and electronic adaptive intervention program, grades 4 and above.* New York: Scholastic.

Palmer, N. (2003). *An evaluation of READ 180 with special education students.* New York: Scholastic.

Papalewis, R. (2003). *Final report: A study of READ 180 in middle schools in Clark County School District, Las Vegas, Nevada.* New York: Scholastic.

Papalewis, R. (2004). Struggling middle school readers: Successful, accelerating intervention. *Reading Improvement, 41*(1), 24–37.

Pearson, L.M., & White, R.N. (2004). *Study of the impact of READ 180 on student performance in Fairfax County Public Schools* (Report prepared for Scholastic, Inc.). New York: Scholastic.

Peterson, C.L., Caverly, D.C., Nicholson, S.A., O'Neal, S., & Cusenbary, S. (2000). *Building reading proficiency at the secondary level: A guide to resources.* Austin, TX: Southwest Educational Development Laboratory.

Policy Study Associates. (2002). *Final report: A summary of independent research on READ 180.* New York: Scholastic.

Scholastic Research and Evaluation Department. (2004a). *Final report: A study of READ 180 with English language learners.* New York: Scholastic.

Scholastic Research and Evaluation Department. (2004b). *Final report: A study of READ 180 at Shiprock High School in Central Consolidated School District on the Navajo Indian Reservation, New Mexico.* New York: Scholastic.

Scholastic Research and Evaluation Department. (2004c). *Impact study: Stages A and B: Irdell-Statesville Schools, North Carolina.* New York: Scholastic.

Scholastic Research and Evaluation Department. (2005). *The compendium of READ 180 research: 1999–2004.* New York: Scholastic. Retrieved May 25, 2006, from http://teacher.scholastic.com/products/read180/research/reports.htm

Taylor, R. (2002). Creating a system that gets results for older, reluctant readers. *Phi Delta Kappan, 84*(1), 85–87.

Thorpe, P. (2003). *Escher's intersecting worlds: Evaluation as a reflection of the evaluator, the evaluator being reflected in the evaluation.* Wichita, KS: Wichita Public Schools.

U.S. Department of Education. (2004, February 13). Department to study technology's role in raising student achievement [Press release]. Retrieved January 14, 2007, from http://www.ed.gov/news/pressreleases/2004/02/02132004.html

White, R.N., Williams, I.J., & Haslem, M.B. (2005). *Performance of District 23 students· participating in Scholastic READ 180*. Washington, DC: Policy Studies Associates.

READ RIGHT

Instructional Approach

The development of the READ RIGHT reading intervention program began in 1978 with three years of research into a variety of fields: reading theory, learning theory, linguistics, language acquisition theory, information theory, communication theory, cognitive psychology, neurobiology, and neuropsychology. The methodology was first developed in 1981 and began to be tested in public schools (elementary through middle school) and community colleges. In 1990, the methodology was used by private industry for adult workforce literacy programs and more than a dozen Fortune 500 companies in the United States, Canada, and China before it was implemented formally in secondary schools. It has been formally implemented with Title I and special education students and with English-language learners (grades 3 and above) since 1990. The READ RIGHT reading intervention program includes everything required to implement it: a 900+-book library, assessment and evaluation systems, student management systems, and monthly reporting of students' progress.

The program is based on the theoretical premise that the brain constructs a separate neural network to guide each process it learns. When an individual wants to read, the brain accesses the neural network built specifically to guide the act of reading, the network operates on the text, and reading happens. Thus, the theory is that the root cause of every reading problem is a network that was built to guide the process of reading but that was built erroneously and operates inappropriately, resulting in inefficient, ineffective reading. It is also theorized that since reading, like all procedural learning, operates primarily below the level of consciousness, processes cannot be directly and explicitly taught. Therefore instruction that structures an environment that compels the brain to rebuild the neural networks that support reading is thought to be most effective. The READ RIGHT methodology is designed to create this kind of environment.

Trained READ RIGHT tutors work with four students in 40- to 60-minute sessions. Each session comprises two components designed to compel the brain to figure out the implicit aspects of the reading process. In the Excellent Reading Component, students are held accountable for reading paragraphs of text excellently. Audiotapes are used to enhance the predictability of the text so the student can achieve the required outcome in spite of the reading problem. During the Coached Reading component students read aloud unfamiliar pages of text to the tutor. The tutor responds with feedback designed to give the students information that will influence their brains to experiment with the implicit aspects of the reading act.

Professional Development

Tutors need not hold a teaching credential but must become READ RIGHT certified. Most importantly, seven weeks of intensive, hands-on (with students) training is provided. The training is spread throughout the school year. A competency-based system leads to READ RIGHT Tutor Certification.

Program Evaluation

The developer of the program collects data from participating sites on an ongoing basis. To date, most evaluation has been internally conducted, but two third-party evaluations have been conducted with favorable results (Litzenberger, 2001a, 2001b). The website lists several case studies of successful READ RIGHT implementation at a variety of schools and also provides a list of secondary schools where the program has been implemented. The program has been successfully replicated in 180+ schools, and on request both quantitative and qualitative data gathered by school personnel are available from each implementation site.

Contact Information

Address: Dee Tadlock
          READ RIGHT Systems
          310 West Birch Street
          Shelton, WA 98584
Phone: 360-427-9440
E-mail: info@readright.com
Website: www.readright.com

Sources

Litzenberger, J. (2001a). *Reading research results: Using READ RIGHT as an intervention program for at-risk 10th graders* (Final report prepared for Kent School District and READ RIGHT Systems). Shelton, WA: READ RIGHT Systems.

Litzenberger, J. (2001b). *Reading research results: Using READ RIGHT as an intervention program for elementary and middle school students, a longitudinal study* (Final report prepared for the Literacy Alliance and Union Gap School District). Shelton, WA: READ RIGHT Systems.

Peterson, C.L., Caverly, D.C., Nicholson, S.A., O'Neal, S., & Cusenbary, S. (2000). *Building reading proficiency at the secondary level: A guide to resources.* Austin, TX: Southwest Educational Development Laboratory.

Tadlock, D. (2005). *Read right! Coaching your child in excellence in reading.* New York: McGraw-Hill.

Instructional Approach

Reading Apprenticeship is an instructional framework developed by the Strategic Literacy Initiative (SLI) at WestEd, designed to improve the literacy achievement of middle and high school students. The Reading Apprenticeship model emphasizes that educators create classrooms of inquiry into content area subjects in which talk centers not only on *what* we read but on *why* and *how* we understand the written information in a specific content area. In other words, teachers learn to change their stance from "conveying content" to supporting students in building independent and flexible use of the strategies and critical stances most helpful to reading and writing within specific content areas.

Because SLI's professional development programs focus on teaching teachers how to teach students to be strategic readers, writers, and learners for specific content areas, implementation of the program does not require revising or adding to existing curricula. The Reading Apprenticeship approach reframes reading and writing in subject areas as strategic activities for engaging with a particular field, a "ways of thinking" in science, math, literature, history, or social science This reconceptualization enables teachers to model and provide guided practice for their students in, for example, reading and writing like an experienced reader of scientific texts. Thus, the apprenticeship model improves on more traditional models in two ways: Students are explicitly trained in the strategies to achieve in a subject area and are actively engaged in the field by participating in metacognitive and critical conversations. In addition, although it has yielded significant growth for students in a wide range of demographic groups, this model is particularly focused on reaching poor and minority youths. One key idea teachers learn in SLI professional development is to look for and build on students' existing knowledge and strengths as strategic and literate young people as a way of bridging from "the known to the new."

Professional Development

SLI supports educators in learning, integrating, adapting, and refining the use of the Reading Apprenticeship instructional framework through publications, materials development, and a variety of professional development opportunities. A model they refer to as "generative professional development" (Greenleaf & Schoenbach, 2004) is at the core of developing educators' ability to implement the SLI/Reading Apprenticeship approach with maximum fidelity (and efficacy) while adapting it to varied contexts. This model of generative professional development emphasizes having educators closely examine their own reading processes, the reading processes of adult peers, the reading processes of students (through case inquiries), and the challenges of varied types of texts. Through this kind of slowing down to look carefully at the complex, invisible, and varied processes involved in reading, educators come to see reading differently; to see and hear students differently; and to change their stance, goals, and classroom practices in relation to reading and writing in content area classes.

SLI offers multiple professional development opportunities ranging from introductory sessions for interdisciplinary teams of teachers to intensive train-the-trainer sessions, to seminars for teacher educators interested in engaging preservice teachers with Reading Apprenticeship (see Braunger, Donahue, Evans, & Galguera, 2004), to training for teaching the ninth-grade Reading Apprenticeship Academic Literacy course. Information on these varied opportunities is available and updated in the Services section of the SLI website.

Program Evaluation

The Reading Apprenticeship program is typically evaluated by its creators using the Degrees of Reading Power (DRP) test (Touchstone Applied Science Associates, 1995). Although students in this program have not been compared to control groups in experimental or quasi-experimental designs, the use of a norm-referenced test allows for some comparison to "normal" growth. In a study of the program's impact on ninth-grade students in one San Francisco school, researchers found that while an average increase of 1–2 DRP raw score points is typical in the norming population, SLI ninth-grade students demonstrated an average increase of about 4 points (Greenleaf, Schoenbach, Cziko, & Mueller, 2001). No teacher effect was found in the study, indicating that results were consistent across classrooms.

Evaluations of the program have been conducted in the Los Angeles Unified School District (LAUSD) and the Bay Area Coalition of Essential Schools (BayCES), also using the DRP. In LAUSD, students improved their DRP scores by an average of nearly 6 points. Similar but slightly less dramatic results were also found in BayCES, where the average gain was about 4 points. The LAUSD results were also disaggregated by language group and demonstrated that limited-English-proficient (LEP) and bilingual students achieved growth that was nearly identical to the overall average. When further disaggregated by language proficiency, bilingual students who were initially fluent in English showed the most growth (mean = 6.4); LEP students showed slightly less, but still impressive, growth (mean = 4.9).

Two new randomized controlled studies of Reading Apprenticeship are being carried out by external evaluators beginning in 2005. One is a National Science Foundation (NSF)–funded study of biology teachers in California high schools. The other is an Institute of Education Sciences (IES)–funded study conducted by Manpower Research Demonstration Corporation (MRDC) and American Institutes for Research (AIR) on the effects of Reading Apprenticeship Academic Literacy, a supplemental literacy program for ninth-grade students based on the Reading Apprenticeship framework.

Contact Information

Address: Dr. Ruth Schoenbach
           Strategic Literacy Initiative, WestEd
           300 Lakeside Drive, 25th Floor
           Oakland, CA 94617
Phone: 510-302-4255
E-mail: rschoen@wested.org
Website: www.wested.org/stratlit

Sources

Braunger, J., Donahue, D., Evans, K., & Galguera, T. (2004) *Rethinking preparation for content area teaching: The Reading Apprenticeship approach.* San Francisco: Jossey-Bass.

Donahue, D. (2003). Reading across the great divide: English and math teachers apprentice one another as readers and disciplinary insiders. *Journal of Adolescent & Adult Literacy, 47*, 24–37.

Greenleaf, C.L., & Mueller, F.L. (2003). *Impact of the Pilot Academic Literacy Course on ninth grade students' reading development: Academic year 1996–1997. A report to the Stuart Foundation.* San Francisco: WestEd.

Greenleaf, C.L., & Schoenbach, R. (2004). Building capacity for the responsive teaching of reading in the academic disciplines: Strategic inquiry designs for middle and high school teachers' professional development. In D.S. Strickland & M. Kamil (Eds.), *Improving reading through professional development* (pp. 97–127). Norword, MA: Christopher-Gordon.

Greenleaf, C.L., Schoenbach, R., Cziko, C., & Mueller, F.L. (2001). Apprenticing adolescent readers to academic literacy. *Harvard Educational Review, 71*(1), 79–129.

Killion, J. (2002). *What works in the high school: Results-based staff development.* Oxford, OH: National Staff Development Council.

Schoenbach, R., Braunger, J., Greenleaf, C., & Litman, C. (2003). Apprenticing adolescents to reading in subject-area classrooms. *Phi Delta Kappan, 85*(2), 133–138.

Schoenbach, R., Greenleaf, C., Cziko, C., & Hurwitz, L. (1999). *Reading for understanding: A guide to improving reading in middle and high school classrooms.* San Francisco: Jossey-Bass.

Strategic Literacy Initiative. (2002a). *Secondary school literacy project: A summary of student outcomes on the Degrees of Reading Power test, academic year 1999–2000.* Oakland, CA: WestEd.

Strategic Literacy Initiative. (2002b). *Summary of the results of the Degrees of Reading Power test: LAUSD Strategic Literacy Network, 1999–2000.* Oakland, CA: WestEd.

Strategic Literacy Initiative. (2004a). *1996–1999 9th grade academic literacy course studies.* Oakland, CA: WestEd.

Strategic Literacy Initiative. (2004b). *1997–2000 A study of teacher learning and student reading outcomes in an SLI professional development network.* Oakland, CA: WestEd.

Strategic Literacy Initiative. (2004c). *1999–2002 Studies of student reading growth in diverse professional development networks.* Oakland, CA: WestEd.

Strategic Literacy Initiative. (2004d). *2001–2004 Increasing student achievement through school-wide reading apprenticeship.* Oakland, CA: WestEd.

Strategic Literacy Initiative. (2004e). *2001–2004 Reading Apprenticeship classroom study: Linking professional development for teachers to outcomes for students in diverse subject-area classrooms.* Oakland, CA: WestEd.

Touchstone Applied Science Associates. (1995). *Degrees of Reading Power Test.* Brewster, NY: Author.

READING IS FAME (GIRLS AND BOYS TOWN)

Instructional Approach

Reading Is FAME consists of a series of four courses for struggling readers in grades 7–12 and is based on Jeanne Chall's stages of reading development. The first course in the series, Foundations of Reading, is designed for students reading below a fourth-grade level and teaches decoding skills, primarily through spelling. The second course, Adventures in Reading, is designed for students reading between the fourth- and sixth-grade levels and focuses on basic vocabulary instruction and increasing fluency. Mastery of Meaning, the third course, is designed for high school students reading between the sixth- and eighth-grade levels; it seeks to further expand vocabulary through increasing background and conceptual knowledge. The final course, Explorations, is designed for high school students reading somewhat below grade level and teaches comprehension (i.e., summarizing) and study skills (i.e., note taking) in the context of content area subjects, such as social studies, science, and the humanities. The program uses a combination of computer activities, oral and silent reading, speaking and writing exercises, and work sheets. Each course offers direct instruction, followed by guided practice and finally independent practice.

Professional Development

Training by Girls and Boys Town Reading Center staff is a prerequisite for purchasing the curriculum. Each course of FAME requires one day of training, and most schools opt to have Foundations and Adventures training first. Mastery and Explorations training often occurs in conjunction with the site's follow-up consultation, a requirement for FAME implementation. It is recommended that consultation transpire after the program has been in use for several weeks. FAME implementation training includes instruction in how to use both curriculum-based and standardized assessment for student placement within the program. In addition, purchase of the curriculum requires an agreement to provide Girls and Boys Town Reading Center with feedback regarding implementation of the program, but this does not necessarily include student data.

Center staff can provide training at any level (i.e., district, program, school, or classroom) and can involve any staff. The training comprises instruction in assessing and placing students in the program and selecting and implementing the various components of the program. Follow-up support is also provided throughout the implementation phase by the trainer. In addition to the direct support of on-site consultation, FAME consultants support sites indirectly via phone or e-mail. This ongoing indirect support is provided throughout the duration of a system's FAME implementation.

Program Evaluation

Evaluation of the FAME program consists solely of internally conducted analyses of standardized test results for students who have participated in the program. Initial testing with the Girls and Boys Town population showed average gains of one grade-level equivalent per semester of instruction. When FAME was taken to a public school setting, similar results were seen. As a result, since 1994, FAME has been implemented in 25 states.

The Girls and Boys Town Reading Center shared with us the results of evaluation data collected from sites implementing the program. These data were collected between 1997 and 2004. Sites ranged from entire districts running dozens of FAME courses to just one school running a single section. Because data submission is strictly voluntary, not all implementation sites were represented in the data. Results are reported as grade-equivalent scores for standardized tests. Since these data were gathered primarily for descriptive purposes, Girls and Boys Town Reading Center did not calculate tests of statistical significance.

On average, participating students made close to a one-year gain in each FAME one-semester course. Foundation students made a 0.9 gain in decoding and a 0.8 gain in vocabulary during one semester. In other words, these students made 7- to 10-month gains in 4 months. Adventures students made a 0.9 gain in decoding and a 0.8 gain in vocabulary, or an 8- to 9-month gain, in 4 months. Mastery students made a 1.0 gain in vocabulary and a 1.3 gain in comprehension; that is, these students made at least a full year gain in 4 months. Explorations students made a 0.9 gain in vocabulary and comprehension, nearly a full year gain in 4 months. These results indicate that FAME students had accelerated growth in reading skills.

Contact Information

Address: Girls and Boys Town National Resource and Training Center
14100 Crawford Street
Boys Town, NE 68010
Phone: 800-545-5771
E-mail: nrtcmarketing@girlsandboystown.org
Website: www.girlsandboystown.org/pros/training/education/FAME_pro
gram.asp

Sources

Curtis, M.E., & Longo, A.M. (1996, April). *Reversing reading failure in adolescents with behavioral disorders.* Paper presented at the annual convention of the Council for Exceptional Children, Orlando, FL.

Curtis, M.E., & Longo, A.M. (1999). *When adolescents can't read: Methods and materials that work.* Cambridge, MA: Brookline.

Curtis, M.E., & Longo, A.M. (2001). Teaching vocabulary to adolescents to improve comprehension. *Reading Online, 5*(4). Available at http://www.reading

online.org/articles/art_index.asp?HREF=curtis/index.html

Killion, J. (2002). *What works in the high school: Results-based staff development.* Oxford, OH: National Staff Development Council.

Longo, A.M., Chmelka, B., & Curtis, M.E. (1997, April). *Teaching basic reading skills to adolescents with behavioral disorders.* Paper presented at the annual convention of the Council for Exceptional Children, Salt Lake City, UT.

Instructional Approach

Originally developed for use with secondary students, Reading Power in the Content Areas (RP) has since been adapted for use with students as young as third grade. RP is a professional development model that trains both academic and vocational teachers across the curriculum in how to integrate reading strategies. Teachers are trained to assess the reading abilities of students as well as to determine the readability of their content area text and materials for their particular students. Teachers are also trained to scaffold their students' reading comprehension and learn how to teach reading comprehension, vocabulary acquisition, and study skills through authentic text. Finally, teachers are trained to plan for classroom implementation of the RP program.

Professional Development

RP recommends that professional development be conducted by a Reading Power certified trainer and overseen by a reading or curriculum specialist within the school. It is also recommended that the training be conducted schoolwide. The training includes instruction in administering and interpreting standardized and informal assessment, how to build vocabulary through the reading of authentic texts, teaching reading comprehension and critical thinking strategies, and planning for implementation of the RP program. Formal training lasts one to two days and follow-up training is recommended.

Program Evaluation

It appears that all evaluation of the RP program has been conducted internally. Evaluation studies validating the program's effectiveness have been done for the U.S. Department of Education through the National Diffusion Network Program Effectiveness Panel. Several of these studies have found that middle and secondary students from a variety of backgrounds have made significant gains on standardized reading measures after participating in RP instruction. The control group in each case was the national norm group for the standardized measure utilized for the evaluation. Information on schools and/or districts that have successfully implemented the program is available on request.

Contact Information

Address: Carol Burgess
            Director, Reading Power in the Content Areas
            16705 12th Avenue North
            Plymouth, MN 55447
Phone: 763-404-1010

E-mail: burge003@umn.edu
Website: no website

Sources

Cushenberry, D.C. (1988). *Comprehensive reading strategies for all secondary students*. Springfield, IL: Charles C Thomas.

Lang, G. (1995). *Education programs that work: The catalogue of the National Diffusion Network (NDN) "Linking the Nation With Excellence."* Longmont, CA: Sopris West. Retrieved April 25, 2006, from http://www.ed.gov/pubs/EPTW/index.html

Killion, J. (1997). *What works in the middle: Results-based staff development*. Oxford, OH: National Staff Development Council.

Killion, J. (2002a). *What works in the elementary school: Results-based staff development*. Oxford, OH: National Staff Development Council.

Killion, J. (2002b). *What works in the high school: Results-based staff development*. Oxford, OH: National Staff Development Council.

Peterson, C.L., Caverly, D.C., Nicholson, S.A., O'Neal, S., & Cusenbary, S. (2000). *Building reading proficiency at the secondary level: A guide to resources*. Austin, TX: Southwest Educational Development Laboratory.

RECIPROCAL TEACHING

Instructional Approach

Reciprocal teaching is a research-designed approach focused on improving strategic reading for comprehension. Reciprocal teaching targets children of any grade level but is typically used with students scoring in the 35th percentile or below on standardized reading measures. It involves explicit instruction in and modeling of a particular set of strategies coupled with increasing opportunities for practice in a collaborative environment. Ideally, it leads students to take ownership of the process of constructing meaning with texts and promotes active processing of text. The strategies supporting the discussion include summarizing (identifying the gist), generating questions to assess one another's understanding of the content, clarifying (words, sentences, and/or concepts), and predicting (based upon the ideas or structure of the text). While the strategies are initially introduced in this order, the goal is for the strategies to be used opportunistically and flexibly.

Reciprocal teaching is best used in a small-group setting of 10 or fewer students so that each participant has the opportunity to take his or her turn leading the dialogue. The teacher initially assumes significant responsibility for leading the dialogue, modeling the use of the strategies for sense making and knowledge building from the text. Students then take turns leading the dialogue while the teacher coaches and instructs as necessary. The discussion leader is responsible for generating the first question (to which others in the group respond), proposing the initial summary (which can be modified by others in the group), identifying clarifications, and venturing the first prediction. While some authors and publishers have chosen to associate the strategies with roles that participants take, reciprocal teaching was not designed in that fashion; rather the idea was that learners experience using a repertoire of strategies to experience how they complement one another and lead one to engage in different ways of processing the text. Ideally, the group is working with text that is accessible but challenging, so that the students are experiencing a genuine need to be strategic in their reading and there is something worth discussing in constructing the meaning of the text.

Professional Development

Because reciprocal teaching is not a purchasable product, no centralized mechanism for professional development is available. Several existing articles and books guide teachers through the theory behind reciprocal teaching and how to effectively implement it (Hager, 2003; McKenna, 2002; Oczkus, 2003).

Program Evaluation

As one of the older reading comprehension interventions designed by researchers, reciprocal teaching has a broad research base supporting its effectiveness (Rosenshine & Meister, 1994). Although originally designed for use with elementary school children scoring at or below the 35th percentile on standardized reading measures, it has been used and found effective in a variety of contexts and for a variety of readers. Reciprocal teaching has been found effective in teaching children with mild disabilities in pullout (Marston, 1995) or inclusive settings (Lederer, 2000), with deaf and hard-of-hearing students (Al-Hilawani, 2003), with high school students (Alfassi, 1998; Westera & Moore, 1995), with bilingual students (Padron, 1992), and even with students learning English as a second language in other countries (Fung, Wilkinson, & Moore, 2002).

Contact Information

Address: Dr. Annemarie Palincsar
University of Michigan
610 East University
Ann Arbor, MI 48109-1259

Phone: e-mail or mail contact preferred

E-mail: annemari@umich.edu

Website: http://edr1.educ.msu.edu/CompStrat/login.asp
(*username: demo; password: demo*)

Sources

Alfassi, M. (1998). Reading for meaning: The efficacy of reciprocal teaching in fostering reading comprehension in high school students in remedial reading classes. *American Educational Research Journal, 35*(2), 309–332.

Alfassi, M. (2004). Reading to learn: Effects of combined strategy instruction on high school students. *Journal of Educational Research, 97*(4), 171–184.

Al-Hilawani, Y.A. (2003). Clinical examination of three methods of teaching reading comprehension to deaf and hard-of-hearing students: From research to classroom applications. *Journal of Deaf Studies and Deaf Education, 8*(2), 146–156.

Fung, I.Y.Y., Wilkinson, I.A.G., & Moore, D.W. (2002). L-1-assisted reciprocal teaching to improve ESL students' comprehension of English expository text. *Learning and Instruction, 13*(1), 1–31.

Goodman, A. (2005). The middle school high five: Strategies can triumph. *Voices From the Middle, 13*(2), 12–19.

Hager, A. (2003). Learning to use reciprocal teaching: One teacher's journey. *Michigan Reading Journal*, 35(3), 25–29.

Kelly, M. (1994). Reciprocal teaching in a regular primary school classroom. *Journal of Educational Research*, 88(1), 53–61.

Lederer, J.M. (2000). Reciprocal teaching of social studies in inclusive elementary classrooms. *Journal of Learning Disabilities*, 33(1), 91–106.

Lysynchuk, L.M., Pressley, M., & Vye, N.J. (1990). Reciprocal teaching improves standardized reading comprehension performance in poor comprehenders. *The Elementary School Journal*, 90, 469–484.

Marston, D. (1995). Comparison of reading intervention approaches for students with mild disabilities. *Exceptional Children*, 62(1), 20–37.

McKenna, M.C. (2002). *Help for struggling readers: Strategies for grades 3–8*. New York: Guilford.

Oczkus, L.D. (2003). *Reciprocal teaching at work: Strategies for improving reading comprehension*. Newark, DE: International Reading Association.

Padron, Y.N. (1992). The effect of strategy instruction on bilingual students' cognitive strategy use in reading. *Bilingual Research Journal*, 16(3–4), 35–51.

Palincsar, A.S. (2003). Collaborative approaches to comprehension instruction. In A.S. Sweet & C.E. Snow (Eds.), *Rethinking reading comprehension* (pp. 99–114). New York: Guilford.

Palincsar, A.S., & Brown, A. (1984). Reciprocal teaching of comprehension-fostering and comprehension-monitoring activities. *Cognition and Instruction*, 1(2), 117–175.

Palincsar, A.S., & Brown, A.L. (1986). Interactive teaching to promote independent learning from text. *The Reading Teacher*, 39, 771–777.

Palincsar, A.S., & Brown, A.L. (1988). Teaching and practicing thinking skills to promote comprehension in the context of group problem solving. *Remedial and Special Education (RASE)*, 9(1), 53–59.

Palincsar, A.S., & Herrenkohl, L.R. (2002). Designing collaborative learning contexts. *Theory Into Practice*, 41(1), 26–32.

Rosenshine, B., & Meister, C. (1994). Reciprocal teaching: A review of the research. *Review of Educational Research*, 64(4), 479–530.

Van Garderen, D. (2004). Reciprocal teaching as a comprehension strategy for understanding mathematical word problems. *Reading and Writing Quarterly*, 20, 225–229.

Westera, J., & Moore, D.W. (1995). Reciprocal teaching of reading comprehension in a New Zealand high school. *Psychology in the Schools*, 32(3), 225–232.

REWARDS

Instructional Approach

REWARDS is a literacy program designed to help students in grades 4–12 learn to decode multisyllabic words and build reading fluency. REWARDS is a supplemental remedial program recommended for intensive use for a short duration. The program contains 20 lessons. The first 12 lessons focus on the prerequisite skills for decoding multisyllabic words, while the final lessons focus on applying a strategy for decoding long words to word lists, sentences, and passages. Students also reread the passages to increase fluency.

Rewards Plus: Reading Strategies Applied to Social Studies Passages and to Science Passages are two supplemental programs consisting of 6 review lessons and 15 additional application lessons. These lessons facilitate transfer of the REWARDS strategy to social studies and science passages. In addition, the application lessons extend students' skills in vocabulary, comprehension, and writing.

Professional Development

The REWARDS program consists of teacher manuals, student workbooks, posters, and demonstration videos. These products are for sale through Sopris West and require little teacher training. The developers of the program are available to provide training. In addition, the program developers have trained many others to be REWARDS trainers. The Sopris West website lists these independent trainers.

Program Evaluation

Program evaluation has been conducted by the developers of the program. Several field tests and pilot studies were conducted that showed student gains on standardized word-attack and word-identification subtests after five weeks of instruction. Two experimental studies have been conducted: one examining the progress of fourth- and fifth-grade students, the other of middle school students (Archer, Gleason, Vachon, & Hollenbeck, 2001; Vachon & Gleason, 2001). In each study, gains were found in students' abilities to decode multisyllabic words, or parts therein, and in correct words read per minute (fluency). An outside study of the program found that seventh-graders who were reading two to four years below grade level made significant gains in six weeks on measures of word-reading efficiency, reading rate, reading accuracy, and reading fluency (Shippen, Houchins, Steventon, & Sartor, 2005). The Florida Center for Reading Research (2004) has also conducted an independent review of the program.

Contact Information

Address: Sopris West
4093 Specialty Place
Longmont, CO 80504
Phone: 800-547-6747
E-mail: customerservice@sopriswest.com
Website: www.rewardsreading.com

Sources

Archer, A.L., Gleason, M.M., Vachon, V.L., & Hollenbeck, K. (2001). *Instructional strategies for teaching struggling fourth and fifth grade students to read long words*. Retrieved July 25, 2005, from http://www.rewardsreading.com/PDFs/Intermediate_Study.pdf

Florida Center for Reading Research. (2004, February). *REWARDS*. Tallahassee, FL: Author. Retrieved January 15, 2007, from http://www.fcrr.org/FCRR Reports/PDF/rewards_report.pdf

Shippen, M.E., Houchins, D.E., Steventon, C., & Sartor, D. (2005). A comparison of two direct instruction reading programs for urban middle school students. *Remedial and Special Education (RASE)*, 26(3), 175–182.

Vachon, V.L., & Gleason, M.M. (2001). *The effects of mastery teaching and varying practice contexts on middle school students' acquisition of multisyllabic word reading strategies*. Retrieved July 25, 2005, from http://www.rewardsreading.com/PDFs/Middle_School_Study1.pdf

Instructional Approach

Saxon's Phonics Intervention is a program developed for struggling older readers (from fourth grade to adult). Designed to be a supplement to a reading curriculum, the program is Orton-Gillingham–based and focuses on explicit and systematic instruction in decoding and spelling. Before instruction begins, students' phonemic awareness and decoding skills are evaluated. The information gained from these formal and informal assessments will enable teachers to customize instruction to address those areas that are deficient. New learning is presented sequentially and reviewed throughout the curriculum, and assessments are incorporated on a regular basis to judge mastery of each concept taught. Teachers are provided with all necessary materials in a scripted teacher's manual, a workbook for each student, and classroom materials, consisting mostly of card decks for the various lesson components (i.e., letter, picture, sight word, affix, and vocabulary decks). The program can be used individually or within a classroom setting.

Professional Development

Saxon Publishers offers a variety of supports for correctly implementing Phonics Intervention. An inservice video is included in the purchase of the program. The inservice video provides teachers with a background of the Saxon pedagogy, as well as the best way to implement the program. Schools can also schedule an inservice with a Saxon consultant. Finally, teachers can receive support from the Saxon School Support Line. This toll-free number allows teachers to talk live with an experienced Saxon teacher to answer questions and provide tips for effective implementation of Phonics Intervention (800-284-7019).

Program Evaluation

This program is based on reading research showing the importance of explicit, systematic, and repetitive instruction in phonics for students with learning disabilities. Saxon purports that all struggling readers will benefit from the same instruction that has proven most effective with students with learning disabilities; however, specific data were not available to substantiate this claim. In an internal report, *Research Support: Phonics Intervention*, Saxon (n.d.) cites the research base for the curriculum and reports anecdotal incidents of improved standardized test scores for students participating in the program. Two newer evaluations have been released and are available at the Saxon website. One describes implementation of the intervention curriculum with teenaged and adult inmates at a correctional facility, but this study did not find statistically significant effects for the Saxon program. The other evaluation report is a summary of several case studies conducted in several states. Although these case studies indicate positive results from using the Saxon program, they were primarily conducted with first-through third-grade students. The one case study conducted with older students was conducted with fourth graders in Ohio, where students had received Saxon phonics instruction since kindergarten. Eighty-two percent of these children passed the state reading test compared with 61% of students across the state (Harcourt Achieve, 2005).

Contact Information

Address: Harcourt Achieve
            6277 Sea Harbor Drive
            Orlando, FL 32887
Phone: 800-284-7019
E-mail: info@saxonpublishers.com
Website: http://saxonpublishers.harcourtachieve.com

Sources

Calhoon, M.B. (2005). Effects of a peer-mediated phonological skill and reading comprehension program on reading skill acquisition for middle school students with reading disabilities. *Journal of Learning Disabilities, 38*, 424–433.

Harcourt Achieve. (2005, March). *Case study summaries of Saxon Phonics and Spelling: Web version.* Orlando, FL: Author. Retrieved May 31, 2005, from http://saxonpublishers.harcourtachieve.com/HA/correlations/pdf/s/Saxon_PhonicSpel_CaseStudiesl_web.pdf

Harcourt Achieve. (2004, March). *A study of the effectiveness of the Saxon Phonics intervention program with adult learners: Web version.* Orlando, FL: Author. Retrieved May 31, 2005, from http://saxonpublishers.harcourtachieve.com/HA/correlations/pdf/s/SaxonPhonicsInt_research_web.pdf

Saxon. (n.d.). *Research report: Phonics intervention.* Orlando, FL: Author. Retrieved April 9, 2004, from http://www.saxonpublishers.com/pdf/research/saxon_phonics_int_research.pdf

SCAFFOLDED READING EXPERIENCE

Instructional Approach

The Scaffolded Reading Experience (SRE) is an instructional approach that is designed to help teachers give students support in reading both narrative and expository texts. SREs have two phases: planning and implementation. When planning, teachers consider their students' strengths and needs, the text to be read, and the purposes for reading. Based on these, the teacher selects supports designed to promote optimal comprehension. Supports are divided into prereading, during-reading, and postreading activities based on when they are implemented.

Prereading activities include motivating students for reading, activating and building prior knowledge, providing text-specific knowledge, relating the reading to students' lives, preteaching vocabulary and/or concepts, suggesting comprehension strategies, prequestioning, prediction, and direction setting. During-reading activities include silent or oral reading by students, teacher read-alouds, guided reading, and modifying the text. Postreading activities include questioning, writing, drama, artistic and other nonverbal activities, application and outreach activities, building connections, reteaching, and general discussion. The full range of activities is not implemented for every text or task. No one element is considered essential; rather, support and the methods of support are adapted from text to text and task to task based on reader needs.

Professional Development

SRE can be learned by teachers through the purchase of a book on implementing SREs (Graves & Graves, 2004). SRE does not offer a formal professional development component. However, its originators do offer a free website compendium of existing SREs. Each SRE is for a specific text and includes an introduction to the text; instructional objectives for the text; the higher-order thinking skills to be targeted; a chronological list of activities; a detailed breakdown of each activity; a list of needed materials; and a list of additional resources, including Internet sites. Anyone may search the database for an SRE by author, title, type of text, grade level, the higher-order thinking skill targeted, or academic subject area. In addition, users may search for a book preview or story map by author or title.

Program Evaluation

So far five studies of SRE's effectiveness have been conducted, three of which have been published. Among the published studies, one was a quasi-experimental study of 50 seventh-grade students in which SRE was found to yield better reading comprehension and attitudes than a traditional approach to teaching short stories (Fournier & Graves, 2002). Another quasi-experimental study found that use of SRE as opposed to a traditional English literature instructional approach resulted in significantly better reading comprehension and higher-order thinking skills use among high school sophomores and seniors (Graves & Liang, 2003). Of the other studies that were presented at professional conferences, one was a quasi-experimental study of SRE's effects on 121 seventh-grade students. It found that both high- and low-achieving students scored higher on multiple-choice and open-response reading comprehension measures and on attitude measures when they received SRE instruction (Cooke, 2002b). Additional studies are underway.

Contact Information

Address: Michael Graves
University of Minnesota
330A Peik Hall
Minneapolis, MN 55455
Phone: 612-625-2390

E-mail: mgraves@umn.edu
Website: www.onlinereadingresources.com

Sources

Cooke, C.L. (2002a, December). *The effects of scaffolding multicultural short stories on students' comprehension and attitudes*. Paper presented at the 52nd annual meeting of the National Reading Conference, Miami, FL.

Cooke, C.L. (2002b). The effects of scaffolding multicultural short stories on students' comprehension and attitudes (Doctoral dissertation, University of Minnesota). *Digital Dissertations*, AAT 3052766.

Fitzgerald, J., & Graves, M.F. (2004–2005). Reading supports for all. *Educational Leadership, 62*(4), 68–71.

Fitzgerald, J., & Graves, M.F. (2003). *Scaffolding reading experiences for English language learners*. Norwood, MA: Christopher-Gordon.

Fournier, D.N.E., & Graves, M.F. (2002). Scaffolding adolescents' comprehension of short stories. *Journal of Adolescent & Adult Literacy, 46*, 30–39.

Graves, M.F., & Avery, P.G. (1997). Scaffolding students' reading of history. *Social Studies, 88*(3), 134–138.

Graves, M.F., & Graves, B.B. (2004). *Scaffolding reading experiences: Designs for student success* (2nd ed.). Norwood, MA: Christopher-Gordon.

Graves, M.F., & Liang, L.A. (2003). On-line resources for fostering understanding and higher-level thinking in senior high school students. In D.L. Schallert, C.M. Fairbanks, J. Worthy, B. Maloch, & J.V. Hoffman (Eds.), *51st yearbook of the National Reading Conference* (pp. 204–215). Oak Creek, WI: National Reading Conference.

Liang, L.A. (2004a, November). *Scaffolding middle school students' comprehension of and response to narrative text*. Paper presented at the annual meeting of the National Reading Conference, San Antonio, TX.

Liang, L.A. (2004b). Using scaffolding to foster middle school students' comprehension and response to short stories (Doctoral dissertation, University of Minnesota). *Digital Dissertations*, AAT 3137184.

Massey, D., & Heafner, T. (2004). Promoting reading comprehension in social studies. *Journal of Adolescent & Adult Literacy, 48*, 26–40.

Rothenberg, S.S., & Watts, S.M. (1997). Students with learning difficulties meet Shakespeare: Using a scaffolded reading experience. *Journal of Adolescent & Adult Literacy, 40*, 532–539.

SOAR TO SUCCESS

Instructional Approach

The Soar to Success program is designed to improve reading comprehension skills for students in third to eighth grades who are reading significantly below grade level. Implementation requires 40 minutes of instruction, five days a week and involves small-group instruction. Since the program is designed to be used with groups of five to seven students, lower gains are expected if the program is used with larger groups. The program is also designed as a supplement to a core reading/language arts curriculum, and the goal is to bring students quickly up to grade level and then out of the program. There is no placement testing as teachers are encouraged to start at the beginning of the curriculum, even if the books seem too easy for students. This is so that students experience success with the program early on and also so that they can practice the new comprehension strategies on simpler reading material. Regular story retellings and oral-reading checks are used by teachers to measure progress.

Each day's activities are designed to be fast-paced and include a lesson focusing on transferable comprehension and decoding strategies, followed by reading from one of a series of Houghton Mifflin trade books leveled for difficulty. Reciprocal teaching and the use of graphic organizers are central comprehension building strategies taught. Home activities are part of the curriculum, and homework activities are included for levels 7 and 8.

Professional Development

The Houghton Mifflin Company does not require professional development to use the curriculum. However, it is strongly recommended by the developer. Training conferences are offered at sites around the United States and can also be scheduled in cooperation with local schools/districts. These Intermediate Intervention Institutes provide two days of intensive training to teachers preparing to use the Soar to Success curriculum as well as instruction on how to choose appropriate books for students at different reading levels. A teacher's manual provides background information and lessons for teaching Soar to Success. Staff development video and other materials are also provided to institute participants.

Houghton Mifflin educational consultants are also available to provide inservice training and offer support to teachers using Soar to Success. This inservice training consists of three-hour sessions introducing the curriculum and teaching strategies for implementation. Educators can become qualified to teach other teachers by using the curriculum for at least a semester and attending a second level of training.

Program Evaluation

The Soar to Success program is based on a two-year national research study, Project SUCCESS. In this study, conducted in 13 classrooms across the United States, students were found to make significant gains in retelling, answering questions, comprehension, and oral reading, but not in a vocabulary subtest, after 76 days of instruction. An executive summary of this report appears in all Soar to Success teacher manuals, and the full report is available from Houghton Mifflin Company.

Since this time, several schools using the Soar to Success curriculum have reported their testing information, and this information is posted online. Although it was based on researched best practices in literacy instruction, to date no outside studies have been conducted on the efficacy of the program. The Florida Center for Reading Research (2004) has conducted an independent review of the program.

Contact Information

Address: Houghton Mifflin Company
            School Division
            Education Place
            222 Berkeley Street
            Boston, MA 02116

Phone: see website for appropriate regional number
E-mail: ask@hmco.com
Website: www.eduplace.com/intervention/soar

Sources

Cooper, J.D., Boschken, I., McWilliams, J., & Pistochini, L. (1997). *Project Success: A study of the effectiveness of an intervention program designed to accelerate reading for struggling readers in the upper grades.* Unpublished manuscript.

Eduplace. (n.d.). *Project Success: Soar to Success test results 1997–1998, 1998–1999, 1999–2000.* Boston: Author. Retrieved June 11, 2005, from http://www.eduplace.com/intervention/soar/testscores/index.html

Florida Center for Reading Research. (2004, June). *Soar to Success.* Tallahassee, FL: Author. Retrieved January 15, 2007, from http://www.fcrr.org/FCRRReports/PDF/soar_success.pdf

Pikulski, J.J. (1994). Preventing reading failure: A review of five effective programs. *The Reading Teacher, 48,* 30–39.

SPELL READ P.A.T.

Instructional Approach

The Spell Read P.A.T. program (P.A.T. stands for Phonological Auditory Training) is built upon the basic underlying assumption that fluency in phonological skills will free a student's mental capacity permitting an unhindered focus on comprehension and vocabulary acquisition. The program is developed from Kay MacPhee's work with hearing-impaired and dyslexic students.

Each Spell Read P.A.T. class includes activities in phonemic and phonetic skill development, spelling, reading, and writing, with phonological automaticity being one of the fundamental goals. The program is delivered in three sequential phases. In the first phase, students are introduced to the 44 phonemes in the English language in a specific order and manner. The objective is to enable each student to achieve mastery or phonological automaticity. The students then progress into the second phase where they are taught secondary spellings for sounds that can be represented by more than one letter or letter combination. More complicated decoding challenges, such as consonant blends and multisyllabic words, are also taught in this phase. The third phase continues multisyllabic decoding instruction by introducing common prefixes and suffixes. The entire program typically requires between 100 and 200 hours of instruction. Materials include instructor manuals and materials, student activity books and manipulatives, and language-rich reading material.

Student skills are assessed prior to training, using the TOWRE (Test of Word Reading Efficiency), in order to benchmark word-level skills and place the students into homogeneous groups of up to five. Ongoing progress assessment uses the standardized tests preferred by the client (e.g., school district). Individual student progress is tracked and supported through an online system. Instructors enter specific student progress data weekly, and this information enables Spell Read P.A.T. to provide detailed program support relating to the fidelity of delivery and/or the progress of individual students, where and when needed.

Professional Development

Purchase of Spell Read P.A.T. includes extensive training for teachers, paraprofessionals, and specialists. Training in the first phase of Spell Read P.A.T. is intensive and takes two weeks. Training in the subsequent phases is brief and occurs later. Ongoing instructor support is also provided.

Program Evaluation

The Spell Read P.A.T. program website specifies that clinical trials and neuroimaging studies have proven the program's effectiveness (as noted on the Spell Read P.A.T. website, www.spellread.com/a/publish/evidence.shtml, on January 27, 2007). Data from one such trial in a Maryland middle school demonstrated that after 100 hours of the program over five months, sixth- and seventh-grade students, on average, improved in their word-reading skills by eight grade equivalents and their comprehension by over three grade equivalents (Torgesen, Rashotte, Alexander, Alexander, & MacPhee, 2003). In another small-scale evaluation, the program was found effective after only 20 hours for incarcerated teenagers (Rashotte, 2001). The one published study of Spell Read P.A.T. demonstrated its effectiveness for improving the phonological awareness, word-reading accuracy, spelling, and comprehension of first- through sixth-grade students (Rashotte, MacPhee, & Torgesen, 2001). Students received approximately 30 hours of instruction in small groups. Gains were maintained when students were tested again two months later. Spell Read P.A.T. is also one of four intervention programs under evaluation by the Power4Kids Research Initiative in a randomized experiment (see www.haan4kids.org/power4kids/exec_summary_0306.html). The study will compare the programs in terms of impact, fidelity of treatment, neurological effects, and cost-effectiveness. The Florida Center for Reading Research also conducted an independent review of Spell Read P.A.T.

Contact Information

Address: P.A.T. Learning Systems, Inc.
2927A Olney Sandy Springs Road
Olney, MD 20832
Phone: 800-493-0098
E-mail: information@spellread.com
Website: www.spellread.com

Sources

Florida Center for Reading Research. (n.d.). *Spell Read P.A.T.* Tallahassee, FL: Author. Retrieved May 31, 2006, from http://www.fcrr.org/FCRRReports/PDF/KaplanSpellRead.pdf

Rashotte, C.A. (2001). *The effectiveness of a phonologically-based reading program on the reading skills of incarcerated youths at Newfoundland and Labrador Youth Centre at Whitbourne*. Retrieved June 15, 2004, from http://www.spellread.com/a/uploads/whitbourne_study.pdf

Rashotte, C.A., MacPhee, K., & Torgesen, J.K. (2001). The effectiveness of a group reading instruction program with poor readers in multiple grades. *Learning Disability Quarterly, 24*, 119–134.

Torgesen, J.K., Rashotte, C.A., Alexander, A.W., Alexander, J., & MacPhee, K. (2003) Progress towards understanding the instructional conditions necessary for remediating reading difficulties in older children. In B. Foorman (Ed.), *Preventing and remediating reading disabilities: Bringing science to scale* (pp. 275–298). Parkton, MD: York.

Torgesen, J., Myers, D., Schirm, A., Stuart, E., Vartivarian, S., Mansfield, W., Stancavage, F., Durno, D., Javorsky, R., & Haan, C. (2006). *National assessment of Title I: Interim report. Volume II: Closing the reading gap: First year findings from a randomized trial of four reading interventions for striving readers*. Washington, DC: National Center for Education Evaluation and Regional Assistance, Institute of Education Sciences, U.S. Department of Education. Retrieved January 14, 2007, from http://www.ed.gov/rschstat/eval/disadv/title1interimreport/vol2.pdf

STRATEGIC INSTRUCTION MODEL

Instructional Approach

The Strategic Instruction Model (SIM) is a comprehensive, two-pronged approach to improving adolescent literacy achievement, offering both a Learning Strategies Curriculum and Content Enhancement Routines. The former focuses on improving the strategic reading and writing of adolescent students by offering struggling students explicit and direct instruction in reading and writing strategies. The latter focuses on helping teachers to reconceptualize how and what they teach.

The Learning Strategies Curriculum is for students who particularly struggle with reading and writing. Students who still struggle with the act of reading words receive intensive interventions in decoding and fluency. Students who have mastered the basics of reading but are still reading dramatically below grade level are taught the skills and strategies that will help them become more efficient and effective readers. These strategies focus on making students more active learners by teaching them how to learn, including ways to organize and monitor their comprehension in various content areas.

Content Enhancement Routines are practices that help subject-matter teachers think about the content they want to convey and how best to convey it, such that all their students have the opportunity to learn. Rather than asking all teachers to become literacy teachers, teachers learn instructional methods that help them present content in a fashion that reaches learners of all ability levels. This is achieved by having teachers reflect on what content they deem to be critical for students to learn, how to optimally organize that content, and how to present the content in such a way that students become actively engaged in learning and exploring complex concepts.

Recognizing that academic interventions alone are not sufficient for student success, SIM also includes components that help students create and participate in productive learning communities, develop appropriate social skills, advocate for themselves and their needs in education conferences, envision positive futures for themselves, and plan how to reach their goals.

SIM is ideally implemented and most effective for students and for whole schools when teachers are afforded sufficient time to plan what and how they are going to teach in a strategic fashion. Teachers must have an opportunity to work with other teachers to coordinate instruction across classes and settings to ensure that critical strategies and behaviors are prompted and reinforced. SIM holds that significant change for students or schools occurs only when teachers are armed with numerous interventions to meet students' diverse needs. SIM encourages general education teachers and specialists to work together to supplement one another's knowledge to promote learning for all students and encourages administrators to play vital roles in SIM implementation. SIM's ultimate goal is to improve adolescent literacy achievement while continuing to offer students of all levels of literacy achievement the same challenging content and curricula.

Professional Development

SIM offers professional development courses for educators of all levels. Professional development institutes occur during the summer months, and certified SIM instructors are available to work with individual schools, districts, or groups of teachers year-round. In addition to professional development opportunities, a variety of materials are available to support teachers, including computer programs and planning tools.

Program Evaluation

SIM has undergone more than 25 years of research and development. During this time, information and research has been published on the program and its components. Among the most recently published studies is evidence that specific content enhancement routines lead to better content knowledge in all students (Bulgren, Deshler, Schumaker, & Lenz, 2000; Bulgren, Lenz, Schumaker, Deshler, & Marquis, 2002) and evidence that specific aspects of the Learning Strategies Curriculum lead to better reading and writing skills among struggling and disabled students (Hock, Pulvers, Deshler, & Schumaker, 2001; Hughes, Ruhl, Schumaker, & Deshler, 2002). Although the program was designed for secondary schools, it has been implemented successfully with middle school teachers as well (Boudah, Deshler, Schumaker, Lenz, & Cook, 1997).

The Florida Center on Reading Research completed an independent evaluation of SIM research in 2006. In addition, a randomized controlled study of the reading interventions of SIM is being carried out by an external evaluator beginning in 2005. This evaluation is funded by the Institute for Education Sciences through a contract to MRDC and American Institutes for Research on the effects. The purpose of this independent evaluation is to determine the effects of SIM as a supplemental literacy program for ninth-grade students.

Contact Information

Address: University of Kansas
Center for Research on Learning
1122 West Campus Road, Room 517
Joseph R. Pearson Hall
Lawrence, KS 66045-3101

Phone: 785-864-4780

E-mail: crl@ku.edu

Website: www.kucrl.org/sim/index.html

Sources

Boudah, D.J., Deshler, D.D., Schumaker, J.B., Lenz, B.K., & Cook, B. (1997). Student-centered or content-centered?: A case study of a middle school teacher's lesson planning and instruction in inclusive classes. *Teacher Education and Special Education*, 20(3), 189–203.

Bulgren, J. (2004). Effective content-area instruction for all students. In T.E. Scruggs & M.A. Mastropieri (Eds.), *Advances in learning and behavioral disabilities: Vol. 17. Research in secondary schools* (pp. 147–174). San Diego, CA: Elsevier.

Bulgren, J.A., Deshler, D.D., & Schumaker, J.B. (1997). Use of a recall enhancement routine and strategies in inclusive secondary classes. *Learning Disabilities Research & Practice*, 12(4), 198–208.

Bulgren, J.A., Deshler, D.D., Schumaker, J.F. & Lenz, B.K. (2000). The use and effectiveness of analogical instruction in diverse secondary content classrooms. *Journal of Educational Psychology*, 92(3), 426–441.

Bulgren, J.A., Hock, M.F., Schumaker, J.B., & Deshler, D.D. (1995). The effects of instruction in a paired associates strategy on the information mastery performance of students with learning disabilities. *Learning Disabilities Research and Practice*, 10(1), 22–37.

Bulgren, J.A., Lenz, B.K., Schumaker, J.F., Deshler, D.D., & Marquis, J.G. (2002). The use and effectiveness of a comparison routine in diverse secondary content classrooms. *Journal of Educational Psychology*, 94(2), 356–371.

Bulgren, J.A., Schumaker, J.B., & Deshler, D.D. (1988). Effectiveness of a concept teaching routine in enhancing the performance of LD students in secondary-level mainstream classes. *Learning Disability Quarterly*, 11(1), 3–17.

Bulgren, J.A., Schumaker, J.B., & Deshler, D.D. (1994). The effects of a recall enhancement routine on the test performance of secondary students with and without learning disabilities. *Learning Disabilities Research and Practice*, 9(1), 2–11.

Center for Research on Learning. (2001). *Strategic Instruction Model: Learning strategies and teaching routines*. Lawrence, KS: University of Kansas.

Clark, F.L., Deshler, D.D., Schumaker, J.B., Alley, G.R., & Warner, M.M. (1984). Visual imagery and self-questioning: Strategies to improve comprehension of written material. *Journal of Learning Disabilities*, 17(3), 145–149.

Deshler, D.D., Schumaker, J.B., Lenz, B.K., Bulgren, J.A., Hock, M.F., Knight, J., et al. (2001). Ensuring content-area learning by secondary students with learning disabilities. *Learning Disabilities Research and Practice*, 16(2), 96–108.

Deshler, D.D., Schumaker, J.B., & Woodruff, S.K. (2004). Improving literacy skills of at-risk adolescents: A schoolwide response. In D.S. Strickland & D.E. Alvermann (Eds.), *Bridging the literacy achievement gap grades 4–12* (pp. 86–104). New York: Teachers College Press.

Duchardt, B.A., Deshler, D.D., & Schumaker, J.B. (1995). A strategic intervention for enabling students with learning disabilities to identify and change their ineffective beliefs. *Learning Disability Quarterly*, 18(3), 186–201.

Ehren, B.J., Lenz, B.K., & Deshler, D.D. (2004). Enhancing literacy proficiency with adolescents and young adults. In C.A. Stone, E.R. Silliman, B.J. Ehren, & K. Apel (Eds.), *Handbook of language and literacy development and disorders* (pp. 681–701). New York: Guilford.

Ellis, E.S., Deshler, D.D., & Schumaker, J.B., (1989). Teaching adolescents with learning disabilities to generate and use task-specific strategies. *Journal of Learning Disabilities*, 22(2), 108–119, 130.

Florida Center for Reading Research. (2006). *Strategic Instruction Model (SIM) and Content Literacy Continuum (CLC)*. Tallahassee, FL: Author. Retrieved January 15, 2007, from http://www.fcrr.org/FCRR Reports/PDF/SIMR.pdf

Hock, M.F., & Deshler, D.D. (2003). Don't forget the adolescents. *Principal Leadership*, 4(3), 50–56.

Hock, M.F., Pulvers, K.A., Deshler, D.D., & Schumaker, J.B. (2001). The effects of an after-school tutoring program on the academic performance of at-risk students and students with LD. *Remedial and Special Education, 22*(3), 172–186.

Hughes, C.A., Ruhl, K.L., Schumaker, J.B., & Deshler, D.D. (2002). Effects of instruction in an assignment completion strategy on the homework performance of students with learning disabilities in general education classes. *Learning Disabilities: Research and Practice, 17*(1), 1–18.

Lenz, B.K., & Hughes, C.A. (1990). A word identification strategy for adolescents with learning disabilities. *Journal of Learning Disabilities, 23*(3), 149–158, 163.

Rademacher, J.A., Schumaker, J.B., & Deshler, D.D. (1996). Development and validation of a classroom assignment routine for inclusive settings. *Learning Disability Quarterly, 19*(3), 163–178.

Rademacher, J., Tyler-Wood, T., Doclar, J., & Pemberton, J. (2001). Developing learner-centered technology assignments with student teachers. *Journal of Computing in Teacher Education, 17*(3), 18–25.

Scanlon, D., Deshler, D.D., & Schumaker, J.B. (1996). Can a strategy be taught and learned in secondary inclusive classrooms? *Learning Disabilities Research & Practice, 11*(1), 41–57.

Schumaker, J.B., & Deshler, D.D. (2003, Spring). Can students with LD become competent writers? *Learning Disability Quarterly, 26*, 129–141.

Schumaker, J.B., Deshler, D.D., Alley, G.R., Warner, M.M., & Denton, P.H. (1982). Multipass: A learning strategy for improving reading comprehension. *Learning Disability Quarterly, 5*(3), 295–304.

Swanson, H.L., & Deshler, D.D. (2003). Instructing adolescents with learning disabilities: Converting a meta-analysis to practice. *Journal of Learning Disabilities, 36*(2), 124–135.

SUCCESS FOR ALL

Instructional Approach

Success for All (SFA) is a comprehensive, schoolwide reform model designed specifically to serve students at risk for academic difficulties. The program has elementary and middle school versions. The SFA program includes curricular change and professional development, as well as organizational changes. Organizational and structural changes for the elementary school version of SFA include a family support program and a 90-minute schoolwide literacy block. During the literacy block, students are grouped across grade boundaries into ability-based classes that maintain an especially low student–teacher ratio. The middle school version requires at least a 60-minute literacy block and does not necessarily include the cross-grade grouping of the elementary version.

The SFA curriculum emphasizes cooperative learning activities, partner reading, story structure, summarization, writing, vocabulary, and direct instruction in reading comprehension skills. At all levels, students read self-chosen books for 20 minutes nightly for homework. Students are assessed every eight weeks to track progress and inform regrouping. Students are also identified in this manner for one-on-one tutoring support. Materials provided include teacher manuals, reproducible instructional materials, and lesson plans. SFA also has a bilingual program with Spanish-language materials for grades 1–5, called *Exitos para Todos*.

Professional Development

Professional development for all faculty, including administrators, is required for SFA implementation. Teachers receive three days of training before instruction begins, and SFA consultants visit SFA schools three times annually for two days. Implementation of SFA also requires a full-time SFA facilitator to ensure smooth running of the program. These facilitators receive extensive training, act as on-site, follow-up trainers, and offer ongoing support in the form of coaching, classroom visits, and meetings. SFA consultants are also available for additional support by phone during the academic year.

Program Evaluation

SFA has undergone intense scrutiny in the field. Its creators have published extensively on its effects (Hurley, Chamberlain, Slavin, & Madden, 2001; Slavin, 2000, 2002; Slavin & Cheung, 2003; Slavin & Madden, 2000, 2001, 2003). These reports and studies support the claim that SFA yields better reading achievement among at-risk students than comparison programs. At least one independent evaluation of long-term SFA outcomes showed that SFA students completed eighth grade with better achievement, fewer special education placements, and fewer retentions than comparison programs with the same educational expense (Borman & Hewes, 2002). The SFA website also offers a listing of independent reviews of its effectiveness (Success for All Foundation, 2003). However, some contend that SFA's results do not show consistent benefits and that students in SFA do not end up reading on grade level (Pogrow, 2000, 2002; Walberg & Greenberg, 1999a, 1999b). Independent analyses comparing schoolwide reform models have shown positive results, but the size of impact has varied (Borman, Hewes, Overman, & Brown, 2003; Legters, Balfanz, & McPartland, 2002; Mason, 2005). The Florida Center for Reading Research has also conducted an independent review of the program, but it has only done so for grades K–3.

Contact Information

Address: Success for All Foundation
200 West Towsontown Boulevard
Baltimore, MD 21204-5200
Phone: 800-548-4998
E-mail: sfainfo@successforall.net
Website: www.successforall.com

Sources

Borman, G., & Hewes, G. (2002). The long-term effects and cost-effectiveness of Success for All. *Educational Evaluation and Policy Analysis, 24*(4), 243–266.

Borman, G.D., Hewes, G.M., Overman, L.T., & Brown, S. (2003). Comprehensive school reform and achievement: A meta-analysis. *Review of Educational Research, 73,* 125–230.

Borman, G., Slavin, R.E., Cheung, A., Chamberlain, A., Madden, N.A., & Chambers, B. (2005a). The national randomized field trial of Success for All: Second-year outcomes. *American Educational Research Journal, 42*(4), 673–696.

Borman, G., Slavin, R.E., Cheung, A., Chamberlain, A., Madden, N.A., & Chambers, B. (2005b). Success for All: First year results from the national randomized field trial. *Educational Evaluation and Policy Analysis, 27*(1), 1–22.

Chambers, B., Cheung, A., Madden, N., Slavin, R.E., & Gifford, R. (2006). Achievement effects of embedded multimedia in a Success for All reading program. *Journal of Educational Psychology, 98*(1), 232–237.

Cheung, A., & Slavin, R.E. (2005). Effective reading programs for English language learners and other language minority students. *Bilingual Research Journal, 29*(2), 241–267.

Daniels, C., Madden, N.A., & Slavin, R.E. (2005). The Success for All middle school: Adding content to middle grades reform. *Middle School Journal.*

Datnow, A., & Castellano, M. (2000). Teachers' responses to Success for All: How beliefs, experiences, and adaptations shape implementation. *American Educational Research Journal, 37*(3), 775–799.

Hurley, E.A., Chamberlain, A., Slavin, R.E., & Madden, N.A. (2001). Effects of Success for All on TAAS Reading: A Texas statewide evaluation. *Phi Delta Kappan, 82*(10), 750–756.

Madden, N.A., Slavin, R.E., Karweit, N.L., Dolan, L.J., & Wasik, B.A. (1993). Success for All: Longitudinal effects of a restructuring program for inner-city elementary schools. *American Educational Research Journal, 30,* 123–148.

Mason, B. (2005). *Achievement effects of five comprehensive school reform designs implemented in Los Angeles Unified School District.* Santa Monica, CA: Pardee RAND Graduate School.

Muñoz, M.A., & Dossett, D. (2004). Educating students placed at risk: Evaluating the impact of Success for All in urban settings. *Journal of Education for Students Placed at Risk, 9*(3), 261–277.

Pikulski, J.J. (1994). Preventing reading failure: A review of five effective programs. *The Reading Teacher, 48*(1), 30–39.

Pogrow, S. (2000). Success for All does not produce success for students. *Phi Delta Kappan, 82*(1), 67–80.

Pogrow, S. (2002). Success for All is a failure. *Phi Delta Kappan, 83*(6), 463–468.

Sanders, W.L., Wright, S.P., Ross, S.M., & Wang, L.W. (2000). *Value-added achievement results for three cohorts of Roots & Wings schools in Memphis: 1995–1999 outcomes.* Memphis, TN: University of Memphis, Center for Research in Education Policy.

Slavin, R.E. (2000). Research overwhelmingly supports Success for All [letter to the editor]. *Phi Delta Kappan, 81*(7), 559–560.

Slavin, R.E. (2002). Mounting evidence supports the achievement effects of Success for All. *Phi Delta Kappan, 83*(6), 469–472.

Slavin, R.E. (2006). *Success for All and academically talented students.* Baltimore, MD: Center for Data-Driven Reform in Education, Johns Hopkins University.

Slavin, R.E., & Cheung, A. (2003). *Effective reading programs for English language learners: A best-evidence synthesis.* Baltimore, MD: Johns Hopkins University, Center for Research on the Education of Students Placed at Risk.

Slavin, R.E., & Madden, N.A. (1999). Effects of bilingual and English as a second language adaptations of Success for All on the reading achievement of students acquiring English. *Journal of Education for Students Placed at Risk, 4*(4), 393–416.

Slavin, R.E., & Madden, N.A. (2000). Research on achievement outcomes of Success for All: A summary and response to critics. *Phi Delta Kappan, 82*(1), 38–40, 59–66.

Slavin, R.E., & Madden, N.A. (2001, April). *Reducing the gap: Success for All and the achievement of African-American and Latino students.* Paper presented at the annual meeting of the American Educational Research Association, Seattle, WA.

Slavin, R.E., & Madden, N.A. (2003). *Success for All/Roots & Wings: 2003 summary of research on achievement outcomes.* Baltimore, MD: Johns Hopkins University, Center for Research on the Education of Students Placed at Risk.

Slavin, R.E., & Madden, N.A. (2006). *Success for All: Summary of research on achievement outcomes* (Revised). Baltimore, MD: Johns Hopkins University, Center for Data-Driven Reform in Education.

Success for All Foundation. (n.d.). *Research.* Towson, MD: Author. Retrieved June 16, 2004, from http://www.successforall.com/resource/researchpub.htm

Success for All Foundation. (2003). *Independent reviews support achievement effects of Success for All: Success for All's strong research base recognized in comparative studies.* Towson, MD: Author. Retrieved June 16, 2004, from http://www.successforall.com/resource/PDFs/410054000_IndependReviews.pdf

Talley, S., & Martinez, D.H. (1998). *Tools for schools: School reform models supported by the National Institute on the Education of At-Risk Students.* Washington, DC: U.S. Department of Education, Office of Educational Research and Improvement.

Walberg, H.J., & Greenberg, R.C. (1999a). The Diogenes factor. *Phi Delta Kappan, 81*(2), 127–128.

Walberg, H.J., & Greenberg, R.C. (1999b). Educators should require evidence. *Phi Delta Kappan, 81*(2), 132–135.

TALENT DEVELOPMENT HIGH SCHOOLS

Instructional Approach

Talent Development High Schools (TDHS) is a comprehensive school reform model for use in middle and high schools predominantly serving at-risk students. A primary goal of the program is to reduce the dropout rate by increasing motivation and this is the focus for curriculum across the content areas. The model also involves implementing changes in school organization, some of which relate to literacy instruction. The literacy curriculum of TDHS is called Strategic Reading, which includes Student Team Literature.

The innovations of the Strategic Reading approach include 90-minute literacy classes, a ninth-grade academy with intensive focus on reading instruction, and a literacy lab for students who are two or more years behind grade level in reading. The 90-minute literacy block in the ninth grade is designed around the premise that reading improves as a result of increased exposure and experience with text of all kinds made up of four components: The first is a 20-minute "reading showcase" in which teachers read aloud to students and model an internal monologue by asking before-, during-, and after-reading questions. The second is a 20-minute "focus lesson" in which teachers offer direct instruction and modeling of a skill or concept that the students will use in independent practice. The third is a 30-minute study of preselected literature by small student teams, in which there is discussion of provided comprehension questions. Teachers prepare the class for the shared reading with relevant background knowledge and vocabulary development. The final 20-minute segment is for students to work independently at workstations on either creative writing and publishing, silent reading, information retrieval, or word games. Complete lessons that follow this sequence are provided to teachers throughout the term.

Literacy support is provided to students who are reading at two or more years below grade level through a literacy lab. Past ninth grade, all students participate in specialized courses like College Prep Reading and Writing and Reading and Writing in Your Career, which are designed to be especially engaging for at-risk students. Assessment is also an important piece of the program. Student performance is measured through standardized testing, and informational teacher assessment is used to measure student progress and determine progress throughout the remainder of the program.

Professional Development

There is a process for becoming a TDHS school. After a school or district has determined that TDHS is a good match for their school(s), the TDHS management team determines whether the school or district has the resources necessary to implement the model at the school in question. Next the school(s) enters into a long-term contract with TDHS in which the school agrees to attend national conferences and institutes and commits to a full year of planning for the implementation of the program in the following year. The model costs US$300 per student to implement fully, which covers the cost of 3.5 coaching staff per school, curriculum materials, and evaluation. In addition, schools must pay for training stipends, additional books and supplies, and the extra teachers required for implementing a block schedule.

Program Evaluation

To date, program evaluation consists of a third-party longitudinal comparative study and several internally conducted analyses of participating schools. The third-party study reported significant improvement in student attendance, promotion, and course passing rates, as well as positive impacts on academic achievement for students with successive years in the TDHS program. Other studies also show improvement in the areas of student motivation, dropout rates, and student retention, including findings that students participating in a TDHS program have made significant gains in reading. Some of these measure gains in terms of passing grades and others measure progress on standardized achievement tests.

Contact Information

Address: Talent Development High Schools
           3003 North Charles Street
           Baltimore, MD 21218
Phone: 410-516-8800
E-mail: bhebron@csos.jhu.edu
Website: www.csos.jhu.edu/tdhs

Sources

American Institutes for Research. (1999). *An educators' guide to schoolwide reform*. Arlington, VA: Educational Research Service.

Balfanz, R., Legters, N., & Jordan, W. (2004). *Catching up: Impact of the Talent Development ninth grade instructional interventions in reading and mathematics in high-poverty schools*. Baltimore, MD: Center for Research on the Education of Students Placed at Risk.

Balfanz, R., & Mac Iver, D. (2000). Transforming high-poverty urban middle schools into strong learning institutions: Lessons from the first five years of the Talent Development middle school. *Journal of Education for Students Placed at Risk, 5*(1–2), 137–158.

Boykin, A.W. (2000). The Talent Development model of schooling: Placing students at promise for academic success. *Journal of Education for Students Placed at Risk, 5*(1–2), 3–25.

Herlihy, C.M., & Kemple, J.J. (2005). *The Talent Development middle school model: Context, components, and initial impacts on students' performance and attendance*. New York: Manpower Demonstration Research Corporation.

Jordan, W.J., McPartland, J.M., Legters, N.E., & Balfanz, R. (2000). Creating a comprehensive school reform model: The Talent Development high school with career academies. *Journal of Education for Students Placed at Risk, 5*(1–2), 159–181.

Kemple, J.J., & Herlihy, C.M. (2005). *The Talent Development high school model: Context, components, and initial impacts on ninth-grade students' performance and attendance*. New York: Manpower Demonstration Research Corporation.

Kemple, J.J., Herlihy, C.M., & Smith, T.J. (2005). *Making progress toward graduation: Evidence from the Talent Development high school model*. New York: Manpower Demonstration Research Corporation.

Killion, J. (1997). *What works in the middle: Results-based staff development*. Oxford, OH: National Staff Development Council.

Legters, N., Balfanz, R., & McPartland, J. (2002). *Solutions for failing high schools: Converging visions and promising models*. Washington, DC: Office of Vocational and Adult Education.

Mac Iver, D.J., Plank, S.B., & Balfanz, R. (1997). *Working together to become proficient readers: Early impact of the Talent Development middle school's Student Team Literature Program. Report no. 15*. Baltimore, MD: Center for Research on the Education of Students Placed at Risk.

McPartland, J.M. (1996). *The Talent Development high school: Early evidence of impact on school climate, attendance, and student promotion. Report no. 2*. Baltimore, MD: Center for Research on the Education of Students Placed at Risk.

McPartland, J., Balfanz, R., Jordan, W., & Legters, N. (1998). Improving climate and achievement in a troubled urban high school through the Talent Development model. *Journal of Education for Students Placed at Risk, 3*(4), 337–361.

McPartland, J., Jordan, W., Legters, N., & Balfanz, R. (1997). Finding safety in small numbers. *Educational Leadership, 55*(2), 14–17.

Plank, S.B., & Young, E. (2000). *Lessons for scaling up: Evaluations of the Talent Development middle school's Student Team Literature program*. Baltimore, MD: Center for Research on the Education of Students Placed at Risk.

Talley, S., & Martinez, D.H. (1998). *Tools for schools: School reform models supported by the National Institute on the Education of At-Risk Students*. Washington, DC: U.S. Department of Education, Office of Educational Research and Improvement.

Useem, E. (1998). *Teachers' appraisals of Talent Development middle school training, materials, and* student progress: *Results from focus groups. Report no. 25.* Baltimore, MD: Center for Research on the Education of Students Placed at Risk.

Useem, E., Neild, R.C., & Morrison, W. (2001). *Philadelphia's Talent Development high schools: Second-year results, 2000–01.* Philadelphia, PA: Philadelphia Education Fund.

THINKING READER

Instructional Approach

Thinking Reader is a computer-based software program designed to improve the reading comprehension of middle school students (grades 5–8) through improved strategy use and motivation. The program was designed by the Center for Applied Special Technologies and Tom Snyder Productions, a leading developer and publisher of educational technology for K–12 classrooms, in collaboration with Annemarie Palincsar. It embeds instruction, modeling, and practice of research-based reading comprehension strategies in authentic, unabridged, core grade-level literature, including *Roll of Thunder, Hear My Cry*; *Esperanza Rising*; *Dragonwings*; and *Tuck Everlasting.*

Using universal design learning technologies, such as text-to-speech software, the program enables students at a wide range of reading levels to read the same text. Other supports include a contextual glossary, with Spanish translations for English-language learners, and universal accessibility features such as adjustable font size, alternative color contrast settings, and keyboard navigation. These supports give students with learning disabilities and limited decoding skills access to the same literature that their peers are reading.

At set points throughout the books, students are prompted to use seven reading comprehension strategies: summarizing, questioning, clarifying, predicting, visualizing, feeling, and reflecting. By clicking on icons, students can remind themselves of what the strategies are and how to use them in general, and they can solicit hints and model answers from animated characters. The models provide students with information about what the character was thinking as well as how the character actually expressed this thinking in his or her answer. These practice opportunities are scaffolded in that teachers can choose among five levels of support that the animated characters can give students. The highest level of support offers students closed-ended questions, whereas the lowest level of support requires students to choose which strategy to use and uses open-response formats. Teachers are able to individualize and adjust student support based on built-in assessments and monitoring systems, as well as teacher-student conferences and classroom observations.

The program is designed to supplement rather than replace classroom instruction. It can be used in a whole-class format as well as in a resource room or literacy lab. Teachers introduce texts and strategies through their normal instructional means, and then students practice strategies and receive further examples and support through the software. Beyond the software, materials include several copies of each novel, a research guide, and a teacher guide that includes reproducible resources. These resources include a Strategy Journal designed for students to use with other texts in order to promote transfer of the strategies to other texts and contexts.

Professional Development

The program is available for purchase without professional development; however, the publisher advocates strongly for the importance of adequate training both in using the program and in reading comprehension strategy instruction. A one-day training workshop covering these topics and classroom management is offered, as are customized training workshops that are adjusted to the purchaser's needs.

Program Evaluation

In a federally funded study, the Center for Applied Special Technology (CAST) evaluated Thinking Reader with students performing below the 25th percentile in reading. After controlling for pretest scores on comprehension and vocabulary, students who used Thinking Reader demonstrated significantly higher gains in comprehension on the test than their peers in a traditional strategy instruction condition. Further studies of the program have not been completed. The Florida Center for Reading Research (2005) has conducted an independent review of the program for grades 6–8.

Contact Information

Address: Tom Snyder Productions
           80 Coolidge Hill Road
           Watertown, MA 02472-5003
Phone: 800-342-0236
E-mail: ask@tomsnyder.com
Website: http://tomsnyder.com/products/product.asp?SKU=THITHI

Sources

Florida Center for Reading Research. (2005, February). *Thinking Reader*. Tallahassee, FL: Author. Retrieved January 15, 2007, from http://www.fcrr.org/FCRR Reports/PDF/ThinkingReaderFinal.pdf

Tom Snyder Productions. (2005). *The research base and evidence of effectiveness for Thinking Reader: Research foundation paper*. Watertown, MA: Author. Retrieved from http://www.tomsnyder.com/reports/TR_White_Paper.pdf

Instructional Approach

Transactional Strategies Instruction (TSI) was developed by the educators at the Benchmark School and in several Maryland county school districts as a more flexible form of comprehension strategies instruction. It has been documented and validated by Michael Pressley and his colleagues (Pressley et al., 1992). As such, TSI is often a component of more comprehensive reading programs (e.g., Project CRISS; see preceding description) and exists in multiple educator-influenced versions (e.g., Students Achieving Independent Learning [SAIL]; Brown, Pressley, Van Meter, & Schuder, 1996). Its flexibility makes it appropriate in small-group or whole-class situations, as well as for use with struggling and learning-disabled students.

TSI is designed to improve reading comprehension by giving students explicit comprehension strategies and developing metacognition. It further is intended to develop the background knowledge and student motivation that promote engaged and effective reading, thereby ensuring use of the strategies and metacognitive stance taught. TSI reading comprehension instruction emphasizes constant student transactions with text where strategies serve as a conduit for the transaction. The strategies teachers use in their instruction vary, but the focus on instrumentality does not.

In this model, teachers explicitly explain, discuss, and model one or more strategies with their classes, often on a daily basis. Students also explain and model strategies, promoting their metacognition and coordinated use of strategies. Teachers act as comprehension coaches during group discussion, promoting student elaboration and explanation (rather than the more traditional teacher initiation and evaluation of student responses). Through various reinforcement techniques, such as attributing student success to effective strategy use, teachers send the message that thoughtfulness about reading is what is valued, rather than right or wrong answers.

Professional Development

TSI is unique in that it has no rigid curriculum or framework and was designed by educators interested in finding more flexible ways to implement comprehension strategies instruction in day-to-day classroom instruction than were offered by researchers (Schuder, 1993). Because transactional strategies instruction is a way of teaching students to become strategic readers, it focuses less on specific strategies and can vary from school to school, and even classroom to classroom.

The most developed version of TSI is SAIL, which is described in various journal articles and presentations. Two articles in an issue of *The Elementary School Journal* include the most extensive description of TSI and SAIL. The analysis of SAIL's genesis from teacher problem-solving gives the best outline of a process by which TSI can be incorporated simultaneously into professional development and curriculum redevelopment (El-Dinary & Schuder, 1994; Schuder, 1993). Another, more general description of how TSI might be implemented is also available and includes examples of appropriate strategies for instruction and suggestions for evaluation of TSI implementation (Casteel, Isom, & Jordan, 2000).

Program Evaluation

TSI has undergone a number of quasi-experimental validations. In one study, students in five second-grade classrooms using SAIL demonstrated better strategy awareness, strategy use, recall of informational reading, and performance on standardized reading tests than did children in five comparison classrooms in the same district receiving traditional reading instruction (Brown, Pressley, Van Meter, & Schuder, 1996).

In a crosscase analysis evaluating teacher reactions to using TSI in grades 1, 3, 4, and 6 teachers appreciated the positive interactions with texts that TSI promoted, its student orientation, and its emphasis on thinking and comprehension (El-Dinary & Schuder, 1993). At the same time, they perceived that it did not emphasize vocabulary enough, did not address decoding adequately, and required substantial time for students to work through a text.

Research on TSI's effectiveness in higher grades has also been conducted. In one study, professional development in TSI for special education teachers serving severely reading-delayed 6th- through 11th-grade students was found to substantially change both teacher and student behaviors during reading instruction, while comparison teachers and students did not change their behaviors during reading instruction (Anderson, 1992). These changes were marked by increased student talk, decreased teacher talk, and greater teacher flexibility. In addition, while both control and experimental groups made substantial improvements on standardized tests, the experimental group made larger gains in reading comprehension.

Contact Information

Address: Literacy Achievement Research Center
Michigan State University
Erickson Hall
East Lansing, MI 48824

Phone: no phone
E-mail: no e-mail
Website: www.msularc.org

Sources

Anderson, V. (1992). A teacher development project in transactional strategy instruction for teachers of severely reading-disabled adolescents. *Teaching and Teacher Education*, 8, 391–403.

Brown, R., Pressley, M., Van Meter, P., & Schuder, T. (1996). A quasi-experimental validation of transactional strategies instruction with low-achieving second-grade readers. *Journal of Educational Psychology*, 88(1), 18–37.

Casteel, C.P., Isom, B.A., & Jordan, K.F. (2000). Creating confident and competent readers: Transactional strategies instruction. *Intervention in School and Clinic, 36*(2), 67–74.

Collins, C. (1991). Reading instruction that increases thinking abilities. *Journal of Reading, 34*, 510–516.

El-Dinary, P.B., & Schuder, T. (1993). Seven teachers' acceptance of transactional strategies instruction during their first year using it. *The Elementary School Journal, 94*(2), 207–219.

Loranger, A.L. (1997). Comprehension strategies instruction: Does it make a difference? *Reading Psychology, 18*(1), 31–68.

Pressley, M. (1994). Transactional instruction of comprehension strategies: The Montgomery County, Maryland, SAIL program. *Reading and Writing Quarterly: Overcoming Learning Difficulties, 10*(1), 5–19.

Pressley, M., El-Dinary, P.B., Gaskins, I., Schuder, T., Bergman, J.L., Almasi, J., et al. (1992). Beyond direct explanation: Transactional instruction of reading comprehension strategies. *The Elementary School Journal, 92*(5), 513–555.

Pressley, M., Schuder, T., Bergman, J., & El-Dinary, P.B. (1992). Teachers in the Students Achieving Independent Learning program: A researcher-educator collaborative interview study of transactional comprehension strategies instruction. *Journal of Educational Psychology, 84*(2), 231–246.

Pressley, M., & Wharton-McDonald, R. (1997). Skilled comprehension and its development through instruction. *School Psychology Review, 26*(3), 448–466.

Schuder, T. (1993). The genesis of transactional strategies instruction in a reading program for at-risk students. *The Elementary School Journal, 94*(2), 183–200.

VOCABULARY IMPROVEMENT PROGRAM

Instructional Approach

The full name of the Vocabulary Improvement Program (VIP) is the Vocabulary Improvement Program for English Language Learners and their Classmates. As its name implies, the program was designed with the vocabulary learning of English-language learners (ELLs) in mind. The program was designed via longitudinal research by Teresa Lively, Diane August, Maria Carlo, and Catherine Snow, among others. VIP targets fourth-, fifth-, and sixth-grade students. The curriculum is designed to provide activities, materials, and scripts that allow all teachers to support their Spanish-speaking ELLs, as well as their native English-speaking students, in the acquisition of specific academic vocabulary and strategies for learning unfamiliar words.

Each grade level of VIP provides teachers with an 18-week curriculum designed to be delivered in 30-minute daily lessons. Each curriculum is divided into eight units, each of which lasts two weeks and relates to an authentic text. Two separate weeks are spent in review of previously taught vocabulary and word-analysis strategies, which are reinforced through engagement in new activities. Strategies taught include inferring meaning from context, from morphology, and from cognates, which are words that have similar spellings and meanings in two languages. The latter is a support targeted to Spanish-speaking ELLs, and an additional support is that taught words are defined in both English and Spanish. Activities are designed to engage students in cooperative work, give students multiple encounters with targeted words, and build word consciousness in a rich language atmosphere.

All necessary materials, including books, assessments, and a teacher's guide, are included with the curriculum. The curriculum for each grade uses a variety of genres to explore thematically related issues such as immigration. Texts include books by children's authors (e.g., Kathryn Lasky, Russell Freedman, and Janet Bode), and newspaper articles from *The New York Times*, as well as diaries and other expository texts. Vocabulary cards illustrate key curriculum words and also provide teachers with multiple definitions and bilingual Spanish–English supports.

Professional Development

Professional development for VIP is not available; however, the teacher's guide is explicit about goals and underlying theories and gives teachers step-by-step instructions for implementing the entire curriculum.

Program Evaluation

Most recently, VIP has been evaluated in a longitudinal study of fifth-grade students. Students receiving VIP instruction showed greater growth than a comparison group in knowledge of taught words, depth of vocabulary knowledge, understanding of multiple meanings for words, and reading comprehension. ELL and native English-speaking students received instruction in heterogeneous classrooms, and ELLs benefited as much as their native English-speaking peers.

VIP was also evaluated in a cross-sectional and longitudinal study of fourth graders in three states over three years. Results demonstrated that when students received the curriculum in fourth and fifth grade, they outperformed similar students in the same school on measures of depth and breadth of vocabulary knowledge over those who received the curriculum for only a year. Both groups improved their reading comprehension but did not differ significantly in their improvement. Finally, ELLs who received two years of instruction benefited more than their English-speaking peers, in effect closing the achievement gap by about half. In contrast, ELLs who received only one year of instruction did benefit from the curriculum, but not more than their English-speaking peers.

Contact Information

Address: Brookes Publishing Co.
           Customer Service Department
           PO Box 10624
           Baltimore, MD 21285-0624
Phone: 800-638-3775
E-mail: custserv@brookespublishing.com
Website: www.brookespublishing.com/store/books/lively-6342/index.htm

Sources

August, D., Carlo, M.S., Lively, T.J., McLaughlin, B., & Snow, C.E. (2006). Promoting the vocabulary growth of English learners. In T.A. Young & N.L. Hadaway (Eds.), *Supporting the literacy development of* *English learners* (pp. 96–107). Newark, DE: International Reading Association.

Carlo, M.S., August, D., McLaughlin, B., Snow, C.E., Dressler, C., Lippman, D.N., et al. (2004). Closing the gap: Addressing the vocabulary needs of English language learners in bilingual and mainstream classrooms. *Reading Research Quarterly, 39*, 188–215.

Carlo, M.S., August, D., & Snow, C. (2005). Sustained vocabulary-learning strategy instruction for English language learners. In E. Hiebert & M. Kamil (Eds.), *Teaching and learning vocabulary: Bringing research to practice* (pp. 137–153). Mahwah, NJ: Erlbaum.

White, C.E. (2001). *Implementation of a vocabulary curriculum designed for second language learners: Knowledge bases and strategies used by monolingual and bilingual teachers.* Unpublished doctoral qualifying paper, Harvard University, Graduate School of Education, Boston, MA.

VOYAGER TIMEWARP PLUS

Instructional Approach

Voyager TimeWarp Plus is an intervention curriculum intended for struggling readers in kindergarten through grade 9 in extended time settings. It provides daily lesson plans with a predictable instructional routine intended to reduce preparation time for after-school teachers. It includes formal and informal assessments so that teachers can match instruction to students needs. Typically, school districts implement the program during the summer months, but some districts use the TimeWarp Plus series in intercessions year-round, Saturday academies, and after-school settings.

Lessons are flexible and can run anywhere from two to four hours daily. TimeWarp Plus offers strategic instruction in five components of reading (phonemic awareness, phonics, fluency, vocabulary, and comprehension), as well as writing. Students participate in a combination of whole-group and small-group activities designed to move students to grade-level proficiency. The four-week series works as an intervention to help struggling readers avoid summer learning loss and master critical reading skills.

Although each of the grade-level curricula covers a wide range of reading and language arts skills, the curriculum also concentrates on specific engaging themes. Each curriculum comes with a library of multiple copies of authentic children's fiction and nonfiction literature, as well as theme-based magazines, student anthologies, and materials for hands-on collaborative activities. For example, in the fourth-grade curriculum students read about and explore ancient Greece. The sixth-grade curriculum focuses on problem solving in a variety of contexts, offers opportunities for students to explore the ancient civilization of China, and introduces critical literacy skills. Finally, the eighth and ninth grades are addressed in a single curriculum that focuses on Native American civilizations and culture and extends content area and critical literacy skills and knowledge.

Voyager also offers several other curricular options, including Voyager Extended Day, Voyager Universal Literacy System, and the Voyager Passport series. Like TimeWarp Plus, Voyager Extended Day is intended for use in out-of-school settings but is designed specifically for use during the school year in after-school hours.

Professional Development

Voyager provides one day of training for the TimeWarp Plus curricula; however, ongoing professional development is available through the company's website and through phone support.

Program Evaluation

Scientific evaluations of the effects of the TimeWarp Plus curricula have been conducted with students at all grade levels in a summer setting. Researchers have documented improved performance on the Voyager Reading Intervention Test and the Stanford Diagnostic Reading Test for a four-week summer program. Comparison groups were not used in these studies; however, effect sizes were calculated using pre- and posttest scores. Effects sizes ranged from .27 to .75, which were considered educationally significant for summer school programs. Numerous study summaries are available on the Voyager website under the tab "Evidence of Effectiveness." These studies have been conducted in Kentucky, Wisconsin, Michigan, Massachusetts, and New York. One independent evaluation by the Wake County Public School System (Paeplow, Baenen, & Banks, 2002) found that students receiving the TimeWarp curriculum on average improved their reading achievement the same as students from the prior year who received a more traditional summer school curriculum, except in middle school grades where students in the traditional curriculum improved significantly more. The Florida Center for Reading Research has completed a review of the Passport program and Universal Literacy System, but it has not conducted an independent review of the TimeWarp program.

Contact Information

Address: Voyager Expanded Learning, L.P.
             1800 Valley View Lane, Suite 400
             Dallas, TX 75234
Phone: 888-399-1995
E-mail: jnowakowski@voyagerlearning.com
Website: www.voyagerlearning.com

Sources

Dossett, D. (1999). *Implementation evaluation—Voyager.* Louisville, KY: Jefferson County Public Schools.

Evaluation Research Services. (1999). *Independent impact study: Rising Stars students in Louisville (KY) make educationally significant gains in reading.* Dallas, TX: Voyager Expanded Learning.

Evaluation Research Services. (2001a). *Independent impact study: Green Bay (WI) students improve reading skills during the summer with Voyager.* Dallas, TX: Voyager Expanded Learning.

Evaluation Research Services. (2001b). *Independent impact study: Hamtramck (MI) students improve reading skills during the summer with Voyager.* Dallas, TX: Voyager Expanded Learning.

Evaluation Research Services. (2001c). *Independent impact study: Lawrence (MA) students improve reading skills during the summer with Voyager.* Dallas, TX: Voyager Expanded Learning.

Evaluation Research Services. (2001d). *Independent impact study: New York City (NY) students improve reading skills during the summer with Voyager.* Dallas, TX: Voyager Expanded Learning.

Evaluation Research Services. (2002a). *Independent impact study: Brooklyn (NY) students make comprehension*

gains with Voyager. Dallas, TX: Voyager Expanded
Learning.

Evaluation Research Services. (2002b). *Independent impact study: New York City (NY) students improve reading scores with Voyager summer intervention.* Dallas, TX: Voyager Expanded Learning.

Paeplow, C.G., Baenen, N.R., & Banks, K.E. (2002). *Voyager Summer Academy—2002 results* (E&R Rep. No. 03.02). Raleigh, NC: Wake County Public School System, Department of Evaluation and Research. Retrieved from http://www.wcpss.net/evaluation-research/reports/2002/0302_voyager.pdf

Roberts, G. (2000, September). *Technical evaluation report on the impact of Voyager summer programs.* Austin, TX: University of Texas.

WILSON READING SYSTEM

Instructional Approach

The Wilson Reading System follows the Orton multisensory approach and was designed to teach adult dyslexics to read. Thus the program is for use with secondary students with severe decoding and spelling difficulties. Students are placed in the program based on their performance on an individualized assessment, which is part of the program and lessons. The program consists of systematic, sequential, and intensive phonics instruction, which is recommended to take place at least two times per week. Instruction should take place individually or in very small groups of students with similar levels of reading performance.

Professional Development

Professional development is not required, and teachers may implement the program simply with the help of an instructor's manual. However, Wilson does offer several options for training: Wilson certified trainers are available to conduct two-day workshops overviewing the curriculum. Wilson also has an online academy, which provides professional development courses, resources, and networking opportunities. College credit is available for teachers participating in Wilson courses. In addition, series of six hour-long videotapes are available, including an overview training workshop. Teachers may also attend intensive training to become a Wilson certified instructor/trainer.

Program Evaluation

There are multiple studies documenting the success of the Wilson Reading System for use with dyslexic or reading-disabled students and/or struggling older readers. In addition to the references listed below, the Wilson Reading System Website lists several references outlining scholarly monographs and state reading initiatives, which support the efficacy of the program as well as internal evaluations and ongoing research studies of the Wilson Reading System. The Wilson Reading System is also one of four intervention programs under evaluation by the Power4Kids Research Initiative in a randomized experiment (as noted on the Spell Read P.A.T. website, www.spellread.com/a/publish/

evidence.shtml, on January 27, 2007). The study will compare the programs in terms of impact, fidelity of treatment, neurological effects, and cost-effectiveness. The Florida Center for Reading Research (2006) has also conducted an independent review of the program.

Contact Information

Address: Wilson Language Training
              47 Old Webster Road
              Oxford, MA 01540
Phone: 508-368-2399
E-mail: info@WilsonLanguage.com
Website: www.wilsonlanguage.com

Sources

Dickson, S., & Bursuck, W. (1999). Implementing a model for preventing reading failure: A report from the field. *Learning Disabilities Research & Practice, 14*(4), 191–202.

Florida Center for Reading Research. (2006). *Strategic Instruction Model (SIM) and Content Literacy Continuum (CLC).* Tallahassee, FL: Author. Retrieved January 27, 2007, from http://www.fcrr.org/FCRR Reports/PDF/wilson.pdf

Mather, N., & Goldstein, S. (2001). *Learning disabilities and challenging behaviors—A guide to intervention and classroom management.* Baltimore, MD: Brookes.

O'Connor, J., & Wilson, B. (1995). Effectiveness of the Wilson Reading System used in public school training. In C. McIntyre & J. Pickering (Eds.), *Clinical studies of multisensory structured language education* (pp. 247–253). Salem, OR: International Multisensory Structured Language Education Council.

Peterson, C.L., Caverly, D.C., Nicholson, S.A., O'Neal, S., & Cusenbary, S. (2000). *Building reading proficiency at the secondary level: A guide to resources.* Austin, TX: Southwest Educational Development Laboratory.

Torgesen, J., Myers, D., Schirm, A., Stuart, E., Vartivarian, S., Mansfield, W., et al. (2006). *National assessment of Title I: Interim report. Volume II: Closing the reading gap: First year findings from a randomized trial of four reading interventions for striving readers.* Washington, DC: National Center for Education Evaluation and Regional Assistance, Institute of Education Sciences, U.S. Department of Education. Retrieved January 14, 2007, from http://www.ed.gov/rschstat/eval/disadv/title1in terimreport/vol2.pdf

Wood, F. (2002). *Data analysis of the Wilson Reading System: Wilson literacy solutions evidence of effectiveness.* Unpublished data compilation report for Wilson Language Training. Retrieved May 31, 2006, from http://www.wilsonlanguage.com/PDF/Evidence_ Data_Analysis.pdf

WRITETOLEARN

Instructional Approach

WriteToLearn is a computer-based reading comprehension and writing instructional tool. Based on the work of Thomas Landauer and his colleagues, WriteToLearn uses latent semantic analysis (LSA) to analyze summaries and essays by students and offers immediate feedback to students and teachers in an aim to improve comprehension and writing quality. Developed for use in grades 4 and higher, WriteToLearn has two parts, Summary Street and the Intelligent Essay Assessor, which are available separately. Envisioned as both an instructional and assessment tool, WriteToLearn provides instant feedback to students and teachers on students' essays and summaries of reading assignments.

Summary Street is a Web-based tool by which students read and then summarize short online texts. Texts include textbooks and supplementary texts in science and social studies. Summary Street instantly compares a student's summary to the original texts using LSA and generates feedback about the student's coverage of the content for each section of a text. The feedback includes information on copying from the text, spelling, redundancy, and irrelevant sentences. The Intelligent Essay Assessor similarly uses LSA to analyze and give feedback on student essays generated in response to online prompts. Feedback addresses overall essay quality and aspects of writing, such as spelling, grammar, and specific writing traits. Writing traits assessed include organization, word choice, conventions, and voice. Scoring and feedback are based on a normative sample of 100–200 real student samples for each passage or prompt and are validated with human scorers. Together, Summary Street and the Intelligent Essay Assessor offer more than 100 reading comprehension passages and 100 essay prompts.

Students using the program log into the program on the Internet, select an assignment (either a text to summarize or a prompt for an essay), enter their work, and receive immediate feedback. In addition to this feedback offered to students, students and teacher can track their progress over time. Teachers can administer specific assignments and can monitor student work individually and by class using a variety of report options.

Professional Development

No information was available on professional development opportunities for WriteToLearn. However, online demonstrations are available on the website, and research articles refer to teacher training in program use.

Program Evaluation

In addition to studies using LSA for other applied purposes (e.g., Foltz, Kintsch, & Landauer, 1998; Landauer & Dumais, 1997), there are several studies documenting the efficacy of WriteToLearn's two components: Summary Street and the Intelligent Essay Assessor. For instance, sixth graders using Summary Street spent more time writing and received better scores on the content represented in their summaries than a comparison group of sixth graders who, given the same amount of time to write and revise their summaries of content area texts, received no automated feedback (Wade-Stein & Kintsch, 2004). Eighth-grade students using Summary Street over a four-week period were similarly compared with students who received the same assignments and writing and revision time of word processors and were found to improve their summary writing and in addition improved their reading comprehension as measured by gist level comprehension questions on a state reading test (Franzke, Kintsch, Caccamise, Johnson, & Dooley, 2005). A wider-scale study of

Summary Street's effects on students in grades 5 through 12 found the program improved summarization and comprehension of all students but had a larger effect on low- and middle-achieving students (Franzke & Streeter, 2006). Additional studies are underway in Chicago high schools and New Jersey middle schools. Research on the Intelligent Essay Assessor program is currently limited to college students; however, findings indicate that program is as reliable as or better than human scorers and that student use of the program to revise essays improves grades and essay quality (Foltz, Gilliam, & Kendall, 2000; Foltz, Laham, & Landauer, 1999; Streeter, Psotka, Laham, & MacCuish, 2002).

Contact Information

Address: Pearson Knowledge Technologies
          4940 Pearl East Circle, Suite 200
          Boulder, CO 80301
Phone: 303-545-9092
E-mail: info@pearsonkt.com
Website: www.pearsonkt.com

Sources

Foltz, P.W., Gilliam, S., & Kendall, S. (2000). Supporting content-based feedback in online writing evaluation with LSA. *Interactive Learning Environments, 8*(2), 111–129.

Foltz, P.W., Kintsch, W., & Landauer, T.K. (1998). The measurement of textual coherence with Latent Semantic Analysis. *Discourse Processes, 25*, 285–307.

Foltz, P.W., Laham, D., & Landauer, T.K. (1999). The Intelligent Essay Assessor: Applications to educational technology. *Interactive Multimedia Electronic Journal of Computer-Enhanced Learning, 1*(2). Retrieved January 26, 2007, from http://imej.wfu.edu/articles/1999/2/04/index.asp

Franzke, M., Kintsch, E., Caccamise, D., Johnson, N., & Dooley, S. (2005). Summary Street: Computer support for comprehension and writing. *Journal of Educational Computing Research, 33*(1), 53–80.

Franzke, M., & Streeter, L.A. (2006). *Building student summarization, writing and reading comprehension skills with guided practice and automated feedback: Highlights from research at the University of Colorado.* Boulder, CO: Pearson Knowledge Technologies.

Landauer, T.K., & Dumais, S.T. (1997). A solution to Plato's problem: The latent semantic analysis theory of the acquisition, induction, and representation of knowledge. *Psychological Review, 104*, 211–240.

Landauer, T.K., Laham, D., & Foltz, P. (2003). Automatic essay assessment. *Assessment in Education: Principles, Policy & Practice, 10*(3), 295–308.

Landauer, T.K., Laham, D., & Foltz, P. (2003). Automatic scoring and annotation of essays with the Intelligent Essay Assessor. In M.D. Shermis & J. Burstein (Eds.), *Automated essay scoring: Cross-disciplinary perspective* (pp. 87–112). Mahwah, NJ: Erlbaum.

Streeter, L., Psotka, J., Laham, D., & MacCuish, D. (2002, December 2–5). *The credible grading machine: Automated essay scoring in the DoD.* Paper presented at Interservice/Industry, Simulation and Education Conference (I/ITSEC), Orlando, FL.

Wade-Stein, D., & Kintsch, E. (2004). Summary Street: Interactive computer support for writing. *Cognition and Instruction, 22*(3), 333–362.

Emerging Adolescent Literacy Programs

Collaborative Reasoning
Center for the Study of Reading, College of Education, University of Illinois,
Urbana-Champaign
http://csr.ed.uiuc.edu/CR/Index.htm

**Evaluating a Multicomponent Reading Program Designed to Address
the Diverse Needs of Struggling Readers in Late Elementary School**
Vanderbilt University
http://peabody.vanderbilt.edu/sped/research.htm

The GIsML Project: Guided Inquiry Supporting Multiple Literacies
Center for the Improvement of Early Reading Achievement, University of Michigan
http://www.umich.edu/~gisml

Improving Reading Comprehension for Struggling Readers
Center for Applied Special Technology (CAST), Inc.
http://www.cast.org/about/news/press/2005-03-30.html

iSTART: Interactive Strategy Training for Active Reading and Thinking
Department of Psychology, University of Memphis
http://csep.psyc.memphis.edu/istart

ITSS: Intelligent Tutoring for the Structure Strategy
College of Education, Pennsylvania State University
http://itss.br.psu.edu/ITSS/pages/index.htm

Quick Reads: A Supplementary/Intervention Fluency Program
Washington Research Institute
http://www.quickreads.org

The Read-Write Cycle (RWC) Project: An Integrated Model for Instruction and Assessment of Reading Comprehension Through Reading and Writing in the Disciplines
University of California, Riverside
http://www.education.ucr.edu/research_and_projects/research_and_projects_snapshot_rws.htm

Science IDEAS: Embedding Knowledge-Focused Reading Comprehension Strategies in Cumulative Content-Area Instruction in Grades 3–5
Florida Atlantic University
http://www.scienceideas.org

SIOP: Sheltered Instruction Observation Protocol
Center for Applied Linguistics
http://www.cal.org/siop and http://www.siopinstitute.net

Strategic Tutoring
University of Kansas, Center for Research on Learning
http://www.kucrl.org/sim/strategies/tutor.shtml

TICA: Teaching Internet Comprehension to Adolescents
University of Connecticut
http://www.newliteracies.uconn.edu/iesproject/index.html

Writing Intensive Reading Comprehension
Graduate School of Education, University of Buffalo
http://www.gse.buffalo.edu/FAS/Collins/images/WIRC.pdf

REFERENCES

Note. Included here is full bibliographic information for the sources cited in the Introduction, Part I, and in the preamble to Part II. Sources for the program descriptions in Part II appear at the end of each program description, but have not been included here.

Achieve. (2005). *Rising to the challenge: Are high school graduates prepared for college and work?* Washington, DC: Author.

ACT. (2005). *Crisis at the core: Preparing all students for college and work.* Iowa City: Author. Retrieved July 31, 2006, from http://www.act.org/path/policy/pdf/crisis_report.pdf

Adelman, C. (2004). *Principal indicators of student academic histories in postsecondary education, 1972–2000.* Washington, DC: U.S. Department of Education, Institute of Education Sciences. Retrieved November 11, 2006, from http://www.ed.gov/rschstat/research/pubs/prinindicat/index.html

Alexander, P.A., & Judy, J.E. (1988). The interaction of domain-specific and strategic knowledge in academic performance. *Review of Educational Research, 58,* 375–404.

Almasi, J.F. (1995). The nature of fourth graders' sociocognitive conflicts in peer-led and teacher-led discussions of literature. *Reading Research Quarterly, 30,* 314–351.

Alvermann, D.E., & Moore, D.W. (1991). Secondary school reading. In R. Barr, M.L. Kamil, P. Mosenthal, & P.D. Pearson (Eds.), *Handbook of reading research* (Vol. II, pp. 951–983). White Plains, NY: Longman.

American Diploma Project. (2004). *Ready or not: Creating a high school diploma that counts.* Washington, DC: Achieve, Inc.

American Educational Research Association. (2004, Winter). English language learners: Boosting academic achievement. *Research Points: Essential Information for Educational Policy, 2,* 1–4. Available at http://www.area.net

Anderson, R.C. (2004). Role of the reader's schema in comprehension, learning, and memory. In R.B. Ruddell & N.J. Unrau (Eds.), *Theoretical models and processes of reading* (5th ed., pp. 594–606). Newark, DE: International Reading Association.

Anderson, D.R., Huston, A.C., Schmitt, K.L., Linebarger, D.L., & Wright, J.C. (2001). Early childhood television viewing and adolescent behavior: The recontact study. *Monographs of the Society for Research in Child Development, 66,* 1–147.

Applebee, A.N., Langer, J.A., Nystrand, M., & Gamoran, A. (2003). Discussion-based approaches to developing understanding: Classroom instruction and student performance in middle and high school English. *American Educational Research Journal, 40,* 685–730.

Astone, N.M., & McLanahan, S.S. (1994). Family structure, residential mobility, and school dropout: A research note. *Demography, 31,* 575–584.

August, D., Carlo, M., Dressler, C., & Snow, C. (2005). The critical role of vocabulary development for English language learners. *Learning Disabilities Research & Practice, 20,* 50–57.

Babbitt, S., & Byrne, M. (1999). Finding the keys to educational progress in urban youth: Three case studies. *Journal of Adolescent & Adult Literacy, 43,* 368–378.

Bain, R. (2006). Rounding up unusual suspects: Facing the authority hidden in the history classroom. *Teachers College Record, 108,* 2080–2114.

Baker, L., & Anderson, R. I. (1982). Effects of inconsistent information on text processing: Evidence for comprehension monitoring. *Reading Research Quarterly, 17,* 281–294.

Bangert-Drowns, R.L., Hurley, M.M., & Wilkinson, B. (2004). The effects of school-based Writing-to-Learn interventions on academic achievement: A meta-analysis. *Review of Educational Research, 74,* 29–58.

Barton, P.E. (2000). *What jobs require: Literacy, education, and training, 1940–2006.* Washington, DC: Educational Testing Service. Retrieved January 12, 2006, from http://www.ets.org/Media/Research/pdf/PICJOBS.pdf

Barton, P.E. (2005). *One-third of a nation: Rising dropout rates and declining opportunities*. Princeton, NJ: Policy Information Center, Educational Testing Service.

Bear, D.R., Invernizzi, M., Templeton, S.R., & Johnston, F. (2003). *Words their way: Word study for phonics, vocabulary, and spelling instruction* (3rd ed.). Englewood Cliffs, NJ: Prentice Hall.

Beck, I.L. (2005). *Making sense of phonics: The hows and whys*. New York: Guilford.

Beck, I.L., McKeown, M.G., Hamilton, R.L., & Kucan, L. (1997). *Questioning the author: An approach for enhancing student engagement with text*. Newark, DE: International Reading Association.

Beck, I.L., McKeown, M.G., & Kucan, L. (2002). *Bringing words to life*. New York: Guilford.

Beck, I.L., McKeown, M.G., Sandora, C., Kucan, L., & Worthy, J. (1996). Questioning the author: A yearlong classroom implementation to engage students with text. *The Elementary School Journal, 96*, 385–414.

Berends, M., Kirby, S.N., Naftel, S., & McKelvey, C. (2001). *Implementation and performance in new American schools*. Santa Monica, CA: RAND.

Berman, I., & Biancarosa, G. (2005). *Reading to achieve: A governor's guide to adolescent literacy*. Washington, DC: National Governors Association Center for Best Practices. Retrieved October 4, 2006, from http://www.nga.org/Files/pdf/0510GOVGUIDELITERACY.PDF

Berninger, V.W., Abbott, R.D., Abbott, S.P., Graham, S., & Richards, T. (2002). Writing and reading: Connections between language by hand and language by eye. *Journal of Learning Disabilities, 35*, 39–56.

Bessai, F., & Cozac, C. (1980). Gains of fifth and sixth grade readers from in-school tutoring. *The Reading Teacher, 33*, 567–570.

Bettinger, E.P., & Long, B.T. (2005). *Addressing the need of under-prepared students in higher education: Does college remediation work?* Cambridge, MA: National Bureau of Economic Research.

Bhabha, H.K. (1994). *The location of culture*. New York: Routledge.

Biancarosa, G., Mancilla-Martinez, J., Kieffer, M.J., Christodoulou, J.A., & Snow, C.E. (2006, July). *Exploring the heterogeneity of English reading comprehension difficulties of Spanish-speaking middle school students*. Presentation to the Society for Scientific Studies of Reading, Vancouver, BC, Canada.

Biancarosa, G., & Snow, C.E. (2004). *Reading next—A vision for action and research in middle and high school literacy: A report to Carnegie Corporation of New York*. Washington, DC: Alliance for Excellent Education. Retrieved October 4, 2006, from http://www.all4ed.org/publications/ReadingNext/ReadingNext.pdf

Biemiller, A. (2003). Oral comprehension sets the ceiling on reading comprehension. *American Educator, 27*(1), 23.

Black, P., & Wiliam, D. (1998). Assessment and classroom learning. *Assessment in Education, 5*(1), 7–74.

Boone, R., & Higgins, K. (2003). Reading, writing, and publishing digital text. *Remedial and Special Education, 24*, 132–140.

Bos, C.S., Anders, P.L., Filip, D., & Jaffe, L.E. (1989). The effects of an interactive instructional strategy for enhancing reading comprehension and content area learning for students with learning disabilities. *Journal of Learning Disabilities, 22*, 384–390.

Boston, C. (2002). The concept of formative assessment. *Practical Assessment, Research & Evaluation, 8*(9). Retrieved July 13, 2004, from http://PAREonline.net/getvn.asp?v=8&n=9

Bridges, W., & Mitchell, S. (2000). Leading transition: A new model for change. *Leader to Leader, 16*, 30–36.

Brinkerhoff, J.D., Klein, J.D., & Koroghlanian, C.M. (2001). Effects of overviews and computer experience on learning from hypertext. *Journal of Educational Computing Research, 25*, 427–440.

Britt, M.A., & Aglinskas, C. (2002). Improving students' ability to identify and use source information. *Cognition and Instruction, 20*, 485–522.

Brown, A.L., Armbruster, B.B., & Baker, L. (1986). The role of metacognition in reading and studying. In J. Orsanu (Ed.), *Reading comprehension: From research to practice* (pp. 49–75). Hillsdale, NJ: Erlbaum.

Brown, A.L., & Day, J.D. (1983). Macrorules for summarizing texts: The development of expertise. *Journal of Verbal Learning and Verbal Behavior, 22*, 1–14.

Brush, T., & Saye, J. (2001). The use of embedded scaffolds with hypermedia-supported student-centered learning. *Journal of Educational Multimedia and Hypermedia, 10*, 333–356.

Bryant, D.P., Vaughn, S., Linan-Thompson, S., Ugel, N., & Hamff, A. (2000). Reading outcomes for students with and without learning disabilities in general education middle school content area classes. *Learning Disabilities Quarterly, 23*, 24–48.

Bulgren, J.A., Deshler, D.D., & Schumaker, J.B. (1997). Use of a recall enhancement routine and strategies in inclusive secondary classrooms. *Learning Disabilities Research & Practice, 12*, 198–208.

Bulgren, J.A., Deshler, D.D., Schumaker, J.B., & Lenz, B.K. (2000). The use and effectiveness of analogical instruction in diverse secondary content classrooms. *Journal of Educational Psychology, 92*, 426–441.

Bulgren, J.A., Lenz, B.K., Deshler, D.D., & Schumaker, J.B. (1995). *The content enhancement series: The concept comparison routine*. Lawrence, KS: Edge Enterprises.

Bulgren, J.A., Lenz, B.K., Schumaker, J.B., Deshler, D.D., & Marquis, J.G. (2002). The use and effectiveness of a comparison routine in diverse secondary content classrooms. *Journal of Educational Psychology, 94*, 356–371.

Bulgren, J.A., Schumaker, J.B., & Deshler, D.D. (1988). Effectiveness of a concept teaching routine in enhancing the performance of LD students in secondary-level mainstream classes. *Learning Disabilities Quarterly, 11*, 3–17.

Bulgren, J.A., Schumaker, J.B., & Deshler, D.D. (1994a). *The concept anchoring routine*. Lawrence, KS: Edge Enterprises.

Bulgren, J.A., Schumaker, J.B., & Deshler, D.D. (1994b). The effects of a recall enhancement routine on the test performance of students with and without learning disabilities. *Learning Disabilities Research & Practice, 9*, 2–11.

Buly, M.R., & Valencia, S.W. (2002). Below the bar: Profiles of students who fail state reading assessments. *Educational Evaluation and Policy Analysis, 24*, 219–239.

Burbank, M.D., & Kauchak, D. (2003). An alternative model for professional development: Investigations into effective collaboration. *Teaching & Teacher Education, 19*, 499–514.

Cain, K., Oakhill, J., & Bryant, P. (2004). Children's reading comprehension ability: Concurrent prediction by working memory, verbal ability, and component skills. *Journal of Educational Psychology, 96*, 31–42.

Calhoon, M.B., & Fuchs, L.S. (2003). The effects of peer-assisted learning strategies and curriculum-based measurement on the mathematics performance of secondary students with disabilities. *Remedial and Special Education, 24*, 235–245.

Campbell, J.R., Kapinus, B.A., & Beatty, A.S. (1995). *Interviewing children about their literacy experiences*. Washington, DC: National Center for Educational Statistics.

Capps, R., Fix, M., Murray, J., Ost, J., Passel, J.S., & Herwantoro, S. (2005). *The new demography of America's schools: Immigration and the No Child Left Behind Act*. Washington, DC: The Urban Institute.

Carbo, M. (1983). Reading styles change between second and eighth grade. *Educational Leadership, 40*(5), 56–59.

Carlisle, J., & Rice, M. (2002). *Improving reading comprehension: Research-based principles and practices*. Baltimore: York.

Carlo, M., August, D., McLaughlin, B., Snow, C.E., Dressler, C., Lippman, D.N., et al. (2004). Closing the gap: Addressing the vocabulary needs of English-language learners in bilingual and mainstream classrooms. *Reading Research Quarterly, 39*, 188–215.

Carnevale, A.P. (2001). *Help wanted...College required*. Washington, DC: Educational Testing Service, Office of Public Leadership.

Carnine, L., & Carnine, D. (2004). The interaction of reading skills and science content knowledge when teaching struggling secondary students. *Reading & Writing Quarterly, 20*, 203–218.

Carver, R.P. (1994). Percentage of unknown vocabulary words in text as a function of the relative difficulty of the text: implications for instruction. *Journal of Reading Behavior, 26*, 413.

Cataldo, M.G., & Cornoldi, C. (1998). Self-monitoring in poor and good reading comprehenders and their use of strategies. *British Journal of Developmental Psychology, 16*, 155–165.

Catts, H.W., Hogan, T.P., & Adlof, S M. (2005). Developmental changes in reading and reading disabilities. In H.W. Catts & A.G. Kamhi (Eds.), *The connections between language and reading disabilities* (pp. 25–40). Mahwah, NJ: Erlbaum.

Chall, J.S. (1996). *Stages of reading development*. New York: McGraw Hill.

Chall, J.S., & Jacobs, V.A. (2003). Poor children's fourth-grade slump. *American Educator, 27*(1), 14–15.

Chall, J.S., Jacobs, V.A., & Baldwin, L.E. (1990). *The reading crisis: Why poor children fall behind*. Cambridge, MA: Harvard University Press.

Chandler-Olcott, K., & Mahar, D. (2003). Adolescents' "Anime"-inspired "fanfictions": An exploration of multiliteracies. *Journal of Adolescent & Adult Literacy, 46*, 556–566.

Cohen, P.A., Kulik, J.A., & Kulik, C.C. (1982). Educational outcomes of tutoring: A meta-analysis of findings. *American Educational Research Journal, 19,* 237–248.

Coiro, J. (2003). Reading comprehension on the Internet: Expanding our understanding of reading comprehension to encompass new literacies. *The Reading Teacher, 56,* 458–464.

Commander, N.E., & Smith, B.D. (1996). Learning logs: A tool for cognitive monitoring. *Journal of Adolescent & Adult Literacy, 39,* 446–453.

Cordova, D.I., & Lepper, M.R. (1996). Intrinsic motivation and the process of learning: Beneficial effects of contextualization, personalization, and choice. *Journal of Educational Psychology, 88,* 715–730.

Cutter, J., Palincsar, A.S., & Magnusson, S.J. (2002). Supporting inclusion through case-based vignette conversations. *Learning Disabilities Research & Practice, 17,* 186–200.

Darling-Hammond, L. (1998). Teacher learning that supports student learning. *Educational Leadership, 55*(5), 6–11.

Darling-Hammond, L. (1999). Target time toward teachers. *Journal of Staff Development, 20*(2), 31–36.

Datnow, A. (2000). Power and politics in the adoption of school reform models. *Educational Evaluation and Policy Analysis, 22,* 357–74.

Day, J.C., & Newburger, E.C. (2002). *The big payoff: Educational attainment and synthetic estimates of work-life earnings.* U.S. Census Bureau. Retrieved March 29, 2006, from http://www.census.gov/prod/2002pubs/p23-210.pdf

Deshler, R., & Smith, K. (in progress). *Organization change and individual transition tool book.* Louisville, KY: Aligna Solutions.

Dillon, A., & Gabbard, R. (1998). Hypermedia as an educational technology: A review of the quantitative research literature on learner comprehension, control, and style. *Review of Educational Research, 68,* 322–349.

Dole, J.A., Duffy, G.G., Roehler, L.R., & Pearson, P.D. (1991). Moving from the old to the new: Research on reading comprehension instruction. *Review of Educational Research, 61,* 239–264.

Donahue, P.L., Voelkl, K.E., Campbell, J.R., & Mazzeo, J. (1999). *The NAEP 1998 reading report card for the nation and the states* (NCES 1999–500). Washington, DC: National Center for Education Statistics, U.S. Government Printing Office. Retrieved June 26, 2006, from http://nces.ed.gov/pub search/pubsinfo.asp?pubid=1999500

Dreher, M.J. (2003). Motivating struggling readers by tapping the potential of information books. *Reading & Writing Quarterly, 19,* 25–38.

Duffy, S.A. (1986). Role of expectations in sentence integration. *Journal of Experimental Psychology: Learning, Memory, and Cognition, 12,* 208–219.

Durkin, D. (1979). What classroom observations reveal about reading comprehension instruction. *Reading Research Quarterly, 14,* 481–533.

Durkin, D. (1981). Schools don't teach comprehension. *Educational Leadership, 38,* 453–454.

Duschl, R., & Hamilton, R. (1998). Conceptual change in science and in the learning of science. In B. Fraser & K. Tobin (Eds.), *International handbook of science education* (pp. 1047–1066). Dordrecht: Kluwer Academic.

Eccles, J.S., Midgley, C., Wigfield, A., Buchanan, C.M., Reuman, D., Flanagan. C., et al. (1993). Development during adolescence: The impact of stage-environment fit on young adolescents' experiences in schools and families. *American Psychologist, 48,* 90–101.

Educational Research Service. (2005). *Salaries and wages paid professional and support personnel in public schools, 2004–2005.* Alexandria, VA: Author.

El-Hindi, A.E. (1997). Connecting reading and writing: College learners' metacognitive awareness. *Journal of Developmental Education, 27*(2), 10–19.

Englert, C.S., & Tarrant, K.L. (1995). Creating collaborative cultures for educational change. *Remedial and Special Education, 16,* 325–336, 353.

Erb, T.O. (1997) Meeting the needs of young adolescents on interdisciplinary teams: The growing research base. *Childhood Education, 73,* 309–311.

Ermeling, B.A. (2005). *Transforming professional development for an American high school: A lesson study inspired, technology powered system for teacher learning.* Unpublished Doctoral Dissertation, University of California, Los Angeles.

Evans, R. (1996). *The human side of school change: Reform, resistance, and the real-life problems of innovation.* San Francisco: Jossey-Bass.

Felner, R.D., Jackson, A.W., Kasak, D., Mulhall, P., Brand, S., & Flowers, N. (1997). The impact of school reform for the middle years: Longitudinal study of a network engaged in Turning Points-based comprehensive school transformation. *Phi Delta Kappan, 78,* 528–532, 541–550.

Fink, R.P. (1995). Successful dyslexics: A constructivist study of passionate interest reading. *Journal of Adolescent & Adult Literacy, 39,* 268–280.

Florida Center for Reading Research. (2006). *Intervention and remedial programs for students above third grade.* Tallahassee: Author. Retrieved October 18, 2006, from http://www.fcrr.org/FCRRReports/CReports.aspx?rep=412

Flowers, N., Mertens, S.B., & Mulhall, P.F. (1999). The impact of teaming: Five research-based outcomes. *Middle School Journal, 31*(2), 57–60.

Fountas, I.C., & Pinnell, G.S. (2001). *Guiding readers and writers, grades 3–6: Teaching comprehension, genre, and content literacy.* Portsmouth, NH: Heinemann.

Fountas, I.C., & Pinnell, G.S. (2006). *Teaching for comprehending and fluency: Thinking, talking, and writing about reading, K–8.* Portsmouth, NH: Heinemann.

Fox, S., Anderson, J.Q., & Rainie, L. (2005). *The future of the Internet.* Washington, DC: Pew Internet & American Life Project. Retrieved October 2, 2006, from http://www.pewinternet.org/pdfs/PIP_Future_of_Internet.pdf

Frey, N. (2002). Literacy achievement in an urban middle-level professional development school: A learning community at work. *Reading Improvement, 39,* 3–13.

Fuchs, L.S., Deno, S.L., & Mirkin, P.K. (1984). The effects of frequent curriculum-based measurement and evaluation on pedagogy, student achievement, and student awareness of learning. *American Educational Research Journal, 21,* 440–460.

Fuchs, L.S., & Fuchs, D. (2002). Curriculum-based measurement: Describing competence, enhancing outcomes, evaluating treatment effects, and identifying treatment nonresponders. *Peabody Journal of Education, 77*(2), 64–84.

Fuchs, L.S., Fuchs, D., Bentz, J., Phillips, N.B., & Hamlett, L. (1994). The nature of student interactions during peer tutoring with and without prior training and experience. *American Educational Research Journal, 31,* 75–103.

Fuchs, L.S., Fuchs, D., & Hamlett, C.L. (1989). Monitoring reading growth using student recalls: Effects of two teacher feedback systems. *Journal of Educational Research, 83,* 103–110.

Fuchs, L.S., Fuchs, D., Hamlett, C.L., Phillips, N.B., & Bentz, J. (1994). Classwide curriculum-based measurement: Helping general educators meet the challenge of student diversity. *Exceptional Children, 60,* 518–537.

Fuchs, L.S., Fuchs, D., & Kazdan, S. (1999). Effects of peer-assisted learning strategies on high school students with serious reading problems. *Remedial and Special Education, 20,* 309–318.

Fullan, M. (1991). *The new meaning of educational change.* New York: Teachers College Press.

Fullan, M. (2001a). *The new meaning of educational change* (3rd edition). New York: Teachers College Press.

Fullan, M. (2001b). *Leading in a culture of change.* San Francisco: John Wiley & Sons.

Fullan, M. (2003). *The moral imperative of school leadership.* Thousand Oaks, CA: Sage Publications.

Gaffney, J.S., Methven, J.M., & Bagdasarian, S. (2002). Assisting older students to read expository text in a tutorial setting: A case for a high-impact intervention. *Reading & Writing Quarterly, 18,* 119–150.

Ganske, K. (2000). *Word journeys: Assessment-guided phonics, spelling, and vocabulary instruction.* New York: Guilford.

Garet, M.S., Porter, A.C., Desimone, L., Birman, B.F., & Yoon, K.S. (2001). What makes professional development effective? Results from a national sample of teachers. *American Educational Research Journal, 38,* 915–945.

Garner, R., & Reis, R. (1981). Monitoring and resolving obstacles: An investigation of spontaneous text lookbacks among upper-grade good and poor comprehenders. *Reading Research Quarterly, 4,* 569–582.

Garner, R., Wagoner, S., & Smith, T. (1983). Externalizing question-answering strategies of good and poor comprehenders. *Reading Research Quarterly, 18,* 439–447.

Gee, J.P. (1996). *Sociolinguistics and literacies: Ideology in discourses.* New York: Falmer.

Genesee, F., Lindholm-Leary, K., Saunders, W., & Christian, D. (2005). English languages learners in U.S. schools: An overview of research findings. *Journal of Education for Students Placed at Risk, 10,* 363–385.

Gentzkow, M., & Shapiro, J.M. (2006). *Does television rot your brain? New evidence from the Coleman study* (Working paper 12021). Cambridge, MA: National Bureau of Economic Research.

Gersten, R., Chard, D., & Baker, S. (2000). Factors enhancing sustained use of research-based instructional strategies. *Journal of Learning Disabilities, 33,* 445–457.

Gersten, R., & Dimino, J. (2001). The realities of translating research into classroom practice. *Learning Disabilities Research & Practice, 16*, 120–130.

Gettinger, M. (1984). Achievement as a function of time spent in learning and time needed for learning. *American Educational Research Journal, 21*, 617–628.

Gettinger, M. (1985). Time allocated and spent relative to time needed for learning as determinants of achievement. *Journal of Educational Psychology, 77*, 3–11.

Gitlin, T. (2001). *Media unlimited.* New York: Metropolitan.

Goldenberg, C. (2006, July). Improving achievement for English language learners: What the research tells us. *Education Week, 25*(43), 34–36.

Goldenberg, C., Saunders, W., & Gallimore, R. (2004). *Settings for change: A practical model for linking rhetoric and action to improve achievement for diverse students.* Final Report to the Spencer Foundation (Grant #19800042).

Goldman, S.R. (2004). Cognitive aspects of constructing meaning through and across multiple texts. In N. Shuart-Ferris & D.M. Bloome (Eds.), *Uses of intertextuality in classroom and educational research* (pp. 313–347). Greenwich, CT: Information Age Publishing.

Graham, S. (2005). Strategy instruction and the teaching of writing: A meta-analysis. In C. MacArthur, S. Graham, & J. Fitzgerald (Eds.), *Handbook of writing research* (pp. 187–207). New York: Guilford.

Graham, S. (2006). Writing. In P.A. Alexander & P.H. Winne (Eds.), *Handbook of educational psychology* (2nd ed., pp. 457–478). Mahwah, NJ: Erlbaum.

Graham, S., & Harris, K.R. (2002). Prevention and intervention for struggling writers. In M.R. Shinn, H.M. Walker, & G. Stoner (Eds.), *Interventions for academic and behavior problems II: Preventive and remedial techniques* (pp. 589–610). Washington, DC: National Association of School Psychologists.

Graham, S., & Perin, D. (2006). *A meta-analysis of writing instruction for adolescent students.* Manuscript submitted for publication.

Graham, S., & Perin, D. (2007). *Writing next: Effective strategies to improve writing of adolescents in middle and high schools: A report to Carnegie Corporation of New York.* Washington, DC: Alliance for Excellent Education.

Greene, J.P., & Winters, M.A. (2005). *Public high school graduation and college-readiness rates: 1991–2002.* New York: Manhattan Institute for Policy Research.

Greenleaf, C.L., Schoenbach, R., Cziko, C., & Mueller, F.L. (2001). Apprenticing adolescent readers to academic literacy. *Harvard Educational Review, 71*, 79–129.

Guthrie, J.T., & Alao, S. (1997). Designing contexts to increase motivations for reading. *Educational Psychologist, 32*, 95–105.

Guthrie, J.T., Alao, S., & Rinehart, J.M. (1997). Engagement in reading for young adolescents. *Journal of Adolescent & Adult Literacy, 40*, 438–446.

Guthrie, J.T., Anderson, E., Alao, S., & Rinehart, J. (1999). Influences of Concept-Oriented Reading Instruction on strategy use and conceptual learning from text. *The Elementary School Journal, 99*, 343–366.

Guthrie, J.T., & Humenick, N.M. (2004). Motivating students to read: Evidence for classroom practices that increase reading motivation and achievement. In P. McCardle & V. Chhabra (Eds.), *The voice of evidence in reading research* (pp. 329–354). Baltimore: Brookes.

Guthrie, J.T., Schafer, W.D., & Huang, C.W. (2001). Benefits of opportunity to read and balanced instruction on the NAEP. *Journal of Educational Research, 94*, 145–162.

Guthrie, J.T., Schafer, W.D., Von Secker, C., & Alban, T. (2000). Contributions of instructional practices to reading achievement in a statewide improvement program. *Journal of Educational Research, 93*, 211–225.

Guthrie, J.T., Hoa, L.W., Wigfield, A., Tonks, S.M., Humenick, N.M., & Littles, E. (in press). Reading motivation and reading comprehension growth in later years. *Contemporary Educational Psychology.*

Guthrie, J.T., & Wigfield, A. (2000). Engagement and motivation in reading. In M.L. Kamil, P.B. Mosenthal, P.D. Pearson, & R. Barr (Eds.), *Handbook of reading research* (Vol. III, pp. 403–422). Mahwah, NJ: Erlbaum.

Gutiérrez, K.D., Baquedano-López, P., Alvarez, H.H., & Chiu, M.M. (1999). Building a culture of collaboration through hybrid language practices. *Theory Into Practice, 38*, 87–93.

Guzzetti, B.J. (2000). Learning counter-intuitive science concepts: What have we learned from over a decade of research? *Reading & Writing Quarterly, 16*, 89–98.

Guzzetti, B.J., Snyder, T.E., Glass, G.V., & Gamas, W.S. (1993). Promoting conceptual change in science: A comparative meta-analysis on instructional interventions from reading education and science education. *Reading Research Quarterly, 28*, 116–159.

Hamilton, M.L., & Richardson, V. (1995). Effects of the culture in two schools on the process and outcomes of staff development. *The Elementary School Journal, 95*, 367–385.

Hamilton, C., & Shinn, M.R. (2003). Characteristics of word callers: An investigation of the accuracy of teachers' judgments of reading comprehension and oral reading skills. *School Psychology Review, 32*, 228–240.

Haney, W., Madaus, G., Abrams, L., Wheelock, A., Miao, J., & Gruia, I. (2004). *The education pipeline in the United States, 1970–2000.* Chestnut Hill, MA: Center for the Study of Testing, Evaluation, and Educational Policy. Retrieved July 1, 2006, from http://www.bc.edu/research/nbetpp/reports.html

Hapgood, S., Magnusson, S.J., & Palincsar, A.S. (2004). Teacher, text, and experience: A case of young children's scientific inquiry. *Journal of the Learning Sciences, 13*, 455–505.

Hart, B., & Risley, T.R. (2003). The early catastrophe: The 30 million word gap by age 3. *American Educator, 27*(1), 4–9.

Hartman, D.K. (1995). Eight readers reading: The intertextual links of proficient readers reading multiple passages. *Reading Research Quarterly, 30*, 520–561.

Hasselbring, T.S., & Goin, L.I. (2004). Literacy instruction for older struggling readers: What is the role of technology? *Reading & Writing Quarterly, 20*, 123–144.

Henk, W.A., & Melnick, S.A. (1995). The Reader Self-Perception Survey (RSPS): A new tool for measuring how children feel about themselves as readers. *The Reading Teacher, 48*, 470–482.

Hiebert, E.H., & Kamil, M.L. (2005). *Teaching and learning vocabulary: Bringing research to practice.* Hillsdale, NJ: Erlbaum.

Hirsch, E.D., Jr. (2003). Reading comprehension requires knowledge—of words and the world: Scientific insights into the fourth-grade slump and the nation's stagnant comprehension scores. *American Educator, 27*(1), 10, 12–13, 16–22, 28–29, 48.

Hirsch, E.D., Jr. (2006). *The knowledge deficit: Closing the shocking education gap for American children.* New York: Houghton Mifflin.

Hock, M.F., Brasseur, I.F., Deshler, D.D., Catts, H.W., Marquis, J., Stribling, J.W., et al. (2006). *What is the nature of struggling adolescent readers in urban schools?* Lawrence: University of Kansas, Center for Research on Learning.

Hock, M.F., Pulvers, K.A., Deshler, D.D., & Schumaker, J.B. (2001). The effects of an after-school tutoring program on the academic performance of at-risk students and students with LD. *Remedial and Special Education, 22*, 172–186.

Hock, M.F., Schumaker, J.B., & Deshler, D.D. (2001). The case for strategic tutoring. *Educational Leadership, 58*(7), 50–52.

Horner, R.H., Sugai, G., & Horner, H.F. (2000, February). A schoolwide approach to student discipline. *The School Administrator, 2*(57), 20–23. Retrieved February 4, 2007, from http://www.aasa.org/publications/saarticledetail.cfm?ItemNumber=3860&snItemNumber=950&tnItemNumber=951

Horton, S.V., Lovitt, T.C., & Bergerud, D. (1990). The effectiveness of graphic organizers for three classifications of secondary students in content area classes. *Journal of Learning Disabilities, 23*, 12–22.

Hull, G.A. (2003). Youth culture and digital media: New literacies for new times. *Research in the Teaching of English, 38*, 229–233.

Ingels, S.J., Burns, L.J., Chen, X., Cataldi, E.F., & Charleston, S. (2005). *A profile of the American high school sophomore in 2002: Initial results from the base year of the Education Longitudinal Study of 2002* (NCES 2005-338). Washington, DC: National Center for Education Statistics, U.S. Government Printing Office. Retrieved June 26, 2005, from http://nces.ed.gov/pubsearch/pubsinfo.asp?pubid=2005338

International Reading Association. (2006). *Standards for middle and high school literacy coaches.* Newark, DE: Author.

Isserlis, J. (2000). Trauma and the adult English language learner. *ERIC Digest* (Report EDO-LE-00-02). Washington, DC: National Clearinghouse for Bilingual Education.

Ivey, G., & Broaddus, K. (2001). "Just plain reading": A survey of what makes students want to read in middle school classrooms. *Reading Research Quarterly, 36*, 350–377.

Ivey, G., & Fisher, D. (2006). *Creating literacy-rich schools for adolescents.* Washington, DC: Association for Supervision and Curriculum Development.

Jimenez, R.T., Garcia, G.E., & Pearson, P.D. (1996). The reading strategies of bilingual Latina/o students who are successful English readers: Opportunities and obstacles. *Reading Research Quarterly, 31*, 90–112.

Johnston, P., & Afflerbach, P. (1985). The process of constructing main ideas from text. *Cognition and Instruction, 2*, 207–232.

Kamil, M.L., Intrator, S.M., & Kim, H.S. (2000). The effects of other technologies on literacy and literacy learning. In M.L. Kamil, P.B. Mosenthal, P.D. Pearson, & R. Barr (Eds.), *Handbook of reading research* (Vol. III, pp. 771–788). Mahwah, NJ: Erlbaum.

Kane, C. (1994). *Prisoners of time: Research, what we know and what we need to know*. Washington, DC: National Education Commission on Time and Learning.

King, J.A. (1994). Meeting the educational needs of at-risk students: A cost analysis of three models. *Educational Evaluation and Policy Analysis, 16*, 1–20.

Klingner, J.K., & Vaughn, S. (2000). The helping behaviors of fifth-graders while using collaborative strategic reading during ESL content classes. *TESOL Quarterly, 34*, 69–98.

Klingner, J.K., Vaughn, S., Arguelles, M.E., Hughes, M.T., & Leftwich, S.A. (2004). Collaborative strategic reading: "Real world" lessons from classroom teachers. *Remedial and Special Education, 25*, 291–302.

Kutner, M., Greenberg, E., & Baer, J. (2006). *A first look at the literacy of America's adults in the 21st century* (NCES 2006-470). Washington, DC: National Center for Education Statistics, U.S. Government Printing Office. Retrieved June 26, 2006, from http://nces.ed.gov/pubsearch/pubsinfo.asp?pubid=2006470

Labbo, L.D., Reinking, D., & McKenna, M.C. (1998). Technology and literacy education in the next century: Exploring the connection between work and schooling. *Peabody Journal of Education, 73*(3/4), 273–289.

Laird, J., Lew, S., DeBell, M., & Chapman, C. (2006). *Dropout rates in the United States: 2002 and 2003* (NCES 2006-062). Washington, DC: U.S. Department of Education, National Center for Education Statistics.

Langer, J.A. (2001). Beating the odds: Teaching middle and high school students to read and write well. *American Educational Research Journal, 38*, 837–880.

Lankshear, C., & Knobel, M. (2002). Do we have your attention? New literacies, digital technologies, and the education of adolescents. In D.E. Alvermann (Ed.), *Adolescents and literacies in a digital world* (pp. 19–39). New York: Peter Lang.

Lawless, K.A., & Brown, S.W. (2003). Introduction: From digital dirt road to educational expressway: Innovations in web-based pedagogy. *Instructional Science, 31*, 227–230.

Leach, J.M., Scarborough, H.S., & Rescorla, L. (2003). Late-emerging reading disabilities. *Journal of Educational Psychology, 95*, 211–224.

Leander, K.M. (2003). Writing travelers' tales on new literacyscapes. *Reading Research Quarterly, 38*, 392–397.

Leander, K., & Lovvorn, J.F. (2006) Literacy networks: Following the circulation of texts, bodies, and objects in the schooling and online gaming of one youth. *Cognition and Instruction, 24*, 291–340.

LEAP for the 21st Century: Spring 2004 criterion-referenced test: State/district/school achievement level summary report: All test takers. (n.d.). Baton Rouge: Louisiana Department of Education. Retrieved July 8, 2005, from http://www.doe.state.la.us/lde/ssa/1891.asp?g=8&t=36

Lederer, J.M. (2000). Reciprocal teaching of social studies in inclusive elementary classrooms. *Journal of Learning Disabilities, 33*, 91–106.

Lee, V.E., Dedrick, R.F., & Smith, J.B. (1991). The effect of the social organization of schools on teachers' efficacy and satisfaction. *Sociology of Education, 64*, 190–208.

Lee, V.E., & Smith, J.B. (1993). Effects of school restructuring on the achievement and engagement of middle grade students. *Sociology of Education, 66*, 164–187.

Lee, V.E., & Smith, J.B. (1996) Collective responsibility for learning and its effects on gains in achievement for early secondary school students. *American Journal of Education, 104*, 103–147.

Lemke, M., Calsyn, C., Lippman, L., Jocelyn, L., Kastberg, D., Liu, Y.Y., et al. (2001). *Outcomes of learning: Results from the 2000 Program for International Student Assessment of 15-year-olds in reading, mathematics, and science literacy* (NCES 2002-115). Washington, DC: National Center for Education Statistics, U.S. Government Printing Office. Retrieved June 26, 2006, from http://nces.ed.gov/pubsearch/pubsinfo.asp?pubid=2002115

Lemke, M., Sen, A., Johnston, J.S., Pahlke, E., Williams, T., Kastberg, D., et al. (2005). *Characteristics of U.S. 15-year-old low achievers in an international context: Findings from PISA 2000* (NCES 2006-010). Washington, DC: National Center for Education Statistics, U.S. Government Printing Office. Retrieved June 26, 2006, from http://nces.ed.gov/pubsearch/pubsinfo.asp?pubid=2006010

Lemke, M., Sen, A., Pahlke, E., Partelow, L., Miller, D., Williams, T., et al. (2004). *International outcomes of learning in mathematics literacy and problem solving: PISA 2003 results from the U.S. perspective* (NCES

2005-003). Washington, DC: National Center for Education Statistics, U.S. Government Printing Office. Retrieved June 26, 2006, from http://nces.ed.gov/pubsearch/pubsinfo.asp?pubid=2006010

Lenz, B.K., & Adams, G.A. (2006). Teacher planning: The cornerstone to accessing the general education curriculum. In D.D. Deshler & J.B. Schumaker (Eds.), *High school students with disabilities: Strategies for accessing the curriculum* (pp. 35–78). New York: Corwin Press.

Lenz, B.K., & Deshler, D.D. (with Kissam, B.R.). (2004). *Teaching content to all: Evidenced-based inclusive practices in middle and secondary schools.* Boston: Allyn & Bacon.

Lenz, B.K., Ehren, B.J., & Deshler, D.D. (2005). The content literacy continuum: A school reform framework for improving adolescent literacy for all students. *Teaching Exceptional Children, 37*(6), 60–63.

Leong, C. K., & Jerred, W.D. (2001). Effects of consistency and adequacy of language information on understanding elementary mathematics word problems. *Annals of Dyslexia, 51,* 277–298.

Lesaux, N.K., & Siegel, L.S. (2003). The development of reading in children who speak English as a second language. *Developmental Psychology, 39,* 1005–1019.

Lesaux, N.K., Lipka, O., & Siegel, L.S. (2006). Investigating cognitive and linguistic abilities that influence the reading comprehension skills of children from diverse linguistic backgrounds. *Reading and Writing, 19,* 99–131.

Leslie, L., & Caldwell, J. (1995). *Qualitative Reading Inventory–II.* New York: Addison Wesley.

Leu, D.J., Jr. (2000). Literacy and technology: Deictic consequences for literacy education in an information age. In M.L. Kamil, P.B. Mosenthal, P.D. Pearson, & R. Barr (Eds.), *Handbook of reading research* (Vol. III, pp. 743–770). Mahwah, NJ: Erlbaum.

Levin, H.M., & McEwan, P. (2001). *Cost-effectiveness analysis methods and applications.* Thousand Oaks, CA: Sage.

Levy, F., & Murnane, R. J. (2004). *The new division of labor: How computers are creating the next job market.* New York: Russell Sage Foundation.

MacArthur, C.A., Ferretti, R.P., Okolo, C.M., & Cavalier, A.R. (2001). Technology applications for students with literacy problems: A critical review. *The Elementary School Journal, 101,* 274–301.

Martin, M.O., Mullis, I.V.S., Gonzalez, E.J., & Kennedy, A.M. (2003). *Trends in children's reading literacy achievement 1991–2001: IEA's study of trends in reading literacy achievement in primary school in nine countries.* Chestnut Hill, MA: Boston College, Lynch School of Education, PIRLS International Study Center. Retrieved June 26, 2005, from http://pirls.bc.edu/pirls2001i/PIRLS2001_Pubs_TrR.html

Mastropieri, M.A., Scruggs, T.E., & Graetz, J.E. (2003). Reading comprehension instruction for secondary students: Challenges for struggling students and teachers. *Learning Disability Quarterly, 26,* 103–116.

Matsumura, L.C., Patthey-Chavez, G.G., Valdes, R., & Garnier, H. (2002). Teacher feedback, writing assignment quality, and third-grade students' revision in lower- and higher-achieving urban schools. *The Elementary School Journal, 103,* 3–25.

Mayer, R.E. (2003). The promise of multimedia learning: Using the same instructional design methods across different media. *Learning and Instruction, 13,* 125–139.

Mayer, R.E., & Moreno, R. (1998). A split-attention effect in multimedia learning: Evidence for dual processing systems in working memory. *Journal of Educational Psychology, 90,* 312–320.

McCombs, J.S., Kirby, S.N., Barney, H., Darilek, H., & Magee, S. (2004). *Achieving state and national literacy goals, a long uphill road: A report to Carnegie Corporation of New York.* Santa Monica, CA: RAND. Retrieved February 4, 2007, from http://www.rand.org/pubs/technical_reports/2005/RAND_TR180-1.pdf

McCrindle, A.R., & Christensen, C.A. (1995). The impact of learning journals on metacognitive and cognitive processes and learning performance. *Learning and Instruction, 5,* 167–185.

McKenna, M.C., & Robinson, R.D. (1990). Content literacy: A definition and implications. *Journal of Reading, 34,* 184–186.

McKoon, G., & Ratcliff, R. (1986). Inferences about predictable events. *Journal of Experimental Psychology: Learning, Memory, and Cognition, 12,* 82–91.

McKoon, G., & Ratcliff, R. (1989). Semantic associations and elaborative inferences. *Journal of Experimental Psychology: Learning, Memory, and Cognition, 15,* 326–338.

McLaughlin, M.W. (1990). RAND change-agent study revisited: Macro perspectives and micro realities. *Educational Researcher, 19*(9), 11–16.

McNamara, D.S., & Kintsch, W. (1996). Learning from texts: Effects of prior knowledge and text coherence. *Discourse Processes, 22,* 247–288.

Moje, E.B., Ciechanowski, K.M., Kramer, K., Ellis, L., Carillo, R., & Collazo, T. (2004). Working toward third space in content area literacy: An examination of everyday funds of knowledge and discourse. *Reading Research Quarterly, 39*, 38–70.

Moje, E.B., Young, J.P., Readance, J.E., & Moore, D.W. (2000). Reinventing adolescent literacy for new times: Perennial and millennial issues. *Journal of Adolescent & Adult Literacy, 43*, 398–410.

Moll, L.C., Veléz-Ibañéz, C., Greenberg, J., Whitmore, K., Saavedra, E., Dworin, J., et al. (1989). *Community knowledge and classroom practice: Combining resources for literacy instruction* (OBEMLA Contract No. 300-87-0131). Tucson: University of Arizona, College of Education and Bureau of Applied Research in Anthropology.

Moreno, R., & Mayer, R.E. (2002). Verbal redundancy in multimedia learning: When reading helps listening. *Journal of Educational Psychology, 94*, 156–163.

Morgan, N. (2001). How to overcome "change fatigue." *Harvard Management Update, 6*(7), 1–3.

Mosborg, S. (2002). Speaking of history: How adolescents use their knowledge of history in reading the daily news. *Cognition and Instruction, 20*, 323–368.

Murphy, C.U., & Lick, D.W. (2001). *Whole-faculty study groups: Creating student-based professional development*. Thousand Oaks, CA: Corwin Press.

Murray, J.D., & Burke, K.A. (2003). Activation and encoding of predictive inferences: The role of reading skill. *Discourse Processes, 35*, 81–102.

Na, L., & Nation, I.S.P. (1985). Factors affecting guessing vocabulary in context. *RELC Journal, 16*(1), 33–42.

Nagy, W.E. (1988). *Teaching vocabulary to improve reading comprehension*. Bloomington, IN: ERIC Clearinghouse on Reading and Communication Skills; Urbana, IL: National Council of Teachers of English; Newark, DE: International Reading Association.

Nagy, W.E., & Scott, J.A. (2000). Vocabulary processes. In M.L. Kamil, P.B. Mosenthal, P.D. Pearson, & R. Barr (Eds.), *Handbook of reading research* (Vol. III, pp. 269–284). Mahwah, NJ: Erlbaum.

Nathan, R.G., & Stanovich, K.E. (1991). The causes and consequences of differences in reading fluency. *Theory Into Practice, 30*, 176–184.

National Association of Secondary School Principals. (2005). *Creating a culture of literacy: A guide for middle and high school principals*. Reston, VA: Author. Retrieved October 4, 2006, from http://www.principals.org/s_nassp/bin.asp?CID=62&DID=52747&DOC=FILE.PDF

National Center for Education Statistics (NCES). (2006a). *The condition of education 2006* (NCES 2006-071). Washington, DC: U.S. Government Printing Office. Retrieved October 30, 2006 from http://nces.ed.gov/pubsearch/pubsinfo.asp?pubid=2006071

National Center for Education Statistics (NCES). (2006b). *The nation's report card: 2005 assessment results, national student groups—Average scale scores and achievement-level results in reading for English language learners*. Washington, DC: U.S. Department of Education. Retrieved November 11, 2006, from http://nces.ed.gov/nationsreportcard/nrc/reading_math_2005

National Commission on Writing. (2004). *Writing: A ticket to work...or a ticket out: A survey of business leaders*. New York: College Board. Retrieved July 31, 2006, from http://www.writingcommission.org/report.html

National Commission on Writing. (2005). *Writing: A powerful message from state government*. New York: College Board. Retrieved July 31, 2006, from http://www.writingcommission.org/report.html

National Education Commission on Time and Learning. (1994). *Prisoners of time: Schools and programs making time work for students and teachers*. Washington, DC.

National Institute of Child Health and Human Development. (2000). *Report of the National Reading Panel. Teaching children to read: An evidence-based assessment of the scientific research literature on reading and its implications for reading instruction* (NIH Publication No. 00-4769). Washington, DC: U.S. Government Printing Office.

National Research Council. (1996). *National Science Education Standards*. Washington DC: National Academies.

Neild, R.C., Stoner-Eby, S., & Furstenberg, F.R., Jr. (2001). *Connecting entrance and departure: The transition to ninth grade and high school dropout*. Working paper commissioned for Dropouts in America conference held January 13, 2001, Cambridge, MA. Retrieved July 12, 2006, from http://www.civilrightsproject.harvard.edu/research/dropouts/dropouts_papers.php

Neuman, S.B., & Celano, D. (2001). Access to print in low-income and middle-income communities: An ecological study of four neighborhoods. *Reading Research Quarterly, 36*, 8–26.

New York City Public Schools Division of Assessment and Accountability. (2000). *ELL Subcommittee research studies: Progress report.* New York: New York City Board of Education. Retrieved September 27, 2006, from http://schools.nyc.gov/daa/ARCHV_reports/ELL_Research_Studies.pdf

Norris, S., & Phillips, L.M. (1994). Interpreting pragmatic meaning when reading popular reports of science. *Journal of Research in Science Teaching, 31,* 947–967.

O'Connor, R.E., Bell, K.M., Harty, K.R., Larkin, L.K., Sackor, S.M., & Zigmond, N. (2002). Teaching reading to poor readers in the intermediate grades: A comparison of text difficulty. *Journal of Educational Psychology, 94,* 474–485.

Orfield, G. (Ed.). (2004). *Dropouts in America: Confronting the graduation rate crisis.* Cambridge, MA: Harvard Education Press.

Organisation for Economic Co-operation and Development (OECD). (2000). *Literacy in the information age: Final report of the International Adult Literacy Survey.* Paris: Author.

Palincsar, A.S., & Dalton, B. (2005). Speaking literacy and learning to technology: Speaking technology to literacy and learning. In B. Maloch, J.V. Hoffman, D.L. Schallert, C.M. Fairbanks, & J. Worthy (Eds.), *54th yearbook of the National Reading Conference* (pp. 83–102). Oak Creek, WI: National Reading Conference.

Palincsar, A.S., & Ladewski, B. (2006). Literacy and the learning sciences. In K. Sawyer (Ed.), *The Cambridge handbook of the learning sciences* (pp. 299–316). Cambridge: Cambridge University Press.

Palincsar, A.S., Magnusson, S.J., Collins, K.M., & Cutter, J. (2001). Making science accessible to all: Results of a design experiment in inclusive classrooms. *Learning Disability Quarterly, 24,* 15–32.

Perfetti, C.A. (1985). *Reading ability.* New York: Oxford University.

Perfetti, C.A., & Bolger, D.J. (2004). The brain might read that way. *Scientific Studies of Reading, 8,* 293–304.

Perfetti, C.A., Britt, M.A., & Georgi, M. (1995). *Text-based learning and reasoning: Studies in history.* Hillsdale, NJ: Erlbaum.

Perie, M., Grigg, W., & Donahue, P. (2005). *The nation's report card: Reading 2005* (NCES 2006-451). Washington, DC: National Center for Education Statistics, U.S. Government Printing Office. Retrieved June 26, 2006, from http://nces.ed.gov/pubsearch/pubsinfo.asp?pubid=2006451

Perie, M., Moran, R., & Lutkus, A. D. (2005). *NAEP 2004 trends in academic progress: Three decades of student performance in reading and mathematics* (NCES 2005-464). Washington, DC: National Center for Education Statistics, U.S. Government Printing Office. Retrieved June 26, 2005, from http://nces.ed.gov/pubsearch/pubsinfo.asp?pubid=2005464

Piaget. J. (1977). *The development of thought: Equilibration of cognitive structures.* New York: The Viking Press. (Originally published in French, 1975).

Pinnell, G. S., & Fountas, I. C. (1998). *Word matters: Teaching phonics and spelling in the reading/writing classroom.* Portsmouth, NH: Heinemann.

Plester, B., Bell, V., & Wood, C. (2006). *Exploring the relationship between text messaging and literacy attainment.* Vancouver, BC: Society for Scientific Studies of Reading.

Pressley, M. (2000). What should comprehension instruction be the instruction of? In M.L. Kamil, P.B. Mosenthal, P.D. Pearson, & R. Barr (Eds.), *Handbook of reading research* (Vol. III, pp. 545–561). Mahwah, NJ: Erlbaum.

Pressley, M., Wharton-McDonald, R., Mistretta-Hampston, J., & Echevarria, M. (1998). Literacy instruction in 10 fourth- and fifth-grade classrooms in upstate New York. *Scientific Studies of Reading, 2,* 159–194.

Pressman, J.L., & Wildavsky, A. (1973). *Implementation: How great expectations in Washington are dashed in Oakland; or, why it's amazing that federal programs work at all, this being a saga of the Economic Development Administration as told by two sympathetic observers who seek to build morals on a foundation of ruined hopes.* Berkeley: University of California Press.

Pribesh, S., & Downey, D.B. (1999). Why are residential moves associated with poor school performance? *Demography, 36,* 521–534.

Quirk, T.J., Trismen, D.A., Nalin, K.B., & Weinberg, S.F. (1975). The classroom behavior of teachers during compensatory reading instruction. *The Journal of Educational Research, 68*(5), 185–192.

Rainie, L. (2006). *Life online: Teens and technology and the world to come.* Speech to annual conference of Public Library Association, Boston, MA. Retrieved October 30, 2006, from http://www.pewinternet.org/ppt/Teens%20and%20technology.pdf

RAND Reading Study Group. (2002). *Reading for understanding: Toward an R&D program in reading comprehension.* Santa Monica, CA: RAND. Retrieved October 2, 2006, from http://www.rand.org/pubs/monograph_reports/2005/MR1465.pdf

Rasinski, T.V. (2003). *The fluent reader: Oral reading strategies for building word recognition, fluency, and comprehension*. New York: Scholastic.

Rasinski, T., Blachowicz, C., & Lems, K. (2006). *Fluency instruction: Research-based best practices*. New York: Guilford.

Raudenbush, S.W., Rowan, B., & Cheong, Y.F. (1992). Contextual effects on the self-perceived efficacy of high school teachers. *Sociology of Education, 65*, 150–167.

Reynolds, P.L., & Symons, S. (2001). Motivational variables and children's text search. *Journal of Educational Psychology, 93*, 14–22.

Rosenshine, B.V. (1978). Academic engaged time, content covered, and direct instruction. *Journal of Education, 160*(3), 38–66.

Rosenshine, B.V., & Stevens, R. (1984). Classroom instruction in reading. In P.D. Pearson, R. Barr, M.L. Kamil, & P. Mosenthal (Eds.), *Handbook of reading research* (pp. 745–798). New York: Longman.

Samuels, S.J., & Farstrup, A.E. (Eds.). (2006). *What research has to say about fluency instruction*. Newark, DE: International Reading Association.

Sandoval, W.A., & Millwood, K.A. (2005). The quality of students' use of evidence in written scientific explanations. *Cognition and Instruction, 23*, 23–55.

Schiefele, U. (1999). Interest and learning from text. *Scientific Studies of Reading, 3*, 257–279.

Schleppegrell, M., & Achugar, M. (2003). Learning language and learning history: A functional linguistics approach. *TESOL Journal, 12*(2), 21–27.

Schoenbach, R., Braunger, J., Greenleaf, C., & Litman, C. (2003). Apprenticing adolescents to reading in subject-area classrooms. *Phi Delta Kappan, 85*, 133–138.

Scholastic Research and Evaluation Department. (2006). *Compendium of READ 180 research* (Report 125916). New York: Scholastic.

Schraw, G., Flowerday, T., & Reisetter, M.F. (1998). The role of choice in reader engagement. *Journal of Educational Psychology, 90*, 705–714.

Schunk, D.H. (2003). Self-efficacy for reading and writing: Influence of modeling, goal-setting, and self-evaluation. *Reading & Writing Quarterly, 19*, 159–172.

Scott, S. (2006). *Examining the role of coaches in low achieving, high poverty elementary schools*. Unpublished manuscript.

Shanahan, C. (2005). *Adolescent literacy intervention programs: Chart and program review guide*. Naperville, IL: Learning Point Associates. Retrieved October 18, 2006, from http://www.learningpt. org/literacy/adolescent/intervention.pdf

Shanahan, T. (2004). Improving reading achievement in secondary schools: Structures and reforms. In D.S. Strickland & D.E. Alvermann (Eds.), *Bridging the literacy achievement gap: Grades 4–12* (pp. 43–55). New York: Teachers College.

Short, D., & Boyson, B. (2004). *Creating access: Language and academic programs for secondary school newcomers*. McHenry, IL: Delta Systems, Inc.

Short, D., & Fitzsimmons, S. (2007). *Double the work: Challenges and solutions to acquiring language and academic literacy for adolescent English language learners: A report to Carnegie Corporation of New York*. Washington, DC: Alliance for Excellent Education.

Soja, E.W. (1996). *Thirdspace: Journeys to Los Angeles and other real-and-imagined places*. Malden, MA: Blackwell.

Spraker, J. (2003). *Teacher teaming in relation to student performance: Findings from the literature*. Portland, OR: Northwest Regional Educational Laboratory.

Stahl, S.A. (2003). Vocabulary and readability: How knowing word meanings affects comprehension. *Topics in Language Disorders, 23*, 241–247.

Stahl, S.A., & Nagy, W.E. (2005). *Teaching word meanings*. Hillsdale, NJ: Erlbaum.

Stanovich, K.E. (1986). Matthew effects in reading: Some consequences of individual differences in the acquisition of literacy. *Reading Research Quarterly, 21*, 360–407.

Staub, D., & Lenz, B.K. (2000). *The effects of strategic tutoring on Casey Family Program foster-care youth*. Lawrence: University of Kansas, Center for Research on Learning.

Stine-Morrow, E.A.L., Gagne, D.D., Morrow, D.G., & De Wall, B.H. (2004). Age differences in rereading. *Memory & Cognition, 32*, 696–710.

Strangman, N., & Dalton, B. (2005). Technology for struggling readers: A review of the research. In D. Edyburn, K. Higgins, & R. Boone (Eds.), *Handbook of special education technology research and practice* (pp. 545–569). Whitefish Bay, WI: Knowledge by Design.

Supovitz, J.A., Mayer, D.P., & Kahle, J.B. (2000) The longitudinal impact of professional development in the context of systemic reform. *Educational Policy, 14*, 331–356.

Taylor, B.M., & Pearson, P.D., Clark, K., & Walpole, S. (2000). Effective schools and accomplished teachers: Lessons about primary-grade reading instruction in low-income schools. *The Elementary School Journal, 101*, 121–165.

Tierney, R.J., & Shanahan, T. (1991). Research on the reading–writing relationship: Interactions, transactions, and outcomes. In R. Barr, M.L. Kamil, P. Mosenthal, & P.D. Pearson (Eds.), *Handbook of reading research* (Vol. II, pp. 246–280). White Plains, NY: Longman.

Tierney, R.J., Soter, A., O'Flahavan, J.F., & McGinley, W. (1989). The effects of reading and writing upon thinking critically. *Reading Research Quarterly, 24*, 134–173.

Troia, G.A., & Graham, S. (2003). Effective writing instruction across the grades: What every educational consultant should know. *Journal of Educational & Psychological Consultation, 14*, 75–89.

Ulrich, D. (1997). *Human resource champions: The next agenda for adding value and delivering results.* Boston: Harvard Business School Press.

Ulrich, D., Zenger, J., & Smallwood, N. (1999). *Results-based leadership: How leaders build the business and improve the bottom line.* Boston: Harvard Business School Press.

Umbel, V.M., Pearson, B.Z., Fernandez, M.C., & Oller, D.K. (1992). Measuring bilingual children's receptive vocabularies. *Child Development, 63*, 1012–1020.

Valencia, S.W., & Buly, M.R. (2005). Behind test scores: What struggling readers *really* need. In S.J. Barrentine & S.M. Stokes (Eds.), *Reading Assessments: Principles and Practices for Elementary Teachers* (2nd ed., pp. 134–146). Newark, DE: International Reading Association.

van den Broek, P. (2001). *The role of television viewing in the development of reading comprehension.* Report from the Center for the Improvement of Early Reading Achievement. Washington, DC: Office of Educational Research and Improvement. Retrieved July 31, 2006, from http://www.ciera.org/library/archive/2001-02/200102pv.pdf

van den Broek, P., Lorch, E.P., & Thurlow, R. (1996). Children's and adults' memory for television stories: The role of causal factors, story-grammar categories, and hierarchical level. *Child Development, 67*, 3010–3029.

van Garderen, D. (2004). Reciprocal teaching as a comprehension strategy for understanding mathematical word problems. *Reading & Writing Quarterly, 20*, 225–229.

Vaughn, S., Klingner, J., & Hughes, M. (2000). Sustainability of research-based practices. *Exceptional Children, 66*, 163–171.

Vaughn, S., Klingner, J.K., & Bryant, D.P. (2001). Collaborative strategic reading as a means to enhance peer-mediated instruction for reading comprehension and content-area learning. *Remedial and Special Education, 22*, 66–74.

Verhallen, M., & Schoonen, R. (1993). Vocabulary knowledge of monolingual and bilingual children. *Applied Psycholinguistics, 14*, 344–363.

Wallace, R.M., Kupperman, J., Krajcik, J., & Soloway, E. (2000). Science on the web: Students online in a sixth-grade classroom. *Journal of the Learning Sciences, 9*, 75–104.

Wheelock, A., & Miao, J. (2005). The ninth-grade bottleneck: An enrollment bulge in a transition year that demands careful attention and action. *School Administrator, 62*, 36–40.

Wiliam, D., & Black, P. (1996). Meanings and consequences: A basis for distinguishing formative and summative functions of assessment? *British Educational Research Journal, 22*, 537–548.

Wiliam, D., Lee, C., Harrison, C., & Black, P. (2004). Teachers developing assessment for learning: Impact on student achievement. *Assessment in Education, 11*(1), 49–65.

Wolfe, M.B.W., Schreiner, M.E., Rehder, B., Laham, D., Foltz, P.W., Kintsch, W., et al. (1998). Learning from text: Matching readers and texts by latent semantic analysis. *Discourse Processes, 25*, 309–336.

Worthy, J., Moorman, M., & Turner, M. (1999). What Johnny likes to read is hard to find in school. *Reading Research Quarterly, 34*, 12–27.

Wright, J.C., Huston, A.C., Murphy, K.C., St. Peters, M., Piñon, M., Scantlin, R., et al. (2001). The relations of early television viewing to school readiness and vocabulary of children from low-income families: The early window project. *Child Development, 72*, 1347–1366.

AUTHOR INDEX

SUBJECT INDEX

Note. Page numbers followed by *f* and *t* indicate figures and tables, respectively.

A

ACADEMY OF READING, 130–132

ACCELERATED READER, 132–134

ACHIEVE3000, 135–136

ACHIEVING MAXIMUM POTENTIAL (AMP) READING SYSTEM, 137–138

ACTION PLANNING, 108–109; template for, 109*t*

ADOLESCENT LITERACY, 1–7; competing media and, 15–16; condition of, 1–3; context dependence of, 31–34; demands on, changes in, 18–19; history of, 14–15; myths of, 11–17; realities of, 17–35; school and district change for, 92–110

ADOLESCENT LITERACY INSTRUCTION: characteristics of, 49–55; in comprehension, 24; content of, 37–48; versus demands, 19–20; supports of, 55–59

ADOLESCENT LITERACY PROGRAMS: core principles for, 98–109; costs of implementing, 61–91; emerging, 229–230; evaluated features, 119–120, 126*t*–127*t*; evaluation criteria for, 115–117; evaluation of, 111–227; included features, 118–119, 124*t*–125*t*; selection criteria for, 113–115; selection of, 88–89; skills, strategies, and knowledge taught, 120–121, 128*t*–129*t*; types of students served by, 118, 122*t*–123*t*

ADVANCED LEVEL: term, 12

ADVANCED LITERACY: demands for, 3–4

ADVANCEMENT VIA INDIVIDUAL DETERMINATION (AVID), 138–140

ADVANTAGE PROGRAM, 130

ADVISORY COMMITTEE, 106, 106*f*

AFTERSCHOOL KIDZLIT, 140–142

ALTERNATIVE LITERACIES, 46–47

AMERICA'S CHOICE, INC., 142

AMERICA'S CHOICE—RAMP-UP LITERACY, 142–145

AMP. *See* Achieving Maximum Potential Reading System

ANCHORING TABLE, 95

ASSESSMENT: formative versus summative, 53; importance of, 34–35; and school reform, 107–109

AUGUST, DIANE, 220

AVID. *See* Advancement Via Individual Determination

B

BACKGROUND KNOWLEDGE: definition of, 22; instruction in, 40–42; and struggle, 22–23

BASIC LEVEL: term, 12

BECK, ISABEL, 183

BELOW BASIC LEVEL: term, 12

BENCHMARK WORD DETECTIVES, 145–146

BERNADINE HIGH SCHOOL: case study of, 93–98; context of, 7, 93

BOSTON HIGHER EDUCATION PARTNERSHIP RESEARCH COLLABORATIVE (BHEPRC), 20

C

CARLO, MARIA, 220

CENTER FOR APPLIED SPECIAL TECHNOLOGIES, 186, 216–217

CHALL, JEANNE, 193

CHANGE: decision making on, stakeholders and, 104–107; term, 99

CHANGE FATIGUE, 98

CHANGE READINESS, 99–104; considerations in, 101*t*

CHANGE STRUCTURE: sample, 106–107, 106*f*

CHOICE: in goal-setting, 51–52

CHURCHILL PREP: context of, 17; decoding instruction at, 39

CLASS SIZE: reduction of, and resources, 64; and struggle, 27

CLC. *See* Content Literacy Continuum

COACHES: literacy, 58–59

COGNATES, 41

COLLABORATIVE LEARNING: text-based, 52–53

COLLABORATIVE REASONING, 229

COMMUNICATION TECHNOLOGY: literacy in, 45–46

COMMUNITIES ORGANIZING RESOURCES TO ADVANCE LEARNING (CORAL), 141

COMPARISON ROUTINE, 95

COMPETING EVENTS: and change readiness, 101*t*, 104

COMPREHENSION: versus fluency, 14; instruction in, 42–43; and struggle, 24–25

COMPUTER LITERACY, 32–33; instruction in, 45–46

COMPUTERS: versus adolescent literacy, 15–16

CONCEPT-ORIENTED READING INSTRUCTION (CORI), 147–149

CONSORTIUM OF POLICY RESEARCH IN EDUCATION (CPRE), 144

CONTENT AREAS: comprehension instruction for, 43; coordination across, 57; literacy instruction in, 19; reading across, 29–31; scaffolding in, 53–54

CONTENT ENHANCEMENT ROUTINES, 95, 208

TEACHER-STUDENT RATIOS: and struggle, 27
TEACHER TEAMS, 56–57
TEACHING FOR TRANSFER, 49–50; evaluation of, 116
TEACHING INTERNET COMPREHENSION TO ADOLESCENTS (TICA), 230
TECHNOLOGY: evaluation of, 116; information and communication, literacy in, 45–46; as tool, 54–55
TEENBIZ3000, 135
TELEVISION: versus adolescent literacy, 15–16
TEST OF WORD READING EFFICIENCY (TOWRE), 206
TEXT SELECTION: diversity in, 51
THINKING READER, 187, 216–217
THIRD SPACE, 31–32, 47
TICA. *See* Teaching Internet Comprehension to Adolescents
TIME: constraints, and struggle, 27–28; for literacy, increased, 55–56; on reading, and fluency, 22, 39; as resource, 64
TOM SNYDER PRODUCTIONS, 187, 216
TOWRE. *See* Test of Word Reading Efficiency
TRACKING, 28
TRANSACTIONAL STRATEGIES INSTRUCTION (TSI), 218–220
TRANSFER: evaluation of, 116; teaching for, 49–50

TRANSITION: versus change, 99
TRITES, RONALD, 130
TSI. *See* Transactional Strategies Instruction
TURNER MIDDLE SCHOOL: literacy coaching at, 59
TUTORING: strategic, 54, 57–58, 230

V

VIDEO GAMES: versus adolescent literacy, 15–16
VISUALIZING AND VERBALIZING (V/V), 165
VOCABULARY: definition of, 22; instruction in, 40–42; and struggle, 22–23
VOCABULARY IMPROVEMENT PROGRAM (VIP), 220–222
VOYAGER EXPANDED LEARNING, 171–172
VOYAGER TIMEWARP PLUS, 222–224
V/V. *See* Visualizing and Verbalizing

W

WILSON READING SYSTEM, 224–225
WORD CALLERS, 14
WRITETOLEARN, 225–227
WRITING: instruction in, 43–45
WRITING INTENSIVE READING COMPREHENSION, 230

To order additional copies of this book:

Order online at **www.reading.org**
Call toll free **800-336-7323**
(Outside the U.S. and Canada call 302-731-1600.)

INTERNATIONAL
Reading Association
800 BARKSDALE ROAD, PO BOX 8139
NEWARK, DE 19714-8139, USA
www.reading.org